ONCE THEY WERE HATS

In Search of the Mighty Beaver

FRANCES BACKHOUSE

ECW PRESS

·TORONTO·

*"A traditional knowledge
of the beaver is the birthright
of every Canadian."*

— Horace T. Martin, *Castorologia*

CONTENTS

INTRODUCTION

The beaver has a major image problem. A chubby rodent with goofy buckteeth and a tail that looks like it was run over by a tractor tire — it's no wonder beavers prefer to work under cover of darkness. They're ungainly on land and ride so low in the water when they're swimming that from a distance they can be easily mistaken for floating deadwood.

At best, some might say, the beaver is an icon of insipidness: although often lauded as a paragon of diligence and industriousness, the beaver could just as well be described as a monogamous, workaholic homebody.

At worst, beavers are embarrassing. Not only has their name been co-opted as smutty slang for female genitalia (a usage that first appeared in print in the 1920s), but they're also wimps in comparison to charismatic national animals like the American eagle, the English lion and China's giant panda.

Unofficially, the beaver has represented Canada since before the country achieved full nationhood. In 1851, 16 years before Confederation, the Province of Canada's newly independent postal system issued its first postage stamp, the Three-Pence Beaver, which depicted the eponymous animal crouched on a bank beside a cascading stream. But when it came to devising a coat of arms for Canada in 1921, the beaver didn't make the cut. In the blunt words of Under-Secretary of State Thomas Mulvey, a member of the design committee, "It was decided that as a member of the Rat Family, a Beaver was not appropriate." (Actually, beavers belong to their own, exclusive family, the Castoridae, and are only distant cousins of rats and other members of the Rodentia order, but such distinctions probably wouldn't have swayed Mulvey.)

The only reason the beaver eventually gained official standing as Canada's national animal may have been that Americans were threatening to usurp the emblem. Apparently no Canadians had noticed when Oregon, long known as the Beaver State because of its fur-trade history, adopted the beaver as a state mascot in 1969. When New York announced plans to do the same a few years later, Canada finally asserted its own claim. In 1975, Parliament passed Bill C-373, "An Act to provide for the recognition of the Beaver (*Castor canadensis*) as a symbol of the sovereignty of Canada."

However, a fancy title doesn't guarantee respect. In 2011, Senator Nicole Eaton stood up in the Red Chamber and called for the beaver to be stripped of its honours and replaced by the polar bear. Canada's symbol of sovereignty was, she said, nothing more than a "dentally defective rat" and a "toothy tyrant" that "wreaks havoc on farmlands, roads, lakes, streams and tree plantations." Her denunciation hinted at a revenge motive, for she also mentioned her ongoing battle to keep beavers from damaging the dock at her summer cottage.

I have never outright scorned beavers, but I did, for a long time, take them for granted and underestimate their worth. "What are you writing about?" friends would ask when they found out I was working on a new book. "Beavers," I'd mutter, in the early days, and change the subject for fear of hearing the word "boring" in response. Yet I quickly came to realize that beavers aren't boring. I just didn't know how fascinating they would turn out to be.

The truth is, the humble and much-maligned beaver is actually the Mighty Beaver, arguably North America's most influential animal, aside from ourselves. For no less than a million years, and possibly as long as 24 million, beavers in one form or another have been sculpting the continental landscape by controlling the flow of water and the accumulation of sediments — filling whole valleys and rerouting rivers, in places. For an equal length of time, they've also been nudging other species down distinctive evolutionary paths, from trees that have developed defenses against the woodcutters to a multitude of plants and animals that rely on beaver-built environments. Beavers even have an exclusive parasite, the louse-like beaver beetle (*Platypsyllus castoris*), which spends its whole life roaming through its host's fur or hiding out in the ceiling of the beaver's lodge.

Two things are behind this far-reaching influence: a unique lifestyle and sheer ubiquity. No other animal in the world lives quite like the woodcutting, dam-building beaver. Although eccentric, this way of life is what makes *Castor canadensis* a classic keystone species — that is, the indispensable creator of conditions that support entire ecological communities; an unwitting faunal philanthropist.

Before the fur trade devastated their population, these ecosystem engineers were extraordinarily abundant and prevalent. Picture at least 60 million beavers (or 400 million if the high-end estimate is correct) spread out across almost every part of the continent. At least 25 million dams. And countless biodiversity hotspots — beaver ponds, beaver wetlands, beaver meadows

— all teeming with life. Today's numbers pale in comparison, but beavers are back on the job in many places.

This book is a journey of sorts, one that meanders through the millennia of castorid existence in the company of paleontologists, archaeologists, First Nations elders, historians, hatters, fur traders, trappers, biologists and, of course, beavers. It begins in the watery realm where *Castor canadensis* once ruled, then plunges back in time to meet the beaver's ancient kin, from lumbering giants to pint-sized burrowers. It explores the perspectives of the beaver's first human acquaintances, peoples who knew this venerated animal by hundreds of different names, and follows the fur-hungry Europeans who arrived at the close of the fifteenth century and fanned out across the continent in ruthless pursuit of the pelts that were to them like brown gold. After tracing the species' nosedive to near extinction and its subsequent revival (one of North America's most notable conservation success stories), we enter the twenty-first century, where the beaver, so long appreciated mainly for its fur and its legendary busyness, is making a comeback as an ecological hero. Its journey is not over, after all, and there are new vistas ahead on our travels together.

For as long as humans have inhabited this continent, beavers have played a significant role in our lives. They have fed and clothed us, inspired spiritual beliefs and cultural traditions, driven the course of history, lent their name to countless landmarks and kept our water reservoirs charged. Until recently, we've tended to overlook this last contribution, but as we struggle to adapt to the vagaries of climate change, water stewardship may prove to be the beaver's greatest gift to us.

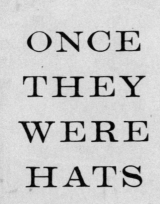

ONCE
THEY
WERE
HATS

others reckon it no more than a hundred Fathom

A View of ye Industry of ye Beavers of Canada in making Dams to stop ye Course of a Rivulet, in order to form a great Lake, about wch they build their Habitations. To Effect this; they fell large Trees with their Teeth, in such a manner as to make them come Cross ye Rivulet, to lay ye foundation of ye Dam; they make Mortar, work up, and finish ye whole with great order and wonderfull Dexterity. The Beavers have two Doors to their Lodges, one to the water and the other to the Land side. According to ye French Accounts

·One·
INTO THE HEART
OF BEAVERLAND

In 1497, when the Anglo-Italian navigator and explorer John Cabot landed on Newfoundland's rocky shores and kicked off the European invasion of North America, beavers inhabited almost all of what we now call Canada and the United States, plus a sliver of Mexico. They ranged from the Atlantic coast to the Pacific and from just south of the Rio Grande to the Mackenzie and Coppermine river deltas on the Arctic Ocean. The only off-limit regions were the Arctic barrens, the parched deserts of the extreme southwest and the alligator-patrolled swamps of the Florida peninsula. Otherwise, wherever they could find water and wood, beavers were present.

Although there are no firsthand written descriptions of North America during the beaver's Golden Age, David Thompson arrived sufficiently early and travelled widely enough to provide a credible report soon afterwards. In 1784, when he was just 14, Thompson sailed from England to Hudson Bay to apprentice as a clerk at a fur-trading post. Over the next three decades, employed first by the Hudson's Bay Company and later by the rival North West Company, he surveyed and mapped one-sixth of the continent. In the course of his work, he walked, rode and paddled nearly 90,000 kilometres, the equivalent of circling the globe twice.

Near the end of his life, Thompson gathered together all of his meticulously kept notebooks and field journals and penned a detailed account of his travels. In it he recalled a time, only a few generations earlier, when "Man was Lord of all the dry land and all that was on it" and beavers reigned over the rest.

"Previous to the discovery of Canada," Thompson wrote, "this Continent from the Latitude of forty degrees north to the Arctic Circle, and from the Atlantic to the Pacific Ocean, may be said to have been in the possession of two distinct races of Beings, Man and the Beaver . . . except [for] the Great Lakes, the waves of which are too turbulent, [the Beaver] occupied all the waters of the northern part of the Continent. Every River where the current was moderate and sufficiently deep, the banks at the water edge were occupied by their houses. To every small Lake, and all the Ponds they builded Dams, and enlarged and deepened them to the height of the dams. Even to grounds occasionally overflowed, by heavy rains, they also made dams, and made the permanent Ponds, and as they heightened the dams [they] increased the extent and added to the depth of the water; Thus all the low lands were in possession of the Beaver, and all the hollows of the higher grounds." In other words, beavers were everywhere.

The stronghold described by Thompson lay north of the fortieth parallel — a line that connects New York City to California's Mendocino County, passing through Pittsburgh, Pennsylvania, and Lincoln, Nebraska, along the way. Yet beavers were far from inconsequential in the southern half of their range. The Sacramento River, for instance, harboured an abundance of famously hefty beavers, especially in the marshlands near the mouth. One visitor to the lower Sacramento Valley in the mid-1800s wrote: "There is probably no spot of equal extent on the whole continent of America, which contains so many of these much sought for animals."

Unfortunately, it was one of the last outposts of the beaver's once-great empire and it, too, would soon fall.

When I first read David Thompson's account of the beaver's glory days, I wished I could have witnessed them myself. The more I learned about that erstwhile watery Eden, which I came to think of as Beaverland, the more I wanted to visit it. Impossible, of course, or so it seemed until I heard about the Beaver Capital of Canada.

Jean Thie, the man who discovered and named the Beaver Capital of Canada (which may well be the Beaver Capital of the World), is a landscape ecologist with a unique hobby. Born and raised in the Netherlands, Thie came to Canada as a 20-year-old graduate student in 1967 and went on to a distinguished career in government. His accomplishments included pioneering the use of geographic information system (GIS) technology in Canada, completing the Canada Land Inventory and directing the National Atlas Information Service. Now, as the president of an Ottawa-based remote sensing and geospatial mapping company, he specializes in contemplating terrain from a bird's-eye view and interpreting it for earthbound mortals. Studying things like permafrost melt and forest cover for government agencies and corporate clients is his job. Cruising virtually over the continent in search of beaver dams and lodges is his private obsession. Instead of playing computer games or watching television to relax, he spends hours at a time poking around on Google Earth and World Wind — scaling up and down, spinning the globe with a click of his mouse — with the sole purpose of exploring beaver haunts.

Thie began pursuing this quirky passion around 2004, in the early days of Google Earth, after he spotted a beaver dam while doing peatland research. Three years later, he zoomed in on the boggy lands at the base of the Pasquia Hills in east-central Saskatchewan and immediately recognized the area as a centre of exceptional beaver activity. He dubbed it the Beaver Capital of Canada.

In the satellite images Thie has posted on his website, the Beaver Capital looks like a moth-eaten blanket. The beaver ponds show up as widely spaced, black rents in the green fabric, their upslope margins ragged and diffuse, their downslope edges defined by the solid curves of the dams. In most of the ponds, a large beige dot punctuates the dark water, as unnatural-looking as the streets and houses in the tiny Cree community of Pakwaw Lake next door. These beaver lodges are no bigger than a single-car garage, but they're easily visible from outer space.

Since 2007, Thie has yet to find such a concentration of beaver dams anywhere else in all his virtual travels around North America. By his count, there are 15 to 20 dams per square kilometre and most of them have an associated lodge. Assuming that the average lodge houses about five beavers (a reasonable supposition), he figures that every square kilometre of these wetlands supports 50 to 100 beavers. Transpose that density to one of our human capitals and we'd have nearly 18,000 beavers wandering the streets of Washington, D.C., or more than a quarter of a million in Ottawa.

The moment I heard of Thie's discovery, I knew I had to go there. It seemed like the perfect place to find out what North America looked like back when beavers ruled. All I had to do was get to Nipawin, Saskatchewan, and follow Highway 55, also known as the Northern Woods and Water Route, until I reached the turnoff to Pakwaw Lake. The irregular polygon that Thie had superimposed on the website photos conveniently straddled the highway and stretched a few kilometres northwest along the Pakwaw Lake access road. I might not even have to get out of my car to see the castorid metropolis.

My journey to the Pasquia Hills began on an overcast July morning after a pleasant night in the Nipawin and District Regional Park campground. Heading east out of town, Highway 55 was a paved two-lane road, the kind of respectable rural thoroughfare that bisects and links small communities all across the prairies. The only indication that I was venturing off the beaten path was a sign on the edge of town: "No services 178 km." No problem, I thought. My destination was only 70 kilometres away and I had a full tank of gas. Not even the darkening sky ahead — slate grey above vibrant yellow canola fields — or the curtains of rain that swept the horizon could spoil my anticipation.

It was evident from Thie's website that he had never actually visited the Pakwaw beavers. (When we spoke later, he confirmed that he conducts all of his beaver research from his home office in Wakefield, Quebec.) Nor was the Beaver Capital marked on any map. But I wasn't worried. I had complete trust in my guide, though I had yet to even exchange emails with the man, and equal faith in Google Earth.

Still, I wasn't at all sure what I would find when I got there. After Jesuit historian Pierre-François-Xavier de Charlevoix toured New France in the early 1720s, he reported that "there are sometimes three or four hundred [beavers] together in one place, forming a town which might properly enough be called a little Venice." Surely an exaggeration, but secretly I was hoping for such a sight.

At first, the vast expanse of open, cultivated land that stretched out on either side of my route made it hard to believe I was on my way to a record-setting beaver colony. Then, about 40 kilometres from the outskirts of Nipawin, the asphalt gave way to gravel, and a long, straight fence that extended as far as I could see both north and south of the road brought the farm fields to an abrupt halt. East of the wire, trees took over — a phalanx of black spruce and tamarack, with flashes of balsam poplar and luminous white birch scattered among their dark ranks. I had entered the Northern Provincial Forest.

It was as if I had driven through a time warp and could suddenly see the land as it appeared to explorer Henry Kelsey when he passed this way in 1690, making history as the first European to enter present-day Saskatchewan. Beavers were plentiful throughout the region then, which was welcome news for Kelsey's employer, the Hudson's Bay Company. After that, it took the fur traders and trappers less than 200 years to wipe them out.

Although the dense forest obscured the lay of the land, the road's occasional undulations hinted at the "knoll and kettle" topography I had read about on Thie's website, and I could picture the depressions filled with fens and bogs. If Thie had been sitting in the passenger seat, he might have pointed out how the highway follows one of the beach lines left by ancient Lake Agassiz and explained how these prominent ice-age features slow the natural drainage. In his absence, my understanding of why the area is beaver heaven came down to this: because of the region's geology, the gently inclined land leading to Pakwaw Lake is one big soggy wetland, irrigated by runoff from the Pasquia Hills.

I was still 30 kilometres from my destination when the first fat raindrops hit my windshield. Minutes later, I was driving through a deluge. I cranked the wipers up to high and halved my speed as the road turned as soft and slippery as cream cheese beneath my tires. I didn't dare pull over onto the weedy strip that passed for a shoulder. If I were to slide into the deep ditch that separated the roadbed from the coniferous wilderness beyond, I might never be found. Except for one 18-wheeler that spewed rooster tails of mud at my little SUV as it roared by, heading west, traffic was nonexistent on this stretch of so-called highway. On the plus side, I was free to weave back and forth across both lanes, aiming for the shallowest trenches.

When I finally reached the Pakwaw Lake turnoff, about an hour after the rain started, it was still pouring. The inter-section marked the centre of my target, but the only pond in sight showed no sign of beaver activity. I crept a few kilometres farther down the highway, hemmed in by stiff, scraggly spruce, then executed a cautious three-point turn in the thick sludge, drove back to the junction and turned right.

The storm had almost sputtered out by then, as had my hopes of finding the beavers. The structures that seemed so obvious from outer space were proving far more elusive at ground level. The terrain was too flat, the vegetation too thick, and there were no sign-posted trails leading to strategically located view-ing platforms. I thought back to the warning a Saskatchewan Tourism rep had given me when I asked about travelling to the Pasquia Hills: "It's pretty wild country," she'd said. "I suppose that's why the beavers like it so much."

I drove slowly down the Pakwaw Lake road and through the village on unpaved and deserted streets — the downpour had apparently chased all the local citizens inside — and turned back towards the highway. Just then, I spotted a dark brown dome a few hundred metres from the road edge, rising out of what appeared to be a grassy meadow fringed with birch trees and tall shrubs. I cranked the wheel to pull over, wriggled into my hooded, face-veiling bug shirt and jumped out, binoculars and camera in hand. Instantly, hordes of mosquitoes and gnats descended upon me, pummelling the mesh around my head and blackening the thin fabric of my pants. Doing my best to ignore them, I started towards the lodge, only to discover that a wide, water-filled ditch blocked my route. There was no point getting wet to my knees wading across it. I was bound to hit deeper water before I got much closer. I could see now that the verdant meadow was an illusion, a marshy moat that afforded the lodge's tenants ample protection against terrestrial invaders like me.

Instead, I returned to the car for my Google Earth print-outs. Bingo! The unreachable dome's position perfectly matched one of the pale dots on the photograph, proof that the satellites weren't lying, even if the rest of the lodges were out of sight. As I stood there studying the dome through my binoculars and savouring my success, a Cree man, the first person I had seen since I turned off the highway, drove by. From his baffled stare I gathered that the Beaver Capital of Canada was not yet a major tourist attraction.

It wasn't a particularly picturesque example of the beaver's art, but I snapped a few photos anyway, thinking of Horace T. Martin, author of the 1892 book, *Castorologia, or The History and Traditions of the Canadian Beaver*. "The beaver lodge," wrote Martin, "is generally included in the list of marvels reserved for the investigation of those who visit beaver districts." That said, he did not recommend the experience, since "no greater disappointment awaits the enquirer than the first inspection of one … [It] is a shock to stand for the first time before a pile of twigs, branches and logs, heaped in disorder on a small dome of mud, and to learn that this constitutes the famous lodge."

Of course, any nineteenth-century sightseer who had read early European accounts of life in North America was bound to be disappointed. The authors of those fanciful reports often represented beaver lodges as multi-storied and many-chambered tenements, designed with "the genius of a clever architect." The illustrators depicted crews of vaguely beaver-like quadrupeds marching along with bundles of lumber balanced on their shoulders, and many commentators displayed equal imagination in describing the beaver's building techniques. Charlevoix, among others, claimed that beavers used their tails as wheelbarrows to transport mud and as trowels to plaster it into onto the exterior walls of their "cabins."

Back in the car, accompanied by the multitude of biting insects that would torment me all the way to Nipawin and beyond, I brooded for a while about my failure to gain admission to the beaver's little Venice. However, by the time I reached the welcome firmness of the paved road, I had decided it didn't matter. The important thing was that such a place remained more than a century after Horace T. Martin's gloomy prognosis that, "As to the ultimate destruction of the beaver no possible question can exist."

Jean Thie's other major beaver discovery is the World's Longest Beaver Dam, which is more famous than the Beaver Capital of Canada and considerably less accessible. No roads lead to this natural wonder. There are no utility corridors or seismic cut lines to follow. No human footpaths either, though moose trails abound. The dam's location, in a remote corner of Wood Buffalo National Park in northern Alberta, is a rarity within North America: undefiled, uninterrupted wilderness, where beavers live exactly the same way they did before Europeans reached the continent.

In 1797, while travelling across the prairies, David Thompson came to a beaver dam that was "a full mile in length" (1.6 kilometres, for the metrically inclined) and wide enough for his horses to walk two abreast. Coming from anyone else, this might seem like hyperbole, but given Thompson's renown as a surveyor, I trust his appraisal. Today, nothing like it exists. In fact, until Thie spotted the Wood Buffalo National Park dam in 2007, the record holder was a 652-metre-long edifice near Three Forks, Montana, documented around 1913 and long since vanished. Nobody has physically surveyed this new find, but Thie has measured it on satellite images. At 850 metres, it's about half as long as the one Thompson crossed.

Wood Buffalo's external relations manager, Mike Keizer, is one of the few people who has seen the mega-dam in person — in his case, from the window of a Cessna airplane. When I called him in 2011, with the naïve notion of arranging a ground-level tour for myself, it quickly became obvious why no one up to that point had managed to get any closer.

The one-hour flight from Fort Smith, Northwest Territories, which is the nearest town, would be the easy part, Keizer said, but would require a pontoon-equipped helicopter, since the lake closest to the dam is too shallow to land a floatplane. After the heartbeat thump of the helicopter's whirling rotors had receded into the distance and my ears had adjusted to the subdued sounds of the boreal forest, I would begin bushwhacking. If I were lucky, I would reach the dam that day. The spongy ground would make for slow going, my boots would be soaking wet the whole time and there would be "mosquitoes by the bucket load."

Would it be worth the effort? I asked. Keizer sounded

doubtful. He facetiously calls the structure "the world's longest beaver dike" because of its low profile. "It's not the Hoover Dam of the beavers," he said, at least not in terms of height. Looking at the photographs and video footage that he and his companions took during their flyover, I had to agree. The only way I could identify the dam's position was by what it separated: scrappy coniferous forest on one side of the meandering line; an irregular semicircle of blue water and bright green aquatic vegetation on the other.

Throughout most of North America, beaver dams rarely rise more than three metres in height or span more than 100 metres, the length of a football field. In the area around Thie's find — an almost imperceptibly sloping alluvial fan at the foot of the Birch Mountains — none of the dams challenge the height records, but lengths of 300 to 600 metres are common. One reason for this exceptional architecture is topography: as run-off from the high ground creeps across the near-level terrain, it inevitably finds its way around the ends of any barrier, forcing the beavers to keep lengthening their dams to corral it.

The other reason is time. By studying old aerial photographs and LandSat imagery, Thie has determined that the beavers began their now-renowned dam in the mid-1970s as two separate dams and have been working on it ever since, a multi-generational effort. He predicts that they'll continue to augment the current structure and eventually, probably within a decade, it will merge with a pair of shorter dams that currently flank it. If that happens, the new, improved version will measure nearly one kilometre from end to end.

We may never again see beaver causeways like the one Thompson crossed, but our maps are rich with reminders of the species' former superabundance. My local landmark is Beaver Lake, one of 79 Canadian and 155 American water bodies that bear the same name. Other beaver-inspired lake names include Beaverhouse, Beaverflood, Beaverjack and Beavertrap, as well as Beaverhide, Beaver Claw, Beaverpaw, Beaverleg, Beaverhead, Beavertail and Beavertooth.

Every Canadian province and territory and every American state except Hawaii has places named for beavers — more than 2,000 altogether, according to the authorities who keep track of geographical names in the two countries. Database convolutions make it hard to determine the exact number, but it's clearly higher than for any other animal. You can't swing a beaver on this continent — if you could even manage to heft one by its flat, scaly tail — without hitting one of its namesakes. Beaver Lake/Pond/River/Creek/Canyon/Mountain/Bluffs/Glacier/Valley/City. Beaver Flats and Beaver Hollow. Beaverlodge, Alberta: home of the world's largest beaver sculpture. Beaver Bottom, Beaver Steady, Beaver Lick, Beaver Medicine Falls. The list goes on.

French-speaking fur traders and settlers knew the beaver as *le castor*. To the Spanish, he was *il castor*. Hence Castorville, Bayou Castor, Lac du Castor Solitaire, Prairie du Castor, Castor Point, Castor Plunge and scores of others.

Most beaver place-names bestowed by the continent's original inhabitants have been erased from both maps and memory. The Dunne-za, also known as the Tsattine ("dwellers among the beavers") and as the Beaver Indians, called the great waterway that flows through their territory the Tsades or "river of beavers." Today, it's known as the Peace River. Other indigenous names are hidden behind translations: Beaver Harbour, Nova Scotia, for example, instead of Kobelawakwemoode, which means roughly the same thing in Mi'kmaq. Among the First Nations names that have endured are many that include *amisk* or *amik*, alternate spellings of the Cree and Anishinaabe word for beaver. Browsing through the list, I noticed Amisk Lake, Saskatchewan, about 120 kilometres north of Pakwaw Lake.

In 1535, during his second voyage to the New World, French explorer Jacques Cartier stopped along the St. Lawrence River at an Iroquoian town called Hochelaga, variously translated as "beaver path" or "at the place of the [beaver] dam." When he returned five years later, the town was abandoned. Cartier's writings were vague about where Hochelaga was, leaving modern archaeologists and historians to argue endlessly about its exact location. The only thing they agree on is that it stood somewhere around the subsequent site of Ville-Marie, the colonial settlement that evolved into Montreal.

Today, the name of Montreal's Hochelaga-Maisonneuve district gives a nod to the city's First Nations roots. Coincidentally, this district is also home to the Montreal Biodôme, where a family of beavers inhabits a fake patch of Laurentian forest. You don't have to churn through hubcap-swallowing mud or brave mosquito-infested muskeg to see them. You just pay your admission and walk inside to join the throngs of visitors who stare through thick plate-glass windows into the underwater realm of the make-believe pond.

Fortunately, vivaria and cartographic commemorations aren't all that's left of Beaverland. *Castor canadensis* has survived to carry on the work of its ancestors, upholding a heritage that may be 24 million years old. It's taken a great deal of adaptation and luck to keep the project going, but beavers are nothing if not persistent.

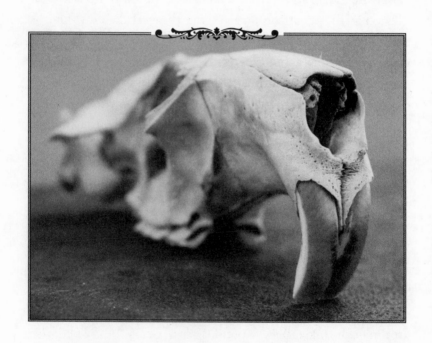

· Two·
ANCIENT ANTECEDENTS

Deep in the cavernous, climate-controlled complex that houses the Canadian Museum of Nature's research collections in Gatineau, Quebec, Natalia Rybczynski held out a barkless, weathered stick for my inspection. The end closest to me was pointed, with shallow furrows carved into the sloping plane of the terminal cut. The corrugations were plainly tooth marks. Beaver tooth marks, to be specific. I had seen countless pieces of wood just like it — except for two notable differences. It was four million years old and had been fashioned by *Dipoides*, an animal that died out two and a half million years ago.

Modern-day beavers belong to a very exclusive club. The family Castoridae contains but one genus out of the roughly 30 (including *Dipoides*) that have existed at one time or another. And that enduring genus, *Castor*, has only two extant species: North America's *Castor canadensis* and the Eurasian *Castor fiber*. As one of the world's experts on the beaver family tree, Dr. Rybczynski, a petite, fine-featured paleobiologist, knows more about the ones that came before than many of us know about the survivors. Now I was to learn some of their secrets.

She reached into the cabinet labelled "Reserved for Natalia's sticks" and selected another specimen. This one was the work of

Castor canadensis. Without their tags, I couldn't have told them apart, but Natalia knew exactly what to look for: the width of the tooth marks; and the angle of the cut surface relative to the long axis. "There's a *Dipoides* angle and there's a *Castor* angle," she told me, and the *Dipoides* cuts are smaller. Subtle but significant distinctions.

In 2001, Natalia had enlisted a pair of beavers named Granby and Cleaver, denizens of the Smithsonian Institution National Zoological Park in Washington, D.C., in a groundbreaking study of beaver woodcutting behaviour. Until then, no one had ever bothered to document how beavers utilize their teeth as tools. Natalia wouldn't have either, if not for *Dipoides*. Seeking insight into the extinct beaver's life, particularly how it might have used trees for food and building material, she decided to compare the woodcutting abilities of *Dipoides* with its latter-day kin.

Natalia's video footage of Granby and Cleaver revealed, among other things, that beavers are not bilateral biters, meaning they don't use their incisors as a pair. "They've got two good strong lower teeth," she said. "Why wouldn't they use them both? But they don't. They just use one and not even the whole tooth. They just use part of that blade edge."

Perhaps if they used two teeth, they'd get fibres jammed between them, she mused. "I'm just imagining that having wood stuck between your teeth could be a problem," she added, making me picture beavers desperately wielding dental floss. "But maybe they don't care. Maybe there are other reasons."

Regardless of why they opt for unilateral cutting, the mechanics of the operation are now clear, thanks to Natalia's video surveillance. The beaver holds the tip of one upper incisor against the wood and employs the sharper-edged lower incisor as the cutting device, sliding it behind the top tooth. To execute this one-sided action, the beaver has to lean its cheek against the wood, or close to it, rather than attacking straight on. Natalia obligingly demonstrated the head-tilted position for me, with a slightly self-conscious giggle, and I suddenly could see why the ends of beaver-cut sticks are sharply angled.

Both *Dipoides* and *Castor* beavers have two basic woodcutting methods. When felling trees or chewing through large-diameter branches, they whittle away at the wood, removing one chip at a time. When bisecting thinner branches, they make a series of overlapping cuts, which leave characteristic impressions: a row of parallel, concave grooves on the part contacted by the curved front of the lower incisor and a matching row of convex ridges on the part shaped by the tongue-side of the tooth.

The concave grooves are the distinctive marks that I had recognized on the two sticks Natalia showed me. I had to admit, however, that I'd never noticed any beaver cuttings bearing convex ridges. That's because the wood on those parts tends to split and break off, producing a point that looks more ragged than sharp, Natalia explained. She has to train her crews to spot the sticks with the "funny, frayed ends."

Despite being more than two million years too late to shoot videos of *Dipoides* beavers, Natalia was able to analyze their technique by measuring their teeth and fossil woodwork. She found they were less capable woodcutters than their modern counterparts.

Dipoides was about two-thirds the size of *Castor canadensis*, with proportionally smaller teeth, but that wasn't its only handicap. Unlike *Castor*'s straight-edged, chisel-like incisors, *Dipoides*' front teeth were strongly rounded, necessitating more overlap between cuts. The extinct beavers also applied less of their tooth width, barely shaving the edge across the wood with each bite. If the two were to face off in a branch-cutting competition, *Castor* would easily win, severing a standard stick with fewer than four cuts. *Dipoides* would need seven or eight bites to do the job.

Natalia's woodcutting study has been a valuable aid to interpreting the hundred or so pieces of *Dipoides*-cut wood that she and her colleagues have dug out of an ancient peat deposit on Ellesmere Island in the High Arctic, a site they call the Beaver Pond. Like the stick she showed me, most of the specimens are stained dark brown from their long entombment in the peat. Otherwise, they are little changed from their original state. "You could still burn this wood," she said.

To light a match to any of it, however, would be a travesty. These are the oldest known examples of trees cut by beavers, as well as the first evidence of wood hewing by any beaver outside of the *Castor* genus, the only group that's still around. According to Natalia, that's of immense consequence. "It's sort of like finding a relative of the Hominid lineage that was making and using fires. No one had talked about *Dipoides* as being a woodcutting animal until this evidence came up, because his teeth are different and he's small and they figured he'd just be kind of like a muskrat."

The Ellesmere Island discovery is a game changer, and not just because it sheds new light on beaver evolution. It also has implications for the flora and fauna that evolved alongside beavers.

Present-day Ellesmere Island is a cold, treeless place, entirely unsuitable for beavers. Four million years ago, however, its climate was much like Labrador's, with warmer temperatures in all seasons. Thick layers of peat preserved the Beaver Pond site from its Early Pliocene heyday until it caught the attention of geologist John Gladstone Fyles in 1961, and they hold a wealth of well-preserved plant material and animal fossils. Based on these clues, paleontologists have recreated the scene in diorama-like detail. The pond, they say, stood in the middle of an open, grassy woodland of larch, spruce, pine, alder and birch. A wide variety of primitive mammals made their homes in this welcoming habitat: bears, wolverines, fishers and badgers; shrews, mice and rabbits; a small canine, a three-toed horse, a deerlet similar to the modern Siberian musk deer. And, of course, the beaver, *Dipoides*.

Natalia first visited the Beaver Pond in 1994 and has since returned four times to spend long days working under the bright Arctic summer sun on the high, windswept hill with its dazzling view of Strathcona Fiord. Over the years, she and other researchers have collected hundreds of bits of bone and tooth from the site. Cleaned, sorted and catalogued, these artifacts now reside in clear Plexiglas boxes, safely tucked away inside stacked grey metal cabinets.

Natalia led me past ranks of these units in one of the museum's high-ceilinged, fluorescent-lit storage rooms, turned down the last aisle and stopped in front of cabinet number 175. She swung the door open and slid out a drawer filled with specimens, some dating back to 1988, when Fyles found the first vertebrate fossils at the Beaver Pond site.

Paper labels inside the lids obscured the contents of most of the boxes. Natalia opened one to give me a better view. Inside, nestled on a layer of cotton batting, lay seven small bones, like sacred relics. They were mahogany-coloured and glossy, as if coated with antique varnish. Reeling off the names, she pointed to each bone as she identified it: femur, pelvis, sacrum, rib, vertebra. Pieces of a puzzle named *Dipoides*.

She lifted another lid to show me a handful of pretzel-thin ribs. "Cute, eh?" The next box contained several jaw fragments studded with teeth, including incisors that match the grooves on the pieces of gnawed wood gathered from the site. These teeth and the hieroglyphics they left behind have played an essential part in Natalia's deciphering of the beaver's complicated history.

The Castoridae originated in North America some time before the end of the Eocene epoch, about 37 million years ago, and spread to Europe and Asia by way of the Beringia land bridge. The fossil record shows that dozens of beaver species have come and gone over the millennia and that the extinct beavers were a diverse bunch. The largest was more than 60 times bigger than the smallest, and they pursued a wide variety of lifestyles. Some lived in underground burrows in arid, open habitats. Others were semiaquatic, dividing their time between land and water. But woodcutting, the activity I had always thought of as quintessential beaver behaviour, was extremely rare. Until *Dipoides* and its chewed sticks turned up on Ellesmere Island, the only beavers known for "tree-exploitation" were members of the *Castor* lineage.

What intrigued Natalia about the Ellesmere Island discovery was that *Dipoides* and *Castor* beavers share their eccentric taste for wood despite being only distantly related. As a rule, biologists don't expect a highly specialized behaviour to evolve twice. That's not, as they put it, parsimonious. A trait is far more likely to arise once, in a common ancestor, and be passed down through gradually diverging lines. And so Natalia set out to pinpoint when beavers began woodcutting by working her way back along the many branches of their family tree. The common ancestor she came up with for *Dipoides* and *Castor* is an unnamed species that lived at least 24 million years ago.

Does it really matter whether beavers first started nibbling on sticks 24 million years ago, as Natalia's research indicates, rather than a mere four million years ago, when *Dipoides* came on the scene? If you're looking at the big picture, it does, especially if those ancient beavers were building dams with their sticks.

"We know that a landscape without [modern] beavers is very different from a landscape with beavers, in terms of the hydrology and the habitats created for other animals," Natalia explained, "so it's a totally different story, evolutionarily, for everyone, not just the beaver."

From this perspective, one of the most exciting finds from the Beaver Pond site is a tangle of beaver-cut tree trunks and branches mixed with cobbles and silt, which strongly resembles the vestiges of a dam. The paleobiologists aren't quite ready to declare the aggregation a beaver dam, but if and when they gather sufficient evidence to make that assertion, it will be "a big deal." Because if *Dipoides* and *Castor* beavers are both dam-builders, this behaviour, like woodcutting, almost certainly originated with their 24-million-year-old progenitor. And the longer that beaver dams have been around, the more liable they are to have affected the evolution of a multitude of species, from aquatic invertebrates and plants to fish, amphibians and wetland-dependent birds and mammals.

There's also the potential impact on species that could be considered beaver prey. Natalia laughs when she calls beavers "tree-predators," but there's serious science behind the characterization. Many plants produce chemicals to make themselves unpalatable, and some have an array of weapons in their arsenal, each one aimed at a particular marauder. The fact that the North American beaver's favourite food-tree, the trembling aspen, responds to intense beaver cutting by sending up shoots with high concentrations of 1,3-disubstituted glycerol in the bark — and that beavers loathe the taste of 1,3-disubstituted glycerol, but not the other anti-herbivore chemicals found in aspen bark — suggests a long-standing relationship between the two adversaries.

"Those poor trees, having to defend themselves," Natalia said, surprising me. I had thought her sympathies would lie with the beavers.

In addition to helping Natalia determine when members of the beaver family likely began exploiting trees, *Dipoides* has also helped her develop a hypothesis about where and how this behaviour originated. The scenario she envisions unfolded in the high Arctic, where harsh winters became the norm during the middle of the Cenozoic era, about 25 million years ago. While many species succumbed to or fled from this new season of snow and ice, the castorids endured, probably thanks to their ability to use trees for food, housing and habitat modification. Under different circumstances, engineering with wood could have been just another bizarre evolutionary experiment that went nowhere. Instead, as the temperature dropped, it became the way of the future.

To understand how climate could have influenced beaver evolution, Natalia looked at how woodcutting enhances winter survival for *Castor canadensis*. One benefit is that it lets beavers hoard sustenance for the months when leafy greens and other choice foods are unavailable. In northern parts of their range, modern beavers build food caches every fall by floating cut branches out into deep water and leaving them to sink. The lowermost branches snag the muddy bottom and secure the raft, while the cap layer, which usually consists of second-rate fodder, stays at the surface and eventually freezes in place. Come winter, whenever hunger strikes, the beavers swim out under the ice and cut a few sticks from the stash, then take them back to the lodge for leisurely dining. The first hard frost of autumn often prompts beavers to begin constructing their caches, perhaps stirring up ancestral memories of the bitter winds that began to blow across the Arctic all those millions of years ago.

Similarly, the increasing severity of northern winters may have favoured the evolution of lodge-construction, a fantastically idiosyncratic approach to creating shelter. To build a lodge, beavers first fell a number of trees near a pond or shallow lake and buck the trunks and limbs into manageable lengths. Then — capitalizing on their ability to stay underwater for periods of up to 15 minutes — they drag these materials into the water and pile them on the bottom, shoving small sticks in between larger ones and filling the gaps with mud and debris, until the mound rises above the surface. Once the pile is sufficiently big and solid, the builders dive back down to the base and perform their most preposterous stunt: gnawing their way up into the woody mass to create an entrance tunnel and carving out their living quarters at the top. These consist of a feeding platform, located just above the waterline, and a slightly higher and roomier chamber where they will raise their kits and spend most of their indoor hours. Finally, they use their front paws to plaster the exposed exterior with mud, which will harden into a concrete-tough casing, leaving a few small holes for ventilation.

Modern beavers don't always live in lodges, though. In areas with only deep lakes or wide, undammable rivers, or when temporary accommodations are required, they make themselves at home in bank dens — simple earthen burrows excavated at the edge of a water body and accessed via the same type of underwater entrance as the classic lodge. Which raises a question: If bank dens are good enough for some beavers, how did the complex and labour-intensive alternative ever catch on? Natalia's answer is that lodges are considerably warmer than burrows and offered a pronounced advantage as the climate cooled at high latitudes during the mid-Cenozoic.

She also suspects that the long-ago big chill bolstered the development of dam-building, a behaviour unique to beavers. In warm weather, the reservoir created behind a beaver dam protects lodge occupants from terrestrial predators, extends the opportunity to get around by swimming (instead of making risky overland excursions) and supports the growth of certain preferred food plants. In winter, dams are even more critical to the beavers' survival: if their home pond freezes solid and they can't leave their lodge or reach their food cache, they're doomed. The prototype beaver dam may be long gone, but its legacy lives on in the DNA of the innovators' descendants.

A little while before I met Natalia Rybczynski, I had come across the work of another researcher who shares her esoteric interest in old pieces of beaver-chewed wood. In Bryony Coles' case, the search is for clues to our human past rather than trying to elucidate beaver evolution and ecological history. Given the overlap in their scholarly pursuits, I was sure Natalia would have heard of the British archaeologist, but she hadn't, so I filled her in and recommended Coles' book, *Beavers in Britain's Past*.

Coles, now an emeritus professor at the University of Exeter, came to the study of beavers by a roundabout route, which began as a passion for prehistoric wood. This interest was sparked in the early 1970s, as she helped extricate a Neolithic plank walkway from a waterlogged peatland known as the Somerset Levels. A few years later, while excavating a 4,500- to 5,000-year-old platform at the same site, Coles and her co-workers unearthed several pieces of willow that bore puzzling cut-marks. They resembled axe or knife facets, but couldn't be replicated with any known stone or metal blade.

Castor fiber hadn't been seen in Britain for centuries, so it took a while for anyone to consider that the mysterious markings might have been made by a beaver, and even longer to get hold of some certified beaver sticks for comparison. As soon as the sample arrived, courtesy of the Chester Zoo, Coles knew she had a match. But that was just a start. She would spend the next 25 years determining the beaver's place in Britain's past, adding to the scientific understanding of modern beavers in the process.

At one time, Eurasian beavers were common in England, Scotland and Wales and throughout continental Europe and northern Asia, but their numbers declined as humans became increasingly efficient hunters. By the Middle Ages, beaver populations had been severely reduced in most regions, and by the end of the 1700s, the species was gone from Britain. A century later, only about 1,200 Eurasian beavers remained, living in a handful of widely separated locations in Western Europe, Scandinavia, Russia and Mongolia.

Coles wanted to know more about the creators of the Somerset sticks, but *Castor fiber*'s untimely downfall had left the species practically unstudied. Geneticists had determined that the Eurasian beaver has 48 chromosomes, compared to the North American beaver's 40, and anatomists had documented a few subtle morphological differences: tail dimensions, skull volume, the shape of the nasal openings in the skull. But the field biologists had largely missed their chance to document behaviour and ecology. Rumour had it that the Eurasian beaver wasn't as much of a lumberjack as its North American cousin and never built dams or freestanding lodges. Some people even claimed that Eurasian beavers never felled trees, but Coles was skeptical. These ideas simply didn't fit with the archaeological evidence. Eventually, she decided she would have to do her own research to settle the question.

In 1997, with *Castor fiber* on the rebound in Europe, Coles launched the Beaver Works Project, centred on two thriving French beaver colonies. For the next few years, she and her hip wader–clad field crew splashed about in Brittany and the Drôme, inspecting beaver infrastructure more closely than anyone else had ever done. They employed archaeological survey methods to map territories and plot the locations of dams, lodges, bank burrows, ponds, bypass channels, canals, overland paths and feeding stations. They dismantled abandoned dams to document their form in painstaking detail, drawing each stick and stone to scale and precisely noting its position. They calculated water volumes, sketched cross-sections of channels and measured pond sediment depths. And above all, they kept trying to picture what these beaver creations would look like if they had been buried for hundreds or thousands of years.

The Beaver Works Project proved that *Castor fiber* can and does construct dams and lodges . . . under the right circumstances. Coles reckons that as hunting pressure in Great Britain, Europe and Asia increased during the Middle Ages, the beaver's survival came to depend on invisibility. Beavers that attracted attention by cutting down trees or building conspicuous structures were killed by humans. Those that foraged more discreetly, while residing in bank burrows and keeping to deep water-bodies that didn't require dams, were more likely to avoid detection. Only in fairly recent times has freedom from persecution allowed the species to reoccupy long-abandoned habitats and resume more high-profile activities.

Taking the insights gained from her French research, Coles started combing through British archaeological and historical records, in search of overlooked or misconstrued beaver evidence. She also began to develop some radical ideas about beavers.

Castor fiber has been around for about two million years (twice as long as *Castor canadensis*) and was present in Britain for most of that time. Like humans and many other animals, beavers retreated to more hospitable environs in Europe at the height of the last Ice Age and returned when the climate moderated. By about 9500 B.C., beavers were back for good.

Coles contends that up until 4000 B.C., beavers had a greater impact on Britain's landscape than humans. While two-legged hunter-gatherers were still sheltering in caves and working with stone tools, beavers were logging forests, modifying hydrological systems and enriching soils through their flooding efforts. And as they shaped the paleo-environment to their own purposes, they created habitats for a long list of other species, to which Coles has rather audaciously added our own. She believes our ancestors were drawn to beaver territories by the wealth of resources and opportunities they offered: plentiful fish and game (including the beavers themselves); dams that could be used as bridges to cross marshes or streams; and ready-made building materials.

Woodcutting was a laborious task for Stone Age, and even Bronze Age, humans, so it made sense for them to let beavers do some of the hard work. The Neolithic platform where Coles discovered her first beaver-gnawed sticks is one of several similar structures that have been found in Britain. Standing on the edge of an island in a marshy wetland, it provided a dry, elevated site for various activities. The platform builders employed both tool-cut and tooth-cut wood in its construction and may have used a collapsed beaver lodge or food cache as the foundation. Now that archaeologists know what to look for, they've found additional pieces of beaver-cut wood in other waterside platforms from the same era, as well as in wooden trackways of the same vintage.

Based on the bits of charred, tooth-marked wood excavated from several archaeological sites, Coles also suspects that ancient *Homo sapiens* burned beaver woodcuttings as fuel. By her calculations, one beaver colony's leftovers could have satisfied one prehistoric human household's firewood needs year-round, even providing woodchips for kindling.

With the rise of agriculture, humans definitely began exploiting another beaver resource: the fertile meadows that were left behind when beavers abandoned their dams and moved on to new territory or when old ponds filled with sediment. Farmers also may have planted crops near active beaver territories so overflow and seepage could help water their fields. It's even possible, Coles speculates, that creative thinkers adapted beaver canals to better serve their irrigation needs and that "some aspects of human water engineering may have been prompted by observation of beaver activity." Humans learning from beavers, in other words.

Likewise, beavers may have helped us figure out the art of coppicing (repeatedly chopping down certain types of trees, such as willow, oak, ash or hazel, to encourage the rapid growth of new stems that grow long and straight, with few side branches). The flexible young shoots produced by coppiced trees are ideal for weaving into baskets, fences and fish traps, while older, sturdier shoots make excellent tool and weapon handles, building poles and walking sticks. Given how common coppiced trees and shrubs are in beaver territories, it's easy to imagine, as Coles has done, that the first people to try this form of woodland management were imitating the original practitioners.

Coles' other provocative (and humbling) conclusion is that it's always going to be tough to distinguish between beaver works and some of the evidence left behind by our own predecessors, because "much of what early hominids achieved" — at least in terms of erecting structures and manipulating the environment — "is within the capabilities of a beaver family."

"It is possible," she wrote, "that, in an archaeological context, the activities of beavers might be misinterpreted as due to humans, and vice versa." That's because, in pre-agricultural times, the two species were both working on the same scale and using the same materials, namely wood, earth and stone.

When I told Natalia about the prehistoric British beavers that had fooled generations of archaeologists, she laughed, but not unkindly. She knows all too well how hard it can be to read those ancient sticks.

Once we had finished with *Dipoides*, we moved on to my other reason for visiting the Canadian Museum of Nature's warehouse, a desire to meet the biggest castorid of all time. *Castoroides*, commonly known as the giant beaver, inhabited North America during the Pleistocene epoch, a period dominated by outsized mammals. These über-beavers appeared on the scene about 1.4 million years ago and departed about 10,000 years ago. They shared the stage with short-faced bears that would have towered over today's largest grizzlies, ground sloths the size of oxen, mastodons, mammoths and sabre-toothed cats. From Florida to the northern Yukon and from New Brunswick to Nebraska, giant beavers wallowed about in swampy habitats across much of the continent. They were particularly abundant just south of the Great Lakes.

Physically, *Castoroides* was like *Castor canadensis* on steroids. A typical modern adult North American beaver is about one metre long from nose to tail tip and weighs 16 to 32 kilograms, about the same weight as a Labrador retriever. The largest giant beavers boasted a total length of about 2.5 metres — almost as long as a Smart car — and a St. Bernard–like mass of at least 60 to 100 kilograms. Some experts figure they may have weighed as much as 200 kilograms, comparable to a large black bear.

Natalia began her paleobiology career under the tutelage of one of the world's foremost authorities on giant beavers, the now-retired Richard Harington, and has been hanging around the Canadian Museum of Nature fossil collections ever since she was in high school in the late '80s. Yet she seemed just as excited as I was when we got to the *Castoroides* cabinets. Although the museum doesn't own a giant beaver fossil skeleton or even a complete skull, it has scads of teeth, many of them collected by Harington himself. Natalia pulled out a drawer filled with dental specimens in Plexiglas boxes and stepped aside so I could peek in. "Aren't they cool?" she said, grinning.

Indeed they were. Mottled in shades of rust and black, the massive, blunt-tipped incisors looked like weathered cast-iron railway spikes that had been heated in a forge and gently bowed, then engraved with a corduroy pattern of narrow, longitudinal ribs. They were as heavy as iron, too, or so it seemed when Natalia let me hold one for a moment.

Measuring up to 15 centimetres long — the length of a dollar bill — these incisors are awe-inspiring, yet paleontologists remain uncertain as to how they were deployed. Some maintain that they weren't sharp enough for woodcutting. Others argue that this must have been their purpose, since *Castoroides* was closely related to *Dipoides* and descended from the same common ancestor that also gave rise to the *Castor* lineage. Unfortunately, there's no concrete evidence that giant beavers shared their relatives' tree-exploiting habits. The smoking gun would be a piece of chewed wood with marks that match the titan's teeth. And so far, nobody's claims to have found such an item have been substantiated.

Ultimately, the solution to this mystery may come from the giant beavers themselves. A few years ago, Michigan State University paleoecologist Catherine Yansa and University of Wisconsin-Whitewater geographer Peter Jacobs radiocarbon-dated dentine from a *Castoroides* tooth and found carbon isotope values that suggest its owner mostly ate submerged aquatic plants. Their results haven't convinced everyone that giant beavers didn't use their teeth for grander feats, but they have enlivened the debate and offered a different way of looking at *Castoroides*.

According to Yansa, these pondweed-gorgers were influential within their communities, but as large-volume nutrient recyclers, rather than tree-felling dam builders. "Ecologically," she says, "the giant beavers were like little hippos."

One certainty is that the modern North American beaver is not a descendent of its hulking relative. *Castor canadensis* made its debut about one million years ago, long before *Castoroides* faded into oblivion. The two frequented the same kinds of forested habitats and perhaps even paddled about in the same waters, but unlike the enigmatic giant beaver, Pleistocene-age *Castor* left proof of its woodcutting proficiency — and its engineering skills.

In the summer of 2005, Natalia, along with a Yukon government paleontologist and a student assistant, made a unique discovery during a fossil-hunting expedition along the Old Crow River in the Yukon Territory, a region renowned for its Pleistocene treasures. While walking across a gravel bar below an eroding riverbank, the trio noticed an odd-looking accumulation of wood protruding from the exposed sediments. The sticks, embedded in a matrix of ancient mud, formed a pyramid-shaped structure that measured about four metres wide at the base. They scrambled up the bank for a closer look and found that much of the wood bore signs of beaver chewing. What they were looking at, they realized, was a remarkably intact fossil beaver dam. Its builders had even incorporated a couple of woolly mammoth foot-bones at the base, the same way modern beavers often place stones in their dams for reinforcement.

Natalia took some of the tooth-marked sticks back to Ottawa and added them to her growing collection at the national museum. She subsequently determined that they're 100,000 to 125,000 years old and were produced by a *Castor* beaver, either *Castor canadensis* or some other member of the genus that has since died out. The Old Crow dam remnants may not be as old or as exotic as the *Dipoides* woodcuttings from Ellesmere Island, but they're an important part of Natalia's ongoing quest to figure out how beavers ended up being as behaviourally "weird" — her word — as they are today.

Castor canadensis may be weird, but no beaver species, living or dead, can match the bizarre habits of *Paleocastor* (which was not represented in the museum's collection, because it never lived north of the forty-ninth parallel). This prairie dog–sized beaver inhabited grasslands in the area of Nebraska, Wyoming and South Dakota about 22 million years ago. Like many primitive castorids, it was an underground burrower, but instead of excavating straight shafts or meandering passageways like the others, *Paleocastor* dug spiral tunnels that drove directly down to their underground dens, two to three metres below the surface. Amazingly, as a result of invading plant roots and silica-rich groundwater, some of these tunnels were preserved as trace fossils: solid, sand-filled tubes that look like enormous pieces of uncooked fusilli pasta.

University of Kansas paleontologist Larry D. Martin examined more than 1,000 *Paleocastor* burrows during his 40-year career, starting in the early 1970s. Based on claw and tooth marks scribbled onto the tunnel walls, he eventually concluded that the beavers scraped away the dirt with their incisors and shovelled it backwards up to the surface with their paws. The diggers were ambidextrous — about half of their burrows twist to the right and half to the left — but once they started in one direction, they were committed. "A burrowing beaver," Martin once remarked in the pages of *Natural History* magazine, "must have fixed its hind feet on the axis of the spiral and literally screwed itself straight down into the ground."

The first scientist to assess these fossils, geologist Erwin Hinkley Barbour, didn't have a clue what he was looking at. In 1891, a Nebraska rancher invited Barbour to check out the strange helical formations found in the Niobrara River valley's eroding cliffs. The locals called these curiosities "devil's corkscrews." Barbour grandly renamed them Daemonelix and pronounced them the remains of enormous freshwater sponges. A few years later, he changed his mind and decided they were casts of some unknown plant's immense taproots. The Nebraska rancher would have gotten much closer to the truth of the devil's corkscrews if he had asked his Lakota Sioux neighbours for their opinion.

Long ago, according to the Lakotas, Water Monsters called *Unktehi* dominated the world. Eventually, these monsters' destructive ways prompted the Thunder Beings to hurl bolts of lightning at them and blast them into stone, but death did not completely defeat the Water Monsters' malevolent power. Evil people learned to use the fossilized *Unktehi* bones to "sting" their enemies, bewitching them or making them fall sick. At that point, the Thunder Beings stepped in again and asked the animals if any of them would give up their lives to counteract the bad medicine of the *Unktehi* bones. When the spiral-tunnelling beavers volunteered, the Thunder Beings turned their bones and burrows to stone, so they would be forever present as a protective force. The Lakota name for the devil's corkscrews was *Ca'pa el ti*: "Beavers' Lodges."

Barbour had noticed fossilized *Paleocastor* skeletons entombed within some of his Daemonelix, but he dismissed their importance. It would be several years before his successors grasped what the Lakotas already understood and more than a decade before the scientific world gave the prehistoric beaver due credit for the fossils.

Just as the Lakota Sioux knew enough about mammalian anatomy to identify *Paleocastor* as a beaver, despite its diminutive stature and subterranean habits, indigenous peoples who stumbled upon *Castoroides* fossils — including those who used the huge incisors as carving tools or wore them as amulets — would have recognized their beaver origins.

Many First Nations have myths and legends about fearsome gargantuan animals that lived long ago: owls large enough to snatch up grown men; monster bears that could chase down all but the swiftest runner; colossal elk that devoured humans; and behemoth beavers that created their own forms of havoc. Adrienne Mayor, a Stanford University research scholar and the author of *Fossil Legends of the First Americans*, believes that stories like these were inspired by the petrified bones of vanished animals. Long before European paleontologists showed up, indigenous North Americans were familiar with fossils and recognized similarities to the bones of living species, she says, which is why extinct animals sometimes appear in traditional First Nations stories.

Mayor also acknowledges the possibility that some of these stories, especially those about giant beavers, may reflect more than just expertise in fossil interpretation. After all, *Castoroides* and North America's earliest human residents shared the continent for many centuries. Maybe these tales actually contain scraps of firsthand knowledge of the long-extinct animals — "a kind of fossil memory," to quote folklorist Jane C. Beck, who was the first to champion this idea.

To illustrate her hypothesis, Beck cited a story told by the Maliseet people of present-day New Brunswick and Maine, in which a giant beaver's towering dam causes massive flooding; when the hero Gluskap tries to catch the perpetrator, the beaver flees eastward, eventually damming the St. Lawrence River and forming the Great Lakes. It is just one of many examples of giant beavers featuring in First Nations lore.

On the opposite side of the continent, in what is now Montana, Kootenai tradition holds that the Flathead River was created by a dam-building giant beaver that reconfigured Flathead Lake. Meanwhile, the Dunne-za of northern British Columbia and Alberta, and the Dene to the north, were being terrorized by predatory giant beavers.

One of the Dene's most important stories recalls a time long ago when giant beavers living in Sahtú (now known as Great

Bear Lake) were constantly harassing their ancestors. The beavers would swim close to canoes and smack the water with their tails, tipping the vessels and causing many people to drown. When the supernatural medicine man Yamoría heard about this situation, he chased the hooligans downstream and killed them. Afterwards, he skinned three of these giant beavers and nailed their hides to the south face of Bear Rock Mountain, above Deh Cho (the Mackenzie River) near Fort Norman, establishing a conspicuous landmark that the Dene have revered ever since.

Clearly, the giant beavers that appear in most of the legends were not strictly modelled on the prehistoric species, but any narrative passed down through so many generations is bound to include some revisions. Besides, mythmakers never let the facts get in their way. If we peel away the symbolism and spirituality of the First Nations giant beaver stories, what we're left with is this: the dizzying possibility of an unbroken chain of spoken words that stretches more than 10,000 years into the past. Like four-million-year-old sticks, fossil legends are an eloquent reminder that beavers have been a powerful force on this continent for a very long time.

·Three·
THE HUNTER
AND THE HUNTED

We don't know precisely when North America gained its first human residents, but we can safely say that *Homo sapiens* and *Castor canadensis* originally met at least 15,000 years ago and that we have a long and intimate history as predator and prey. Five hundred years ago, the nature of this relationship changed dramatically, as foreign economic incentives and technology rewrote the rules of engagement. For both the hunter and the hunted, the consequences were severe.

The traditional beliefs of North America's First Nations, which are as varied as the people with whom they originated, share an overarching worldview. This foundational perspective emphasizes interdependence, informed by the knowledge that all entities have power that can either help or hinder humans. In some cultures, including those of the Tlingit, Tsimshian, Haida, Huron-Wendat, Haudenosaunee, Anishinaabe, Menominee and Mojave, beavers were — and are — linked to clans or similar social divisions. Other peoples simply regarded beavers as part of a cosmology in which every living and nonliving thing was imbued with spirit.

Most, if not all, groups had species-specific precepts governing the treatment of prey remains, which served as a kind of social contract: animals would willingly give themselves up to hunters who demonstrated respect for their prey by following the rules and would withhold themselves from anyone who violated them. An obligation to return beaver bones to the water was common, as was a belief in some form of reincarnation.

Some of the most valuable insights into the pre-colonial relationship between humans and beavers come to us through stories that have been passed down and preserved against all odds. This one, told by the Omaha, serves as a protocol reminder, as well as explains a peculiar anatomical feature of beavers.

One time, the story goes, the trickster Ictinike went to visit his wife's grandfather, the Beaver. The Beavers had no food to serve him, so their youngest child volunteered to be eaten. The Beaver killed his son and the Beaver's wife dutifully boiled the body. As she placed the meal before their guest, the Beaver warned Ictinike that he mustn't break any of the bones. No one noticed when the perpetual troublemaker bit down hard on one small bone and cracked it in two. After the meal, the Beaver gathered the bones, wrapped them in a skin and plunged them into the water outside the lodge. Moments later, the youngster emerged from the pond, miraculously whole and alive. His father asked how he was. Fine, he replied, except that Ictinike's careless chewing had broken one of his toes. Since then, all beavers — *zhábe* to the Omaha — have had one split toe on each hind foot.

In the Anishinaabe story, "The Woman Who Married a Beaver," the woman's *amik*-husband and children repeatedly go off with humans and are killed by them, yet never really die. The husband and children are fond of the humans and visit them often, returning home each time laden with gifts of tobacco, clothing, pots and knives. But the woman is forbidden to go with them. Eventually, her husband passes on (presumably from old age), and she goes back to live with her own people, bearing the message that they must never speak ill of a beaver. Those who observe this injunction will be well loved by the beavers and able to kill them whenever they need to, she says. Contempt will lead to hunting failure.

Relationship is at the heart of both of these parables, a cross-species bond that is almost unfathomable to those of us not brought up in a world where the boundaries between human and non-human are semi-permeable. Hoping to understand it better, I went to meet a woman who had her own stories to tell.

One of Ida Calmegane's favourite Tlingit songs includes the line, "We will open again this box of wisdom left in our care." As I sat in her living room in the southern Yukon village of Tagish, I felt like she had opened her box of wisdom just for me, and I was grateful for that honour.

Born on October 21, 1928, Ida is the snowy-haired matriarch of the Tlingit Deisheetaan clan and a repository of a vast amount of traditional knowledge. I had come to see her, because the beaver, *s'igèdí* in Tlingit, is the Deisheetaan crest animal.

Entering the Calmeganes' living room was like walking into a family reunion. Framed photographs of children, grandchildren, great-grandchildren, elders, siblings, cousins and adopted clan members filled the walls: department store portraits; snapshots of hunters skinning caribou; proud capped-and-gowned university graduates; uniformed sports teams lined up in orderly rows; a serene baby nestled in Santa Claus' arms. The heat radiating from the woodstove was welcome on this cool May morning, but the greatest warmth in the room came from Ida herself, a short, comfortably plump 83-year-old with a gentle voice and a down-to-earth manner that immediately put me at ease.

Once we were settled side by side on the blanket-covered couch, I asked Ida if she could explain what the beaver means to the Deisheetaan. "I'll try," she replied, and she launched into a story about her maternal great-great-great-grandmother, a Tlingit woman from the village of Angoon on Admiralty Island, just south of present-day Juneau, Alaska. It was a long time before she even mentioned the word "beaver."

"This Alaska chief had four daughters and didn't want them to marry locally, so they married inland," Ida began. One daughter went to Telegraph Creek, on the Stikine River in what is now British Columbia. The other three went to Tagish, Teslin and Ross River in the Yukon. Ida's ancestor was "the one that got married to here, to Tagish," a phrase that embraced both the place and the people. The four unions reinforced well-established relationships between the coastal Tlingit and their inland trading partners. They also forged lasting cultural bonds. "You follow your mother's clan," Ida explained, as she concluded her story. "That's how we became Deisheetaan."

The Tagish and the Tlingit both organize their societies on the basis of matrilineal descent. Everyone is born into their mother's moiety and is expected to marry into the opposite kinship division. The Tagish call the two moieties Wolf and Crow (or sometimes Raven) and recognize six clans within them: Daklaweidi and Yan Yedi in the Wolf moiety; Deisheetaan, Ganaxtedi, Kookhittaan and Ishkahittan in Crow. Ida's great-great-great-grandmother's name has been forgotten, but not the identity she brought with her from the coast.

In the late 1890s, the Klondike gold rush transformed this corner of the world, sweeping across the land with the speed and ferocity of an out-of-control wildfire. As the stampede gathered momentum, Ida's grandparents, Maria and Tagish John, moved to Dyea, Alaska, the jumping-off point for fortune-seekers heading to the gold fields by way of the Chilkoot Trail. The arduous 53-kilometre-long trail up the precipitous Chilkoot Pass and over the Coast Mountains to the headwaters of the Yukon River had long been a First Nations trade route. Klondikers who lacked the muscle to shoulder their own gear and supplies or the patience to make the many trips required to move it all up the trail, hired Tlingit and Tagish men and women to carry their packs, either to the summit or the entire distance. Ida's grandparents were young and strong and knew a good opportunity when they saw it.

"Grandma used to talk about it all the time. She said they'd go in the morning, and they would come back in the evening, because they were coming back without any packs. She said 'There was easy money!'" Ida smiled and drew out the word "easy," the way Maria must have done when she told the story. "They got 50 cents a pound, and knowing Grandma, she would have at least taken 100 pounds, I think, so that would be 50 dollars a load, and they went just about every day for about six weeks or so."

Later, looking at a photograph of Maria on Ida's wall, I could hardly imagine that tiny woman carrying such loads. But the weight of the stampeders' packs was nothing compared to the emotional burden she would soon have to bear. In 1897, she had four children: a four- or five-year-old, a set of three-year-old twins and an infant who was about eight months old. Whenever she was on the trail, she left her brood in her mother's care, not realizing the danger they were exposed to in Dyea. Along with easy money, the outsiders had also brought deadly foreign viruses to the north.

"That fall, her babies all died." Ida paused and repeated the words, softly, with an edge of sadness that erased the 115 years that had elapsed since the event. "Yeah, her babies all died."

At the same time, significant cultural losses were also slamming every First Nations community within reach of the Klondike. Not everyone who came north was in pursuit of gold. Some, including the Anglican missionaries who set up in Carcross, near Tagish, in 1901, were prospecting for souls. Convinced that it was their Christian duty to rescue the Indians from their primitive religions, the evangelists didn't hesitate to eliminate symbols of those beliefs. In Tagish, two important buildings may have been among the casualties.

Before the gold rush, Ida told me, Tagish boasted two wooden clan houses, each fronted by a pole displaying the relevant moiety and clan figures: Wolf and Eagle for the Daklaweidi; Raven and Beaver for the Deisheetaan. According to the stories Ida had heard, "The Anglican Church, when they started, they tore the clan houses down and then later on they used the logs for firewood. Because they didn't understand the culture, you know, and they thought that people were worshipping the animals." The actual relationship was incomprehensible to minds moulded by nineteenth-century Christianity.

"We believe that there's a spirit in everything," Ida said, "and that's where the missionaries made a mistake. They tried to make us into different people."

After they lost their first family, Maria and Tagish John moved back to Tagish and had six more children, four of whom reached adulthood. The third child was Ida's mother, Angela, born in 1902. Angela John, later Angela Sidney, lived to 89 and was one of the last fluent speakers of Tagish. For decades, she worked tirelessly to preserve her people's language and culture, receiving the Order of Canada in 1986 for her efforts. Ida's own knowledge of Tagish and Tlingit traditions owes much to her mother's inspiring influence. It is also grounded in her grandmother's teachings.

At birth, Ida explained, she was given Maria's two Tlingit names: Ła.oos Tláa and Ḵaax̱'anshi. "Because I had her names, she really took an interest in my upbringing. She talked to me about medicines, and she used to take me out when I was just that big" — Ida held out her hand, a little above knee height — "before I started school. We used to go running our snares every day, early in the morning after breakfast."

The doting grandmother showed her namesake how to set snares for rabbits and squirrels and how to skin the animals they caught. And every night, she told bedtime stories to young Ida and her siblings. Much of the time, she talked to them in Tagish, while other family members generally spoke Tlingit.

Before Ida left home to attend the nearby residential school, she was proficient in both languages. Once there, her older sisters made sure she never forgot about the school's English-only rule. "Whenever I came up to them, the first thing they said to me was 'Don't talk Indian.'" She was never beaten for slipping into her mother tongue, but she knew children who were. Back at home during school holidays, Ida's opportunities for speaking Tagish were limited as her grandmother often stayed with other relatives. Eventually, all of her Tagish words slipped away, and she stopped speaking the language altogether.

Ida hung onto her Tlingit language-skills, however, and grew up proud of her heritage, due in large part to her father. Although he was Daklaweidi, George Sidney regularly reminded his children of their matrilineal pedigree. "When we came home to visit, Dad always talked to us and he always told us, you got to remember you're Deisheetaan, you got really good blood. And he'd tell us who our ancestors were. He'd just go right down: you are the great-great-great-granddaughter of the biggest chief on the coast, he said, and he would tell us who that was. And he said, you've got to remember that and you've got to behave like good people."

As we talked, my eyes kept returning to Ida's necklace, which featured a palm-sized figure carved out of wood and overlaid with bone (or perhaps mammoth-tusk ivory, which northern gold miners regularly unearth). It had six legs and a longitudinally divided tail, but it was obviously a beaver, shown from a topside perspective. I had admired the necklace when I arrived, and Ida had told me it originally belonged to her mother. Then our conversation moved on, before I could ask about the unusual anatomy. Finally, the discussion came back around to clan crests, and Ida told me her story of the Deisheetaan beaver.

"The people were really hungry," she said. "They couldn't find any game. It was cold, and you know when you walk on the snow it makes a big noise, and they couldn't sneak up to anything, so they were all starving. And the chief of the clan went out himself, and he set a net for beaver. He set the net up across this creek and caught this beaver. Just two claws on each hand was caught in the net. And he went over there and that beaver tried talking to him. He was a medicine man and he was head of the clan too. And that beaver started talking to him and told him 'If you let me go, I'm going to give you good luck.'"

She hesitated momentarily. "I'm not really sure about that part. I'm not sure if he killed him or not. But anyway, that beaver had two tails — the tail was split like that." She gestured towards her necklace. "And his claws was gold, he had golden claws. That was a special beaver. And he told [the chief], from now on, this is going to be your crest; you're going to use this crest. And that's why inland Deisheetaan people, we use that split-tail beaver."

Later, she elaborated, explaining that the beaver gave the chief explicit instructions about where to find caribou and advised him to feed his people bowls of boiled caribou blood before giving them any meat, since they hadn't eaten solid food for so long. "So he did everything he was supposed to do, and he saved that whole tribe."

When Ida finished recounting the story, she asked if I wanted to see her vest. Of course I did, so off she went to find it. A few minutes later, she emerged from her bedroom wearing a magnificent red blanket-style vest over her black T-shirt. A line of lustrous white buttons ran along the bottom, up the front edges and around the neck. A stylized black raven's wing, outlined in sequins, was appliquéd to each front panel. On the back, a brown beaver extended from Ida's shoulder blades to her waist. Opalescent sequins bordered its outstretched form; brown beading gave it claws, eyes and whiskers; and pale beads sketched a crosshatched pattern across the two tails. Like the beaver on her necklace, this one had an extra pair of hind limbs. "Why six legs?" I asked, but she didn't know. That's just how it always is.

I had read that the Deisheetaan also have a song about the beaver. "My cousin Mark can sing that really good," Ida said, when I asked her about it. "I know it a little bit." But when she tried to sing the song for me, the words wouldn't come to her, so we talked about other things for a while. Song ownership, for one. Only the Deisheetaan can sing the beaver song, she explained. "We sing it when we have a potlatch" — a ceremonial gathering featuring gift giving, feasting and storytelling through song and dance.

As we chatted, Ida was reminded of a song that had belonged to her father, written for him by her uncle. "We were supposed to go there at Christmastime one year and we never made it," she recalled. "My uncle was really very fond of my father, and because we never came that time, he made that song for my dad. It says . . ."

Suddenly, she switched from speaking in English to singing in Tlingit, her voice clear and strong, her body motionless and her gaze directed straight ahead, as though focused on a point far beyond the living-room wall. The song lasted barely a minute, but when it ended, I was so enthralled that all I could manage was mumbled thanks.

"I never sing that song to just anybody," Ida said, "but I just thought I'd sing it to you."

After translating her father's song for me, line by line, she sang another. However, since the beaver song continued to elude her, she suggested we listen to a recording of her older brother singing it, to get her started. She dug through a stack of old CDs, holding them out so I could read the labels that confounded her aging eyes, until we found "Songs sung by Pete Sidney recorded 1992."

If Ida's singing voice was water, a pristine northern lake glinting in the sun, Pete's was pine smoke, or rather the memory of pine smoke, woven into the fabric of an old plaid jacket. As he sang, she interpreted some of the lyrics and filled in the storylines. "*This is my father's country*, he says, *it's okay if I die here*." And during another: "That guy who made that song, he was in love with a Raven girl. He's saying, *I'm going to go to bed now and they're going to hear me crying there*." Near the end of the recording, Pete sang a few numbers in English: "Big Rock Candy Mountain" and "Yodelling Cowboy" and a love ballad that I didn't recognize. But the beaver song wasn't there.

Nevertheless, listening to Pete's CD had brought it back to Ida. She sat up tall and started singing with the same intense concentration as the first time. Part of her seemed to be somewhere else, drawing the carefully enunciated words and the rising and falling notes out of the past.

When she finished, she turned to me and began the tricky task of rendering Tlingit words and concepts into English. "They say, *my uncles, they made a,* um, *a clearing space. This beaver, somebody caught this baby beaver and tamed it and they used to let it out and it used to swim around out in front of their place. And then, you know they always like to dig and stuff, and here that little beaver, he start digging underneath the town. He dug all out underneath the town and one day, he,* um, *he slapped his tail"* — she clapped her hands — "*and the whole town fell in the lake and everybody drowned, eh.* That's what they say. And that's the beaver song."

This beaver-generated catastrophe, I found out later in our conversation, occurred at a place called Basket Bay. Following the flood, the survivors — there were some, after all — moved to Angoon, the eventual birthplace of Ida's great-great-great-grandmother. There was a lot of history in that beaver song. A song that a long-ago Tlingit bride had carried from the coast and taught to her children. A song that has survived starvation winters and devastating epidemics, narrow-minded missionaries and potlatch-banning governments. I was deeply touched by Ida's generosity in sharing it with me.

Like the beaver song, Ida's story about how the beaver became the Deisheetaan clan animal also held a lot of history, hearkening back to the time when animals talked to humans, as well as highlighting a method of beaver hunting that was once common all across North America. Less than a month after my visit with Ida, I found myself at the Canadian Museum of Civilization, in Ottawa, looking at exactly the kind of net that had captured the golden-clawed beaver.

The museum has far more artifacts than it can publicly display at any one time, so I had arranged for a behind-the-scenes look at a selection of beaver-related items that were normally in storage. On a sweltering late-June day, Collections Information Liaison Nathalie Guénette ushered me into the viewing room, where a gust of artificially cooled air, spiked with the smoky smell of tanned hides, welcomed us. It was the antithesis of a regular museum gallery; just a stark, brightly lit space with the articles I had asked to see laid out on folding tables. A typed catalogue card accompanied each item.

The museum's collection of beaver nets includes examples made by Cree, Algonquin, Dene and Tahltan peoples. The one I'd chosen to examine came from Northern Tutchone territory in the central Yukon, not far from Ida's home. I wasn't allowed to touch any of the artifacts, but Guénette could. With gloved hands, she partly unwrapped the bulky roll of century-old caribou-skin cord from its protective plastic wrapping and spread it across the table.

Although there wasn't room to extend the net to its full two-by-three-metre span, I could see how the net-maker had configured the thin rawhide strips into a loose lattice, secured by small, tight knots. A bone toggle threaded onto one cord reminded me of a domino: a smooth rectangle with angled corners and a pattern of reddened lines and dots cut into one face. A couple of caribou hooves were also tied to the net; their purpose, the collector had noted, was to "rattle as soon as the beaver moves the net and warn the hunter that the beaver is there, as he has to be pulled out very quickly or he bites his way out of the net."

In parts of eastern North America, the cordage for beaver nets was made from plant fibres, but regardless of materials, all of the versions were used in similar ways. In winter, hunters chopped holes in the ice to place their nets in the water, often baiting them with aspen branches. Sometimes, they placed them in front of lodge exits and broke into the house to drive out the inhabitants. As soon as a beaver swam into the net and became entangled, the hunter pulled it to the surface and dispatched the animal with a club or other weapon.

Chopping a hole in a beaver lodge, a structure built to defy bears, wolverines and wolves as well as humans, is no easy undertaking, particularly in winter, when the mud-plastered exterior is frozen. Bank dens, however, often have relatively thin roofs. Hunters living in some areas, including western Manitoba and around Lake Superior, used keen-nosed dogs to detect beavers hiding in bank dens. Others looked for subtle signs of occupancy, such as ripples near the entrance. Once they had located their quarry, they blocked the opening with stakes and hacked through the roof of the burrow. They then either clubbed or speared the beaver or reached in and grabbed it with a crooked stick or — incredibly — with their hands. Severe bite wounds were an occupational risk.

Traditional beaver-hunting technology also included traps, and the museum had models of two kinds. One, made in 1912, was a scaled-down version of a Huron deadfall trap, used for catching beavers on land. The other was a small wooden replica of a *kuatagen*, created by a James Bay Cree man in 1962. According to the catalogue card, this type of trap was "used when [a] hunter has no beaver net." It consisted of a semicircle of sticks driven into the bottom of the pond to create an underwater palisade, with a carefully positioned trigger stick set near the back of the curve; a plank door would fall into place when an unsuspecting beaver swam into the trap and bumped the trigger. I stared at it for several minutes, awed by the knowledge and skill that went into building and operating such a system.

Throughout North America, indigenous peoples killed beavers for meat and fur, and often used other body parts as well; how important beavers were to a particular group's diet and material culture depended on their availability. Archaeological evidence of this predator-prey relationship includes the knife-scarred bones of beavers butchered 3,700 years ago and fragments of beaver pelt wrapped around a copper axe in a 2,500-year-old burial mound, both unearthed near Lake Huron. The chances of finding any older relics are remote, since all animal remains eventually decay into oblivion unless mummified, fossilized, frozen into the permafrost or preserved by contact with copper objects or campfire ash.

Still, we can reasonably assume that beaver hunting goes back to the earliest days of human presence on the continent. For one thing, beaver is premium fare. Not only does it provide three times more calories than most other red meats, its fattiness offers spin-off benefits. In the absence of fats or carbohydrates, humans can't properly assimilate the protein in the lean flesh of animals such as caribou and moose, so fat-rich beaver meat — roasted, boiled or smoked — was likely a critical food for many people, especially in winter and early spring, when most other animals are at their leanest.

The museum artifacts I had selected for my private viewing represented only a small sampling of indigenous uses of this versatile animal, but they made me realize how central beavers were to many First Nations cultures. An Ojibwa beaver-bone tool for making cord. A Dogrib wood-handled chisel for snowshoe frame construction, fashioned from a piece of beaver jawbone with the incisors still in place. A set of Coast Salish beaver-tooth gambling dice. A Dunne-za necklace of nearly 50 translucent, sepia-toned beaver claws strung onto cotton thread, with yellow glass seed beads as spacers. A Chipewyan bag for carrying meat and bannock, stitched out of caribou hide and the soft skin of a beaver kit. A Tahltan ground-squirrel fur head-band adorned with dangling beaver-pelt pendants. Hats and mitts made in whole or part from beaver fur, and fur-trimmed footwear in a range of styles. A Nlaka'pamux boy's winter belt, a kind of kidney warmer, consisting of a broad section of beaver pelt and four hide ties to snug it around the waist. Each object spoke uniquely to the long association between humans and beavers on this continent.

With the arrival of the fur-mad strangers from across the water, beaver pelts took on new significance for the continent's original citizens. The transformation began slowly in the late 1400s, as French, Portuguese, Spanish and English cod fisher-men and whalers ventured into the waters off the east coast of North America and engaged in casual trade with people they met, exchanging knives and other small items for furs. Although these transactions were merely a sideline, the seafarers found eager buyers with ready cash whenever they returned to their home ports. Before long, ships were sailing across the ocean spe-cifically to load up with New World furs, notably beaver, which was highly sought after for making hats.

As the fur trade moved inland, more and more First Nations were sucked into the vortex of the mercantile imperialism that propelled it. Those who lived close to trading hubs participated either as producers who obtained pelts through their own hunting and trapping efforts or as intermediaries who travelled to remote areas and purchased furs, which they then sold to the Europeans. But the fur frontier was never static. The obliteration of local beaver populations constantly pushed the leading edges westward and northward (and southward, though to a lesser extent, since southern beaver pelts were of lower quality). As well, European traders who resented giving up any profits to First Nations middlemen started moving into the hinterland and dealing with the suppliers directly.

By the early 1600s, the French, English and Dutch all controlled significant fur-trading operations in North America and were engaged in fierce competition with each other. Their rivalries fuelled hostility between their various indigenous trading partners, aggravating pre-existing animosities and creating new ones. Among the most dramatic manifestations of this political upheaval were the Beaver Wars, a series of seventeenth-century conflicts also known as the Iroquois Wars or the French and Iroquois Wars. While the fighting had multiple causes, it was fundamentally a struggle for control over resource wealth, with the resource in question being beaver pelts. For nearly 40 years, starting in 1628, members of the Dutch-allied — and later, English-allied — Iroquois (Haudenosaunee) Confederacy, which then included the Mohawk, Oneida, Onondaga, Cayuga and Seneca, repeatedly attacked the Huron-Wendat and other nations that supported the French fur trade. By the time the hostilities ceased, the Haudenosaunee had devastated, dispersed or absorbed most of their First Nations neighbours. Meanwhile, the British had ousted the Dutch from their New Netherlands colony and renamed it New York.

The end of the 1600s saw the rise of the *coureurs de bois*, independent, itinerant French traders who travelled deep into the interior in search of furs, as well as the founding of what would eventually become the dominant North American fur-trading enterprise. In 1670, England's King Charles II issued a royal charter that established the Hudson's Bay Company — more formally designated "the Governor and Company of Adventurers of England, Trading into Hudson's Bay" — and awarded its bearers exclusive trading rights to the entire Hudson Bay drainage basin, a territory known as Rupert's Land. In exchange, any time the king or his heirs and successors entered Rupert's Land, the company was to hand over two black beavers and two elk. Neither Charles II nor his immediate followers ever ventured across the Atlantic to collect this nominal rent. In fact, the first time the HBC was required to pay up was in 1927, when the Prince of Wales stopped in Winnipeg en route to his cattle ranch in Alberta.

Rupert's Land encompassed nearly 40 percent of what now constitutes Canada, but it took a while for the company to reap the benefits of this largesse and rise to the top of the business. With France refusing to recognize England's right to dish out such deals, the Hudson's Bay Company and its French rivals vied continuously for territory and furs until the signing of the Treaty of Paris in 1763. After that, traders of Scottish and English descent took over the French system and competition intensified. The North West Company, created in 1779, soon emerged as the Hudson's Bay Company's most formidable opponent and the struggle for supremacy lasted until 1821, when the two finally amalgamated under the older firm's name.

Other corporate players in the North American fur trade during the eighteenth and nineteenth centuries included the

Montreal-based Michilimackinac Company; John Jacob Astor's American Fur Company and its subsidiary, the Pacific Fur Company; the Missouri Fur Company, which operated out of Spanish-ruled St. Louis, on the Mississippi River; and numerous smaller ventures.

Except for the predominantly white "Mountain Men" (autonomous trappers who plundered the American Rocky Mountain region from 1825 to 1840, congregating once a year to sell their furs and replenish their supplies at a gathering known as a rendezvous), the hunters and trappers who supplied beaver and other pelts to these companies were mainly aboriginal or Metis. Some participated enthusiastically, others grudgingly, in response to forces beyond their control. Regardless of their motivation, in the end they all suffered similar consequences, for few of the advantages that individuals and communities gained from their involvement in the fur trade were lasting.

At first, the economic benefits of the fur trade went to those on both sides of the transactions, and even favoured the suppliers at times. In 1634, a Montagnais (Innu) acquaintance of Father Paul Le Jeune "jokingly" told the Jesuit priest: "The Beaver does everything perfectly well, it makes kettles, hatchets, swords, knives, bread; and, in short, it makes everything." The man showed Le Jeune "a very beautiful knife" and said, "The English have no sense; they give us twenty knives like this for one Beaver skin."

On the whole, however, the First Nations had more to lose than to gain, a situation that became increasingly evident as the pressure to kill beavers at an unsustainable rate mounted. An old Cree man whom explorer David Thompson met on the prairies in 1797 put it this way: "We are now killing the Beaver without any labor, we are now rich, but [shall] soon be poor, for when the Beaver are destroyed we have nothing to depend on to purchase what we want for our families, strangers now over run our country with their iron traps, and we, and they will soon be poor."

The Europeans had begun importing wrought iron and steel traps to North America around the early 1600s, but these devices were not widely used for trapping beavers until the next century. The turning point came with the introduction of what Thompson called the "infallible bait of Castorum."

Castoreum (as we now spell it) is an aromatic, yellowish brown fluid produced by the concentration of urine in the beaver's castor glands, which lie between the kidneys and the bladder. Beavers of both sexes, but especially males, mark their territories by squirting castoreum onto scent mounds — piles of mud dredged up from the bottom of their ponds and placed in strategic locations on land — or, less conspicuously, onto bunches of grass that they have twisted together. Sometimes they anoint the same site repeatedly, adding more mud each time and creating enormous, car tire–sized monuments.

Beavers have an acute sense of smell (much more useful than sight for an animal that is mostly active at night and spends its days in a dark lodge), and the scent of an intruder's castoreum is like a red flag to a beaver. Residents are quick to investigate any alien scent-mound that shows up in their territory, first sniffing it and then pawing at the mud and obscuring the offending odour with a shot of their own. Which is what makes castoreum such an infallible lure.

Although native North Americans would have known about the beaver's scent-marking behaviour, the use of castoreum to entice beavers into traps appears to have been a European innovation. The oldest written record of anyone deploying the deadly combination of steel and castoreum in North America dates back to 1728 and the observations of Virginia surveyor William Byrd II. The local Indians caught beavers by laying snares near their dams, Byrd wrote, but "the English hunters have found out a more effectual method," for which he provided explicit instructions: squeeze "the juice" out of both "the large pride of the beaver" and "the small pride" (presumably, the castor gland and anal gland, respectively); mix the liquid with powdered sassafras bark; and "place this bait conveniently for your steel trap." Other writings mention Mohawks in the mid-1700s who baited both wooden and steel traps with castoreum, while continuing to use more conventional hunting techniques, such as setting nets, on occasion.

The prevalence of steel traps increased once North American blacksmiths started manufacturing them during the 1700s, though the early versions weren't necessarily an improvement on indigenous technology. Many were prone to breaking, particularly in cold weather, and they weighed three to four kilograms apiece. Then, in 1823, a teenager from New York State revolutionized the business.

Sewell Newhouse was only 17 when he began making leg-hold traps in his father's smithy and selling them to his Oneida Community acquaintances, but he clearly had talent. His designs quickly gained a reputation for being lightweight, meticulously made and reliable. However, they were not widely available until 1850, when Newhouse joined a newly formed utopian community and turned his business over to the collective. By the 1860s, the Oneida Community was selling thousands of machine-made Newhouse traps annually, in eight sizes, and the Hudson's Bay Company was one of their largest customers. The Oneida Community's mass production of high-quality leg-hold traps led the way in the final phase of the continental beaver slaughter, and other manufacturers followed suit. Trappers who combined this easily portable, efficacious equipment with an irresistible dose of castoreum could extend their traplines over a wider area and more easily target lone beavers, picking off the last survivors from nearly extinguished populations.

In the late 1400s, when the first beaver pelts were being carried across the Atlantic in ships laden with dried codfish and whale oil, North American peoples spoke some 400 distinct languages. Between them, they had hundreds of names for the animal that was about to shape their destiny, more than one per language in many cases. Vuntut Gwich'in speakers from the northern Yukon, for example, could talk about beavers in general (*tsèe*) or distinguish a one-year-old beaver (*neezhìi*) from a two-year-old (*ch'aachìi*) or a three-year-old (*ch'edoovìi*). The largest beavers were *ch'ichoo*, and compound words specified sex: *tsèe dinjii* for male beavers; *tsèe tr'ik* for females.

This nuanced lexicon survived because the Vuntut Gwich'in were among the last indigenous groups to encounter Europeans. We can only guess how many words for beaver in other languages have disappeared. But there's no question that the beaver's extirpation from most of North America was a cultural, as well as an economic, loss for many First Nations — like the death of a relative or a beloved and respected member of a close-knit community.

The Dene, who know the beaver as *tsá*, have a story about the time the culture hero Yamoría changed himself into a beaver and went to live with a beaver family to study their ways. A year later, Yamoría resumed his human form and returned to the Dene to share his new knowledge. The most important lesson he conveyed was that the beavers always planned ahead and stockpiled food during summer and fall to see them through winter. When the beavers disappeared from the land, such opportunities for learning ceased.

No one knows how many beavers inhabited North America before Europeans arrived. All we have are educated guesses that range from a cautious 60 million to a mind-boggling 400 million. Regardless of the starting point, the population decline over the next four centuries was clearly precipitous. By the early 1700s, there wasn't a beaver to be found in Massachusetts, where the Pilgrims had financed their quest for religious freedom by shipping tons of beaver skins back to England, and other traders had scooped up any beavers they missed. Before the end of the eighteenth century, the species was also gone from Connecticut, and over the next 50 years, it vanished from Vermont, New Jersey, Ohio, Pennsylvania and New Hampshire. The dam-builders somehow managed to maintain a toehold in New York, Wisconsin, Minnesota and the British territories to the north, but they were so scarce it was as if they didn't exist.

Out West, the losses followed close behind. In 1843, American naturalist and artist John James Audubon travelled nearly 3,000 kilometres up the Missouri River from Saint Louis to Fort Union to collect specimens for an illustrated book on the mammals of North America, his last great work. Despite the assistance of a skilled trapper, Audubon failed to obtain, or even see, a single beaver during his eight-month journey. In just a decade and a half, the renegade Mountain Men had all but annihilated the region's beavers.

By the start of the twentieth century, *Castor canadensis* had been purged from most of the continent, and the species' official status throughout most of its historic range was either absent or rare. In all of North America, the number of survivors was likely in the low hundred thousands — less than one percent of the most conservatively estimated original population. Many observers believed that complete extinction was possible, if not inevitable. For once, the doomsayers were wrong.

·*Four*·
BACK FROM THE BRINK

Even as Three-Pence Beaver postage stamps started rolling off the presses in 1851 and circulating the globe, affixed to Canadian envelopes and postcards, the species that had inspired the image was fading into oblivion. This vanishing act, like the simultaneous disappearance of many other species, provoked alarm and nostalgia among certain spectators, including Henry David Thoreau.

On March 23, 1856, Thoreau complained to his journal that the widespread eradication of native wildlife had diminished the New England landscape: "When I consider that the nobler animals have been exterminated here, — the cougar, panther, lynx, wolverene, wolf, bear, moose, deer, the beaver, the turkey, etc. etc., — I cannot but feel as if I lived in a tamed, and, as it were, emasculated country," he wrote. Surprisingly, at least from a twenty-first-century perspective, the animals he mourned most were not the charismatic carnivores, but the moose and the beaver, in whose absence "the forest and the meadow now lack expression."

Conservationist sensibilities like those expressed by Thoreau gained traction over the next half-century and eventually inspired an eccentric Englishman named Archibald Stansfeld

Belaney, better known as Grey Owl, to take up the beaver's cause. He wasn't the only person involved in pulling the beaver back from the brink. He may not even have been the one who did the most good. But he remains the most famous: the patron saint of beaver conservation. With that in mind, I decided to make a pilgrimage to his grave site, deep in the boreal forest of northern Saskatchewan.

For years, I had dismissed Belaney as a cultural imposter, bigamist, negligent father and alcoholic, the author of obsolete nature books that I had never bothered to read and, more recently, an excuse for Pierce Brosnan to shave his chest and look pensive in a critically panned Hollywood biopic that I never got around to seeing. In reality, I discovered, he was an oddly likeable character, despite all his flaws.

Archibald Belaney was born in Hastings, England, in 1888, and raised by his two spinster aunts. When he was about two, the Belaney family sent the boy's ne'er-do-well father packing and relieved his teen-aged mother of his care. The aunts gave young Archibald a stable, comfortable home and a good education, but their stern, Victorian style of child rearing did nothing to alleviate his feelings of abandonment. A moody loner, he mostly kept company with his menagerie of small animals, which included snakes and hedgehogs, and entertained himself by roaming the woods and reading about North American tribes. With school-mates, his favourite pastime was playing "Red Indians."

At 17, after two years of unsatisfying clerical work in a lumberyard, Belaney left England in search of adventure in Canada. He settled near Lake Temagami in northern Ontario, shortened his name to Archie and started studying for his new life as a woodsman. His teachers were seasoned trappers and hunting guides, including the family of a young Ojibwa woman named

Angele Egwuna, whom he met in 1908, married in 1910 and deserted in 1911, shortly after their first daughter was born.

Belaney began reinventing himself as soon as he arrived in Canada. Initially, he merely hinted at having Native heritage. Later, he developed an elaborate story about being the Mexican-born son of a Scottish frontiersman and an Apache woman. He let his hair grow down to his shoulders and habitually wore a fringed buckskin vest and moccasins. He couldn't completely erase his English accent, so he told people that during his teens he had travelled to Britain as a member of Buffalo Bill's Wild West Show. Those who knew him during the early days of this masquerade didn't necessarily believe him — and with his thin face and slightly aquiline nose, he looked nothing like his new Ojibwa friends — but as the years went on, he refined his act. He dyed his brown hair black, darkened his skin with henna and endeavoured to develop the kind of solemn countenance that he (and many of his later fans) thought epitomized the Apache. He even practised his expressions in the mirror.

After he left Angele, Belaney remained in northern Ontario, working as a fire ranger in summer and running a trapline in winter. He also took up with Marie Girard, a Metis woman. It's unclear whether he knew she was pregnant when he went off in 1915 to enlist in the army and support Canada's war effort. Certainly, he made no effort to stay in touch with her while he was overseas. When he returned two years later, he discovered that Marie had died of TB and that he had a son, but he didn't try to see the child or offer any financial support to the woman who was caring for him.

In April 1916, while Belaney was fighting with the Canadian Expeditionary Force in Belgium, a bullet blew off one of his toes and parts of two others, an injury severe enough to get him invalided back to England. During his convalescence, he reunited with a former sweetheart, Ivy Holmes, and married her in February 1917. Seven months later, he sailed back to Canada, ostensibly planning to send for his new bride as soon as he was resettled. Yet he hesitated, for if Ivy joined him in northern Ontario, she would inevitably learn about his previous liaisons. Moreover, it would be impossible for him to maintain his false persona. After several years apart, Belaney finally wrote and told Ivy about his marriage to Angele Egwuna, which he had never legally terminated. Humiliated by his duplicity, she immediately filed for a divorce.

In the summer of 1925, Belaney found his muse, a young Mohawk woman named Gertrude Bernard, who inspired his conversion from beaver slayer to beaver protector. They met at a resort on Lake Temagami, where he was working as a guide and she as a waitress. Belaney, almost 37, was charmed by the vivacious 19-year-old with stylishly bobbed, thick black hair. She, in turn, was enthralled by his striking looks and inimitable style. Had Gertrude known that Belaney had recently visited Angele and left her pregnant with another child that she would end up raising on her own, she might have been less impressed.

Gertrude was set to begin studies at a finishing school in Toronto that fall, but the sparks that flew between her and Belaney sent that plan up in smoke. By midwinter, she had joined him on his trapline. The following summer, a friend of theirs, an Algonquin chief, performed an unofficial marriage ceremony for them and they considered themselves wed.

During their first few years together, Belaney worked as a fire ranger in the summer and spent the winters trapping, the main occupation he had pursued since his arrival in Canada. Despite his childhood love of animals, his desire to emulate his idols had overridden any reservations he might have had about killing game. However, he drew the line between "clean trapping," as practised by his mentors, and the "unsportsmanlike methods" of incompetent amateurs who paid no heed to sustaining populations or minimizing suffering. Then, in 1928, he suddenly decided to stop trapping beavers, the mainstay of his livelihood.

Belaney wrote about his abrupt change of course in his second book, *Pilgrims of the Wild*, and numerous magazine articles. Gertrude later told her version of the events in her memoir, *Devil in Deerskins*. Their accounts don't match precisely, but the basic storyline is the same: innocent, town-raised Mohawk girl falls in love with hard-bitten, half-breed trapper; is appalled when faced with the bloody reality of his profession; talks him into adopting two beaver kits after he kills their mother; and, with the help of the adorable waifs, convinces him to renounce beaver trapping altogether.

The first glimmerings of a conservationist philosophy may have prompted this about-face. Certainly Belaney came to believe, as he later wrote, that "Beaver stood for something vital, something essential in this wilderness, were a component part of it; they *were* the wilderness. With them gone it would be empty; without them it would be not a wilderness but a waste." But there was another factor that neither he nor Gertrude mentioned: by the time he hung up his beaver traps, he knew he didn't have much of a future as a trapper.

In 1925, the Ontario government had banned everyone except "resident Indians" from trapping beavers and otters. In response, Belaney and many other disqualified trappers relocated to Quebec, where they overran unprotected First Nations lands and increased pressure on that province's beaver populations. Belaney despised the "get-rich-quick-vandals who, caring for nothing much but the immediate profits, swept like the scourge they were across the face of northern Canada" after the war. He considered himself a professional trapper — a "dyed-in-the-wool genuine woodsman." But that self-definition wasn't going to prevent him from losing his beaver-trapping privileges if Quebec implemented the same kind of restrictions that Ontario had, which seemed likely.

Although it was a convenient time to swear off beaver trapping, Belaney still needed to earn a living. He decided to try to find a safe haven where his two rescued beavers could breed in peace and start repopulating the wilds, while he would continue to earn money by trapping other animals. Unfortunately, the part of Quebec that he chose as his new base had almost no furbearers left. He and Gertrude were scraping by on his army disability pension when a new opportunity presented itself.

In a rare letter to his mother, Belaney had voiced his concerns about Canada's vanishing wilds and she, moved by this lament, sent it to England's *Country Life* magazine. The editor responded by inviting him to expand the letter into an article. Published in 1929, it brought Belaney some desperately needed income and a request for a book on the same subject. He immediately started working on *The Men of the Last Frontier*, which hit the bookstores late in 1931. By then, he had adopted the name Grey Owl, and his beaver conservation campaign had gained significant momentum. (In his second book, he introduced readers to his "wife" Anahareo, a purely fictional name that he had dreamed up for Gertrude and which she happily used in public during the rest of their years together.)

While waiting for the book to come out, Belaney, writing under his alias, started submitting articles to *Canadian Forest and Outdoors* magazine. James Harkin, Canada's national parks commissioner and an ardent conservationist, read the first piece in the spring of 1930 and immediately arranged for a camera crew to visit Grey Owl's backwoods home and document his work. The resulting nine-minute black-and-white silent movie, *The Beaver People*, was the world's first professional filming of beavers in a natural setting.

Sadly, however, the orphaned kits that had first won Grey Owl's sympathies did not live long enough to perform for the cameras or share the limelight with him and Gertrude. McGinnis and McGinty had disappeared in the spring of 1929, undoubtedly killed for their pelts.

Harkin was so pleased with the film and the public's response to it that he offered Grey Owl a job as the "caretaker of park animals" (which really meant "beaver promoter") at Riding Mountain National Park in Manitoba. Despite his worries about losing his independence, Grey Owl accepted. A steady paycheque and support for his endeavour were only part of the attraction. He and Gertrude, heartbroken by the loss of their first charges, also hoped that their replacements, Jelly Roll and Rawhide, would be safer in a park.

Soon after arriving at Riding Mountain in the spring of 1931, Grey Owl realized that the lake where he had been installed didn't have sufficient water for the beavers. That fall, he and Gertrude transferred to Prince Albert National Park in Saskatchewan, along with Jelly Roll, Rawhide and the four kits Jelly Roll had delivered that spring. Their new home, which the couple dubbed "Beaver Lodge," was a small log cabin, built to Grey Owl's specifications, beside Ajawaan Lake.

Prince Albert National Park superintendent James Wood shared Harkin's belief in the conservation benefits of recruiting Grey Owl and his beavers. Having noticed many old dams throughout the park, Wood was sure the area had been "infested with beavers at one time." Re-establishing the species "would mean storage of large amounts of water . . . thereby providing additional facilities for fire fighting." He had already introduced one pair of beavers during the park's first four years of existence, and they and their offspring were thriving.

In contrast, J.C. Campbell, the park service's national director of publicity, considered the appointment a superb opportunity to promote the park. As he confidently proclaimed upon Grey Owl's arrival at Ajawaan, "there is no doubt he [has] the greatest publicity value of anything we have ever done."

Eighty years later, at the Prince Albert National Park visitor centre in Waskesiu, I paid my backcountry camping fee and collected the permit that officially blessed my pilgrimage to Ajawaan, along with a brochure about my destination. The cover quote was from Grey Owl himself: "Far enough away to gain seclusion, yet within reach of those whose genuine interest prompts them to make the trip, Beaver Lodge extends a welcome to you if your heart is right." I was pretty sure my heart and mind were appropriately primed. Whether the rest of my body was up to the 40-kilometre round-trip trek was another matter.

During Grey Owl's time at Beaver Lodge, a steady stream of admirers visited the cabin every summer. In 1936 alone, somewhere between 600 and 1,000 people showed up, hoping to meet the park's legendary beaver man and his supporting cast. Then, as now, the trip began with a 32-kilometre drive on a gravel road from Waskesiu, the park's tourist hub, to the south end of Kingsmere Lake. Beyond there, nearly all of the 1930s excursionists travelled the length of the lake by motor launch or canoe, then either walked the final three kilometres to the cabin or carried their canoes over a 600-metre portage and paddled across Ajawaan Lake.

The water route to Beaver Lodge is still popular, but I opted to go on foot. Although it was the height of summer, I had the trail to myself, which suited me fine. My route followed Kingsmere's eastern shore, winding through the forest and offering occasional views of the lake. Shadowy, moss-carpeted stands of black spruce alternated with sunlit groves of white birch and trembling aspen, brightened by flamboyant orange prairie lilies and other wildflowers. Birds flicked through the foliage and tossed shiny melodies into the air. To scare off any bears that might be in the area, I sang too, with silent apologies to Grey Owl, who had abhorred any "jabbering" on the trail. I'm sure he would have felt the same about off-key renditions of old campfire songs, though "Land of the silver birch, home of the beaver" seemed appropriate to the circumstances.

Weighed down by my fully loaded backpack and sweating inside the compulsory bug shirt that swathed my upper body in mesh, I trudged along. Recent storms had dropped countless trees across the path; I climbed over most of them and belly-crawled under the rest. Five hours after leaving the parking lot, I arrived at my campsite.

After I set up camp, I strolled down to the narrow strip of beach, where a merciful breeze kept the mosquitoes at bay. There was no one else around, so I stripped off my clothes, walked into the lake with all the eagerness of a baptismal candidate and floated in the cool water until I felt restored. I spent most of the remaining hours of the day on the beach. From where I sat, the whole world was water and sky, divided by a thin, dark line of trees on the far horizon. For company, I had a couple of common loons and a quartet of white pelicans. Evening brought cumulus clouds of biblical proportions piled up to the northeast. Golden beams angled down from their rosy undersides, pointing towards distant, hidden Ajawaan Lake.

The next morning, carrying only a light daypack, I set off for Beaver Lodge, about seven kilometres away. The wind had picked up overnight, and I could hear waves crashing against the shore, even when I couldn't see the water. I was glad not to be in a canoe. At the north end of Kingsmere Lake, the trail ran along the beach for a short distance, then turned towards Ajawaan. As I left Kingsmere behind, the forest closed around me and the sound of the breakers faded.

A low rise of land separated the two lakes and as I descended the long wooden stairway on the far side, Ajawaan came into view. It was as if I had entered another world: there were no sprawling vistas here, no views beyond the tall trees that wrapped so close on every side that the wind barely ruffled the water or disturbed the lily pads floating on its surface. Small, deep and sheltered, Grey Owl's chosen lake was ideal for beavers.

The trail continued through the forest for a while, then suddenly emerged into a lakeside clearing, where a small log cabin stood with one end almost touching the water. The place was deserted, yet didn't feel forsaken. After all my reading and viewing of old film-footage, I could easily imagine the welcome I would have received in the 1930s. If I had come by canoe, it would have gone something like this:

A tall, lean, buckskin-clad man stands motionless by the cabin and watches our progress across the lake so intently that I feel self-conscious about the way I handle my paddle. He doesn't smile as he doffs his wide-brimmed felt hat in greeting, but his blue eyes (strange for an Indian, I might think) are kind when he extends his hand to steady my step over the gunnel. He checks that none of us is wearing perfume, aftershave or talcum powder, since scented products aggravate the beavers, then summons the "Little Brethren of the Wilderness" whom we've heard so much about. At his call, Jelly Roll and Rawhide come swimming up and clamber onto shore. Ignoring me and the other day-trippers, they toddle straight over to Grey Owl and sit up and beg like portly dogs. He pulls apple slices from his pocket, and, later, peanuts, though Jelly Roll won't take hers unless they are already shelled. The time passes quickly as they perform their little tricks and let us rub their heads. Then we must bid our host farewell and start making our way back to town.

Since I was too late for that scenario, I walked over to the cabin and let myself in. The one-room building held none of Grey Owl's personal effects except an autographed canoe paddle, but the idiosyncratic layout shouted his name. Nearly a third of the space, at the end closest to the lake, was dirt, separated from the rest of the plank-covered floor by knee-high log walls. The centre of the square was filled with mud and sticks — the remains of a three-metre-wide lodge that once filled the enclosure and extended out over the water next to the cabin.

In Grey Owl's day, Jelly Roll, Rawhide and a series of kits with names like Wakinoo, Sugar Loaf and Buckshot, occupied this private apartment year-round. A plunge hole in the dirt floor led to a tunnel that passed under the building wall and into the lake. Since this was the only entrance to the lodge, the beavers were cut off from human company when the lake was frozen. In summer, they enjoyed free access to the cabin through the front door, which they learned to open, but not to close.

Reading Grey Owl's books or watching the grainy black-and-white film footage of him and Anahareo playing with the beavers, I envy their closeness to these animals. Intelligent, playful and affectionate, his protégés exhibited "the mischievous proclivities of a monkey combined with much of the artless whimsicality of a child." They were also keen conversationalists who employed an expressive repertoire of murmurs, mutters, whimpers and sharp exclamations to communicate with each other and their human associates.

These portrayals of beavers as lovable characters with distinct personalities were effective in promoting their cause, yet Grey Owl's feelings for them were much more than just part of his act. The truest thing in those old movies may be the look on his face when he's with the beavers: the tenderness with which he bottle-feeds tiny, fuzzy kits; his frank pleasure when he wrestles with one of the adults. This was a man who spent his whole life avoiding real intimacy with humans. With the beavers, he was able to let down his guard and experience unreserved affection. Jelly Roll, he once admitted, filled "some need in my life of which I had been only dimly conscious heretofore."

Beavers may not be obvious candidates for domestication, but Grey Owl wasn't the first person to have one as a pet. Tamed beavers show up in various First Nations narratives, such as the song Ida Calmegane sang for me about the beaver that flooded the village of Basket Bay. A Lakota story, "Double-Face Tricks a Girl," tells of a young woman who impulsively elopes with a mysterious suitor and discovers that he's a monster. Fortunately, she has brought along her pet beaver and this little *waniyanpi yuha*, or "kept alive one," helps her escape from her fiendish husband. First, the beaver cuts down trees and builds a bridge so the fleeing pair can cross a deep lake that blocks their route. Then he gnaws the logs in two as Double-Face teeters across them, casting their pursuer into the water and to his death. When the girl arrives home with the beaver in her arms, her relieved and elated parents forgive her indiscretion and give her saviour a hero's welcome. "The 'kept-alive' beaver was so greatly loved, highly praised, and even spoiled," the story ends, "that they say he felt like the best person in that whole camp."

During the late 1700s, Hudson's Bay Company fur trader and explorer Samuel Hearne also fell under the beaver's spell. In his *Journey to the Northern Ocean*, Hearne wrote of keeping "several of them till they became so domesticated as to answer to their name, and follow those to whom they were accustomed, in the same manner as a dog would do; and they were as much pleased at being fondled, as any animal I ever saw." During the summer, the beavers occupied a house Hearne had built for them. The rest of the year, they lived in his sitting room, "where they were the constant companions of the Indian women and children."

Whenever the women and children were absent for a prolonged period, Hearne's beavers exhibited "great signs of uneasiness, and on their return shewed equal marks of pleasure, by fondling on them, crawling into their laps, laying on their backs, sitting erect like a squirrel, and behaving to them like children who see their parents but seldom." During winter, the beavers ate the same fare as their keepers. They were particularly fond of rice and plum pudding.

The deeper I dug, the more instances of beaver fostering I discovered. One early nineteenth-century fur trader's favourite pet beaver "used to lie before the fire as contentedly as a dog." And, while yachting on the St. Lawrence River in 1873, Lady Harriot Dufferin, wife of Canada's third Governor General, "bought two little beavers from the Indians, to keep as pets on board." The beavers were housed in a barrel on deck. "[We] amuse ourselves with giving them baths and feeding them," Lady Dufferin wrote in her journal on June 27. Ten days later, amusement had turned to worry, as the beavers refused to come out of their hutch and looked ill. After that, she didn't mention them again.

The most famous of those who have taken beavers into their homes since Grey Owl's day are two women who both turned their properties into beaver sanctuaries and wrote books about their experiences. In the 1940s, Dorothy and Al Richards built an addition on their old farmhouse in the New York Adirondacks and installed a pair of beavers, so she could study them year-round. The room held a swimming pool, filled by water piped in from a creek, and had a wall of windows facing into the house, where Dorothy sat every day, observing the beavers. In the evening, she would invite them to join her and Al in their living room.

Audrey Tournay's relationship with beavers began in the 1970s, when the southern Ontario high school teacher took in an injured kit. Over the next 30 years, she rehabilitated dozens of rescued beavers, often giving them the run of her house and sometimes sharing her bed with them.

By all reports, cohabitation with beavers requires considerable compromise. Their many foibles include persistent chewing on wooden furniture and purloining of all kinds of household objects, which they incorporate into their many indoor construction projects. Grey Owl's beavers considered a blanket-covered bed the perfect place to stand and squeeze the water out of their fur after swimming. They also regularly climbed onto his bunk and slept beside him, snoring in his ear. Once, they stole a manuscript off his desk and dragged it into their lodge. He successfully retrieved it, but it took him days to reassemble the 400 unnumbered pages in the correct order.

When Gertrude came home from hospital with the couple's newborn daughter, Shirley Dawn, in September 1932, she moved into a separate cabin on a knoll behind Beaver Lodge — a decision prompted by Jelly Roll's strong defensive streak and occasional nips at strangers. In *Pilgrims of the Wild*, Grey Owl made light of the potential risk. The only precaution he took was to never leave the baby unattended within reach of the beavers, since "Jelly's habit of appropriating articles which she takes a fancy to, might result in us having to open the beaver house and rescue a very wet and outraged young woman from the ministrations of her triumphant abductor."

Gertrude and the baby returned to the main cabin once the lake froze and the beavers were shut out. That was the only winter the family spent together. Grey Owl's growing obsession with his beaver crusade left no room for close relationships, which he had never been good at anyway. From the summer of 1933 onward, he and Gertrude increasingly went their separate ways and fought frequently when they were around each other. In the fall of 1936, they parted permanently. A couple of months later, Grey Owl (who had still not divorced Angele Egwuna) walked down the aisle with Yvonne Perrier, a French-Canadian woman he had met the previous spring while promoting his cause.

After looking around the main cabin, I climbed the 22 steps to the upper residence, now just an empty shell, and then took a well-worn path leading into the trees along the ridgeline. It was time to pay my respects to the dead.

Grey Owl kept up a punitive pace during the final years of his life. He wrote dozens of magazine articles, as well as three books, published in 1934, 1935 and 1936. He starred in and served as head beaver-wrangler for nine films shot between 1930 and

1937. And he never missed an opportunity to proselytize in person, whether to lecture hall audiences, politicians or canoe-loads of Beaver Lodge visitors. In 1935, he travelled through Great Britain for four months on a wildly popular non-stop speaking tour. Two years later, he returned for a triumphant three-month encore that included a Royal Command Performance at Buckingham Palace. Then, as soon as he got back to North America, he embarked on three gruelling months of travel and public speaking that took him from New York City to Regina.

On April 7, 1938, an exhausted and ailing 49-year-old Grey Owl returned alone to Beaver Lodge. Three days later, he telephoned park headquarters to say he was seriously ill. A warden went straight to the cabin and took him to the hospital, where he was diagnosed with pneumonia. He died on April 13.

News of Grey Owl's great ruse broke on the same day he passed away. Three years earlier, a northern Ontario newspaper reporter had uncovered the truth about his identity, but the paper's editor refrained from publishing an exposé, in deference to Grey Owl's work. The moment the editor heard that Grey Owl was dead, he retrieved the completed feature from his files and fired up the printing presses. The North Bay *Nugget*'s scoop immediately gained worldwide attention and became a bigger story than his death. Public reaction to the shocking revelations ranged from denial to anger to good-humoured acceptance.

On April 15, following a funeral service in Prince Albert, Grey Owl's flag-draped coffin was loaded onto a sled and pulled by a pair of draft horses across the frozen lakes to be interred, according to his wishes, on the hill behind Beaver Lodge. At the head of his grave, the mourners planted a plain cross with two names written on it: "A. Belaney" on the horizontal and "Grey Owl" on the vertical.

I had no trouble finding the grave site, but all traces of Archibald Stansfeld Belaney, including the cross, were gone. In its place was a fieldstone marker with a brass plaque that gave only his assumed name and the dates of his birth and death. I'm sure Belaney himself would have approved of this deception.

Grey Owl is not alone in this peaceful spot. The woman who was instrumental in bringing him here is buried almost within arm's reach and their daughter lies between them, their graves identified with the same minimalism as his. "Anahareo — June 18, 1906–June 17, 1986." "Shirley Dawn — August 23, 1932–June 3, 1984." No mention of the husbands' surnames that replaced Belaney. I don't know who decided on the wording and how it came to be that Anahareo, rather than Grey Owl's last partner, shared this private cemetery with him, but it seems fitting.

Later, as I sat on the porch of the main cabin and watched for beavers, it occurred to me that the little family grouping on the hill was lacking two members. What had happened to Jelly Roll and Rawhide when they lost their benefactor? Why were there no plaques for them? When I got back to town, I found partial answers in the park archives.

Inquiries about the two pet beavers from concerned members of the public began pouring into the park almost immediately upon Grey Owl's passing. The sentiments expressed by Mr. and Mrs. C. Gordon of Victoria, British Columbia, were typical. "Since the death of Grey Owl, we have been wondering what will become of his friends Jelly Roll and Rawhide, that have found a place in the hearts of all lovers of animals, who have read the stories of Grey Owl," they wrote to superintendent Wood on April 17. "Having through his special care, lost some of their natural instincts of self protection, as he himself states, is there at the Park, someone who will provide for their care as he did?"

Although Wood promised the Gordons and other letter-writers that the beavers would be well looked after, his superiors were decidedly cool to the idea of spending any more money on an endeavour now tainted by the disclosure of Grey Owl's fakery. They had been paying Grey Owl $110 a month whenever he was in residence at Beaver Lodge. Eliminating his unique position as caretaker of park animals would save them more than a thousand dollars a year, a substantial amount during the Depression. And wages weren't the only cost associated with maintaining this tourist attraction. It wasn't unusual for Grey Owl's monthly grocery order to include 50 pounds of rice, 40 loaves of whole wheat bread, 10 pounds of peanuts, five crates of apples and a box of chocolate bars — with most of these provisions destined for the beavers.

Grey Owl's will asked his employers to care for Jelly Roll and Rawhide until they died. The National Parks Bureau controller ruled otherwise. His orders were to quietly cut off the beavers' support system and leave them to fend for themselves, which he was confident they could manage. To avoid any accusations of neglect, the park hired a beaver caretaker for the summer of 1938.

In late August, park warden Roy Hubel reported to the superintendent on the situation at Beaver Lodge. Jelly Roll and her newest litter were doing fine, he wrote, but no one had seen Rawhide since the beginning of the month. According to the caretaker, a young man who had filled in for Grey Owl when he was away the previous year, Rawhide had been acting "queer" before he disappeared and "seemed very indifferent to any food he placed before him."

Hubel wasn't optimistic. Rawhide, he noted, "was an unde-monstrative type of beaver and may for all we know have missed the Grey Owl more than we imagined. One cannot gage the feelings of animals, so for all we know Rawhide in his loneliness may have gone off to seek his old friend." Jelly Roll, on the other hand, had her kits to tend to "and tho she showed more affec-tion possibly it was all on the surface, like some people, and not from the heart."

Given that beavers mate for life, Jelly Roll's presence should have been enough to keep Rawhide from leaving, so when he didn't reappear by the next spring, he was presumed dead. The longevity record for wild beavers is 21 years, but most live to about half that age and that's only if they make it past adoles-cence. Maybe Rawhide's time had simply come; after all, both he and Jelly Roll were nine when Grey Owl died. Or maybe grief really did hasten his demise.

If a male beaver loses his mate, he usually abandons his home territory and goes looking for an unattached female. A female beaver that is left alone normally stays put and waits for another male to join her. True to form, Jelly Roll remained at Ajawaan throughout the summer of 1939 and would still come to one warden's calls. The following winter, after hearing rumours that her erstwhile pet was in "mighty poor shape," Gertrude wrote and asked permission to go to Beaver Lodge so she could replenish the underwater food cache and keep the cabin heated with the wood stove. The answer was a brusque refusal.

How long Jelly Roll lived and whether she re-mated is a mystery. As late as 1941, fans were still writing to the park to ask about the beavers' welfare and receiving glib assurances that Rawhide and Jelly Roll had "reverted to their wild state, but can still be seen by parties visiting the lake." Like everything to do with Grey Owl, the legend was more important than the facts.

I didn't see any beavers at Beaver Lodge. They might have appeared if I had stayed into the evening, but I wasn't brave enough to hike back to camp in the dark. I did, however, find a long fern-topped dam on the creek that connects Ajawaan Lake to Kingsmere. A deep pond spread out behind the dam, its margins thick with cattails, tall grass and shrubs. My splashing approach through the wet ground on the downstream side of the dam startled a white-tailed deer that was drinking at the edge the pond. It jerked its head up and bounded away into the forest. I saw no beavers, but plenty of evidence of their presence. Could they be distant descendants of Jelly Roll and Rawhide? I wanted to believe so, and the odds seemed good.

Many myths circle Grey Owl's memory. One is that he single-handedly saved the beaver by creating a groundswell of sympathy for the beleaguered species and compelling the governments of the day to institute protective measures. In fact, beaver conservation efforts go back as far as the early nineteenth century. After the Hudson's Bay Company and the North West Company amalgamated in 1821, the new governor of the expanded enterprise, George Simpson, introduced a number of major policy changes, including measures designed to arrest the beaver's precipitous decline. Between 1821 and 1850, Simpson imposed a series of beaver quotas on HBC opera-tions in the Canadian western interior. He also established trapping seasons for beavers in this region and banned agents at the affected posts from buying the skins of beaver cubs and summer-killed adults, whose fur was of little commercial value anyway. The regulations were unpopular with many of the traders and most of the trappers, but they did produce some positive, though temporary, results.

Unfortunately, at the same time, Simpson was doing his best to liquidate beavers elsewhere in his domain. With the British and the Americans unable to agree on ownership of the Oregon Territory, Simpson was eager to consolidate the Hudson's Bay Company's position in the area and discourage American competitors. To do that, he planned to create a "fur desert" south and east of the Columbia River, which would safeguard the abundant fur resources to the northwest and the ocean ports at the mouth of the river. "An exhausted frontier," he reasoned, "is the best protection we have against the encroachments of rival traders."

The frontline in this battle for fur supremacy was the Columbia River's largest tributary, the Snake River, which Simpson deemed "a rich preserve of Beaver . . . which for political reasons we shall endeavour to destroy as fast as possible." Starting in the early 1820s, the company sent out a series of trapping parties comprised of 100 or more men who scoured the region for furs. By the mid-1830s, the Snake brigades had emptied the buffer zone of most of its valuable wildlife. The frustrated American fur traders gave up on the Oregon Territory's beavers and turned their attention to the emerging buffalo robe trade instead.

A century after Simpson's attempts to "nurse" certain beaver populations back to health (while pulling the plug on others), the Hudson's Bay Company was involved in another, more successful, beaver conservation scheme.

This effort was initiated by James Watt, the factor at Rupert House on James Bay, who could not stand idle when he found himself overseeing a beaver wasteland. In the winter of 1928–29, trappers brought in only four beaver pelts from the surrounding

25,000 square kilometres, an area that had yielded 2,000 pelts in 1920, the year Watt had arrived at the trading post. After a quarter-century of operating within the fur-trade economy established by the Hudson's Bay Company, the local Cree (today recognized as the Waskaganish First Nation) were suddenly faced with poverty and starvation. One couple lost all 13 of their children in a single year, and their situation was not exceptional. Faced with this crisis, Watt extended far more credit than he was authorized to offer and pleaded with his superiors for help. They shrugged off his concerns.

In March 1929, two Waskaganish men showed up at the trading post and reported that they had found an occupied beaver house 50 kilometres away. They had come for traps so they could kill the two tenants. Watt suggested a radical alternative: he would buy both the lodge and the beavers, provided they and their progeny were left in peace to reproduce until the population had recovered. The men accepted his proposal, and Watt repeated the deal the following winter, when another pair of beavers that had escaped the holocaust were found. His plan was to keep on buying active lodges, with his own money, until there were enough beavers to support trapping again.

Watt's strategy drew on principles of sustainability that he'd learned from the Cree, so it wasn't hard to convince them to participate. The challenge was preventing outsiders from coming in and taking every beaver in sight. Watt decided he needed to convince the Quebec government to establish a zone in which only the Waskaganish Cree could trap beavers.

Maud Watt, who had supported her husband's efforts from the beginning, agreed that the request would have to be made in person. And since she spoke French and he didn't, she proposed to travel to the provincial capital and do the asking. On a paralyzingly cold January day in 1930, Maud, along with her two young children and a pair of Cree guides, set off by dogsled for the nearest railway station, 560 kilometres away. A month later, she met with government officials in Quebec City, who acquiesced to her fervent pleas.

The 18,600-square-kilometre Rupert House Beaver Preserve achieved exactly the results the Watts had hoped for. Although James' employers were initially furious at him for acting independently, they quickly came onside and even issued special tokens to help keep track of the number of beavers within each family's traditional hunting territory. By 1940, the beaver population within the preserve had grown to more than 4,000, and the Cree were allowed to resume limited trapping. As the beavers multiplied, the quotas grew too.

James Watt died of pneumonia in 1944, but his legacy lived on. By then, the Rupert House Preserve beaver population had topped 13,000, and the Hudson's Bay Company, working with various government agencies, had established several more sanctuaries modelled on his innovative concept. Finally, more than three centuries into the fur trade, the traders had figured out how to manage their most lucrative resource.

Various motives drove the conservation efforts of the early twentieth century. George Simpson was concerned about profits. The Watts were compelled first and foremost by compassion for the Cree. And Grey Owl's crusade, in which beavers were the messengers as much as the message, was principally about defending his cherished wilds, though he was also spurred by his sentimental attachment to his pets. To these reasons, another pair of pioneering beaver conservationists, Eric and Lillian Collier, added what we might now call the ecological imperative.

Like Archibald Belaney, Eric Collier left a dull office job and emigrated from England to Canada at 17. Collier arrived in 1920, 14 years after Belaney, and headed straight for his cousin's cattle ranch in central British Columbia. A year later, the lanky teen decided ranching was too tame for his tastes and set off on horseback in search of other opportunities. His next stop was the tiny community of Riske Creek on the Chilcotin Plateau, a high, arid tableland bounded by the Coast Mountains to the east and the Fraser River to the west. Thrilled by the vastness of this sparsely populated landscape, he took a job at the Riske Creek trading post and roadhouse. For the next few years, he spent his working days behind the counter or in the livery barn and his leisure time hunting for deer and grouse and exploring his new surroundings.

In spring 1922, Collier discovered Meldrum Creek. At that point, the meandering 62-kilometre-long watercourse was little more than a trickle that linked a series of stagnant, half-empty lakes. Here and there, the creek left the forest and passed through wide, grassy openings — beaver meadows, as he had learned to call them — but the only beaver dams he saw were broken and the grass was parched. Though the creek was clearly ailing, Collier recognized the valley's potential and began fantasizing about building a home there.

That dream took on a new dimension in 1927, the day Lillian Ross and her grandmother, Lala, walked into the trading post. While Lillian, a petite, freckle-faced brunette, immediately caught Eric's eye, he was also fascinated by the old Tsilhqot'in woman, partly because she was the most ancient person he had ever met. Age had blinded her, etched deep wrinkles into her face and washed all the colour from her waist-length braids. She spoke only broken English and might never have exchanged more than a few words with Eric, if not for his curiosity about her history and his attraction to her granddaughter. The eager suitor soon became a regular visitor to Lala's cabin and spent many hours talking with her and Lillian, whom he married in 1928.

Lala was born near Riske Creek around 1830. She had led a conventional Tsilhqot'in life, travelling the Chilcotin Plateau with her family in an annual round of hunting, fishing and gathering, until she married a white settler at age 15. Her knowledge of the land was deep and comprehensive, and to Eric's delight, she had many childhood memories of Meldrum Creek, which lay within her family's traditional hunting grounds. He listened in awe as she described the thousands of Canada geese that once settled on the lakes during migration, the skyline-obscuring flights of ducks that lifted from the marshes at sundown and the beaver ponds teeming with enormous trout, while minks and otters lounged on top of the lodges. None of that existed anymore.

Lala firmly placed the blame for the creek's decrepitude on the trappers who had eradicated beavers from the region. Years later, in his memoir, *Three Against the Wilderness*, Eric recalled her words: "[S]'pose you take all beaver, [by and by] all water go too. And if water go, no trout, no fur, no grass, not'ing stop." This simple lesson in ecology, which explained concepts that academics were still decades away from defining scientifically, resonated with Eric. He also appreciated her proposed remedy — that he and Lillian should go and live on Meldrum Creek and "give it back the beavers." He realized this was "a questionable venture" and couldn't be attempted until he had enough savings to quit his job, but he was excited by the prospect. Luckily, Lillian shared his enthusiasm.

On a sunny June morning in 1931, one year after Lala's death, the Colliers loaded their few possessions and their toddler son, Veasy, into a horse-drawn wagon and headed north from Riske Creek to begin their new life. A few days later, they reached the place where Meldrum Creek enters Madden Lake on its way to the Fraser River.

To get to their homestead, the Colliers followed a rough track worn by cowboys driving their cattle from their summer range to the forest clearings where the herds wintered and fed on wild hay. Some of these wild hay meadows were relics from the distant past, part of the natural habitat mosaic created by the beaver cycle. Others were the recent work of trappers who had chopped gaps in dams so they could catch the beavers when they came to make repairs; once all the dam-builders were dead, the ponds emptied.

Beaver meadows like these proliferated all across North America in the wake of the fur trade and proved a boon to colonists. As the English traveller Henry Wansy noted during an excursion to the eastern United States in 1794, the fertile, treeless expanses left behind by exterminated beavers gave early settlers a tremendous advantage, especially in heavily forested regions. "It is a fortunate circumstance to have purchased lands where these industrious animals have made a settlement," Wansy wrote. "At some of them, there have been four ton of hay cut on an acre."

The Colliers, however, needed only enough hay for a few horses. Eric had secured trapping rights to the Meldrum Creek watershed and aspired to support his family by harvesting furs.

In 1931, muskrat pelts were fetching between 80 cents and a dollar, and minks were worth $15 to $20. A good winter of trapping would easily exceed his trading post wages of $40 a month plus board. However, with no beavers around to dam the creek and create marshes, there was hardly a mink or muskrat to be found anywhere within his 600-square-kilometre domain.

In spring 1932, the Colliers decided that the only way to revitalize Meldrum Creek was to repair the neglected dams. The first one they tackled was more than 100 metres long and nearly two metres high. Eric and Lillian spent weeks felling and bucking trees, dragging the logs into place and hauling wheelbarrow loads of dirt for mortar. During the next rain, the old pond began to refill, much to their relief. Soon afterwards, the first ducks splashed down and long-dormant cattails started sprouting.

Over the next decade, the family rehabilitated some two dozen dams, creating ponds and wetlands that were rapidly populated by water-loving plants and animals. But the Colliers knew their facsimile dams weren't as sturdy or well maintained as the originals. With every storm, they worried about structural failure and downstream devastation. Fortunately, help arrived before any disaster occurred.

In fall 1941, a provincial game warden who had heard about the Colliers' endeavour arrived unexpectedly with two pairs of beavers from a game reserve 400 kilometres north. The warden's car — the first motor vehicle to reach the homestead — had suffered two blow outs, a broken spring, fender damage and a radiator leak on the way from Riske Creek. His passengers, however, were fine. They trundled out of their tin travelling cases, slipped into the water and promptly took over upkeep of the dams. Within a few years, their offspring had recolonized Meldrum Creek and begun dispersing across the Chilcotin Plateau.

It would be years before Eric could bring himself to set any beaver traps, even though he would have welcomed the revenue from their pelts. His labours had given him an acute appreciation of the beaver's importance, and he preferred to leave the expert dam-builders to do the work. Eventually, they became so numerous that he felt obliged to trap some of them, "just to hold their numbers in check." However, he still maintained that beavers did "far more good in the water than as fur on some woman's back."

During the 1940s, while continuing to make his living as a trapper and hunting guide, Eric began writing newspaper and magazine articles, and in 1949, he became the first non-American winner of *Outdoor Life* magazine's Conservation Award. That success prompted him to embark on a book, which recounted — with some literary licence — the family's homesteading adventures and beaver-reintroduction efforts. First published in 1959, *Three Against the Wilderness* was subsequently translated into at least seven languages and became an international bestseller.

The memoir also turned out to be Eric's farewell to Meldrum Creek. Veasy had already left home, and his aging parents were finding wilderness living difficult to handle on their own. In 1960, the Colliers returned to Riske Creek, and Eric died there six years later.

Access to the old Collier homestead has improved since 1941, but it's still not easy to reach. When I visited in 2011, it took me two attempts to find the place. The best part of the route from Riske Creek was the rutted gravel road at the beginning. On the last stretch — an indefinite grassy trail periodically interrupted by muddy craters — I crept along cautiously, until a fallen tree too big to drag out of the way forced me to park my car and cover the final kilometre on foot. With the sun warming my back and Meldrum Creek in sight, the walk was pure pleasure.

The deep, clear waterway that paralleled the track couldn't

have been more different from the parched channel Collier encountered in 1922. Sparkling in the sun, it reflected the cloudless sky and the multitude of greens along the creek's borders: brooding conifers and blithe aspens farthest out; willow thickets and chartreuse grasses in the middle range; and cattails crowding in to frame the open water. In one spot, where the water spread out behind a low dam, the surface was strewn with cattail leaves, like leftovers from a Palm Sunday procession.

The day before, I had seen the same thing on a nameless lake farther upstream, where I had stopped because I'd spotted a lodge. Beavers aren't usually active in the middle of the day, so I didn't expect to see any, but when the car door thumped closed, I heard a heavy splash. A moment later, a beaver's flat head broke the surface, elevated just enough to reveal ears and eyes. A swimming beaver is normally a lot like an iceberg: most of its mass is hidden. But from my vantage on the high bank, I could see the whole animal, until it disappeared into a thick stand of cattails. A few minutes later, I spotted it again, crouched at the edge of the pond, eating one of these plants.

In cartoons, beavers live on nothing but tree-food. In reality, their diet includes plenty of non-woody plants, when they're available, though tree bark and the underlying cambium layer provide essential nourishment, especially in winter. Biologists call beavers "choosy generalist" herbivores, meaning that they'll eat anything from ferns to fruit but have local and seasonal favourites. On the Chilcotin Plateau in late July, cattails were clearly one of the preferred items.

As I watched, the beaver briskly stripped the long, strap-like leaves from the cylindrical stem. Then, like a picnicker tackling a cob of corn, it grasped the stalk in its front paws and began nibbling. When it had devoured that stem, it slid back into the water. The nearest cattails quivered briefly and the beaver clambered back onto the shore holding the next course.

The last time the beaver dove, its mouth was full of cattail leaves. For a moment, I could see it moving underwater, the bottle-green blades streaming out like satin ribbons on either side of its stocky brown body.

I wasn't going to get that lucky two days in a row. After studying the cattail feeding area on Meldrum Creek for long enough to convince myself that no beavers lurked there, I continued down the trail to the homestead. Like all the other lakes strung along the Meldrum watercourse, Madden is long and skinny. It cinches in even tighter by the mouth of the creek, forming the wedge of level ground that the Colliers claimed in 1931.

When I came out of the trees and saw an old, weathered barn and horse corral, I knew I'd arrived. Just beyond them lay Madden Lake, along with the original one-room log cabin and its four-room replacement, built in 1946. The cabins stood on a notch of land that was hardly bigger than a football field, the shore an easy stone's throw from either one.

I entered the newer building through the half-open back door, alarming the swallows that had built their mud nests inside. They zoomed past my head as I walked through the empty rooms to stand in the front doorway. The view, dominated by the twinned blues of lake and sky, was magnificent. How gratifying it must have been for the Colliers to watch the lake level creep back up after they'd rebuilt the dams.

Water lilies — another of the choosy generalists' preferred foods — massed at the edge of the lake, their yellow flowers thrust up like defiant fists above the flat, floating leaves. Beavers feast on this plant's plump rhizomes when they're fresh and juicy and often store them in food caches for winter consumption. They also eat the lily pads — rolled up like fat green cigars, according to Eric Collier.

He credited the beavers with reviving Madden Lake's water-lily population, which was sparse when the lake first refilled. Every year in late summer, the beavers devoured the seed capsules, digested their soft outer rinds and excreted the ripe, undamaged seeds into the lake. Meanwhile, as they dredged mud from the bottom of the lake for their construction projects, they were unintentionally preparing the seed bed.

Seeing the lilies reminded me that beavers also inadvertently propagate willows and certain other woody plants. When beavers imbed uneaten sticks into dams or lodges or leave them lying on moist soil, the cuttings sometimes sprout roots and grow. Some of the shrubby vegetation I had seen earlier along the creek might well have been started this way.

From the homestead, I counted three lodges and suspected there were more out of sight farther down the lake. With vigorous stands of aspen growing all along the shore and an abundance of cattails and water lilies, there was no shortage of beaver provisions. And beavers weren't the only animals that were thriving there. Red-winged blackbirds belted out territorial songs from the cattails, a pair of loons floated serenely in the middle of the lake and an immense number of Canada goose droppings and moulted feathers littered the ground around the cabins.

Later, driving back along the grassy trail, I rounded a corner and came upon a pair of stilt-legged, long-necked birds whose heads would have reached my chest if I stood beside them. The moment I spotted them, they spread their cape-like wings, took a few loping strides and lifted off, leaving me with a blurred impression of rust-tinged grey bodies, white cheeks and bright red crowns. Sandhill cranes! Not exactly a rarity, but scarce enough in British Columbia to be of official concern. They need wetlands for nesting, and habitat loss has taken a toll on their numbers. In returning beavers to Meldrum Creek, the Colliers gave the valley back to a whole suite of species, including streamside willows, pond plants, trout, otters, geese, loons and, not least of all, these cranes, whose trumpeting calls are as iconic as the gunshot crack of a beaver tail striking flat water.

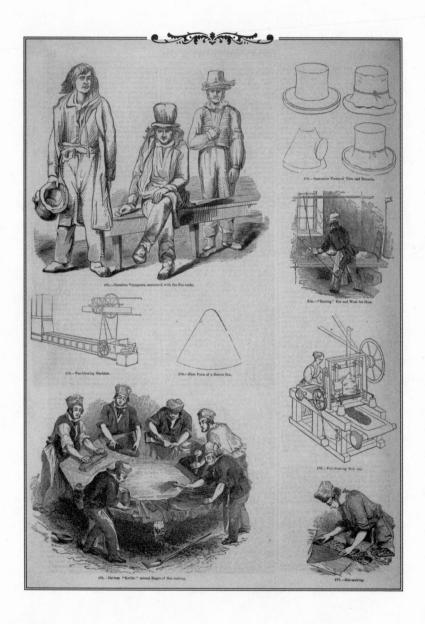

571.—Canadian Voyageurs, connected with the Fur-trade.

573.—Successive Forms of Hats and Bonnets.

574.—"Bowing" Fur and Wool for Hats.

575.—Fur-blowing Machine.

576.—First Form of a Beaver Hat.

572.—Fur-shaving Machine.

573.—Hatters' "Kettle:" several Stages of Hat-making.

577.—Hat-making.

·Five·
HATS

It's common knowledge that the nearly terminal decline of the beaver's North American empire was precipitated by a mania for beaver hats — and this much is true. The popular corollary to this historical tale attributes the beaver's subsequent salvation to the universal abandonment of beaver hats in favour of silk imitators. This idea that a whim of fashion brought the beaver-fur trade to a sudden and permanent halt is, in fact, a misconception. During Bryce Nimmo's seven years as president of Smithbilt Hats in Calgary, Alberta, he often encountered surprise that beaver hats still exist, as well as confusion about what they look like. "Everyone thinks, when you say beaver hat, they're going to see fur, like a Davy Crockett," he told me. Actually, a traditional beaver hat looks nothing like the raccoon-fur, tea-cozy-style headgear made famous by the legendary American frontiersman.

I was talking with Nimmo on the last day of June 2011, eight days before the start of the Calgary Stampede, modestly billed by its organizers as The Greatest Outdoor Show on Earth. From the opening parade on the first Friday to the final fireworks 10 days later, the Stampede brings a blizzard of white cowboy hats to the city's streets, continuing a Calgary tradition launched by Smithbilt's founder and a savvy mayor in the 1940s. The

Stampede is always like Christmas for Smithbilt, but in 2011, the level of excitement was even higher than usual. The company's master hatter had just put the finishing touches on a pair of white cowboy hats that would be presented to Prince William and the Duchess of Cambridge the following week — Calgary's equivalent of giving visiting dignitaries the keys to the city.

The Smithbilt hat-making tradition began in 1919, when Morris Shumiatcher, a 27-year-old Russian Jewish immigrant, bought the fledgling Calgary Hat Works and renamed it Smithbilt, after changing his own surname to Smith. Although he later reverted to Shumiatcher, the corporate moniker endured. Under Smith/Shumiatcher's direction, the company quickly established a reputation for making high-quality dress hats, as well as more practical wide-brimmed hats for working cowboys and ranchers. "Keep A Head With Smithbilt," exhorted a half-block-long sign painted on the side of one of the firm's original stores.

Smithbilt Hats remained a family business until 2002, then floundered for several years after the Shumiatcher descendants sold it. In 2006, a group of Calgary-area investors came to the rescue. The new owners overhauled some of the business practices, but altered none of the fundamental hat-making procedures. If Morris Shumiatcher were to rise from the dead and walk into the Smithbilt workshop today, he would feel right at home.

Smithbilt's current location, like the previous two, is close enough to the Stampede grounds that you can practically smell the livestock pens and sizzling burgers during rodeo season. Perched on the edge of a busy road, the one-storey industrial building is unpretentiously signed and nondescript. As I pulled into the gravel parking lot behind the loading bays, I couldn't have guessed that I was about to enter a shrine to one of the West's most belòved symbols.

The front door opened into a small showroom and sales area, presided over by a large friendly black dog with floppy ears. Brightly lit wall mounts and vertical racks scattered across the plank floor displayed a wide array of headwear: classic black top hats and equestrian dressage hats; bowlers and fedoras in a range of hues, sporting contrasting or matching grosgrain hatbands, a few with jaunty feathers tucked into the ribbon; a multitude of variously styled and coloured cowboy hats — white for the good guys, black for the bad, greys and browns for those on the fence and hot pink for the wild ones. Framed photographs of Smithbilt-wearing politicians, bronco-riders and other celebrities overlooked the merchandise. Country music played softly in the background.

Alerted to my arrival by the jangle of the cowbell that graces the front door, Bryce emerged from his office, wearing an ivory button-down shirt, stonewashed jeans and stylish cowboy boots. He greeted me with a solid handshake and introduced me to his canine companion, Derby. With a smoothness born of years of corporate-boardroom experience, he gave me a quick rundown of the company's history, then motioned me through an open doorway at the back of the showroom.

Our first stop was by a bank of high wooden shelves heaped with round-crowned, flaccid-brimmed hats that looked like something a groovy flower-child might have worn to Woodstock. At first glance, I thought they must be rejects. It turned out they were "hat bodies," waiting to be brought to life.

Smithbilt's felted hats, Bryce explained, are made from either fur (beaver or rabbit or a blend of the two) or sheep's wool. Fur is superior to wool, and pure beaver is unsurpassed. The differences originate during the felting process, when the fibres are wetted, agitated, condensed and pressed into sheets of robust, pliable fabric. All of these fibres are covered with microscopic scales that intermesh during the felting process; those on the rabbit and beaver hairs are tipped with barbs, which grab each other and hook together tenaciously. The longer the barb, the tighter the bond and the stronger the felt's "memory" — which is why beaver, with its exceptionally long barbs, is the fur of choice.

"A wool hat doesn't keep its shape in weather. It just folds," Bryce said. "But beaver's great. The best hat we ever could make is beaver."

Of course, premium quality comes at a cost, so most customers choose wool over fur or a mix of beaver and rabbit over pure beaver. The blends are graded according to the percentage of beaver fur they contain, which then determines the x-factor of the finished hat. Felt made with 20 percent beaver fur produces a 20x hat, and the price rises along with the grade.

"Most of the dress hats are rabbit," Bryce said. "I generally don't sell a pure beaver fedora, because there isn't a huge demand. We've made some. We've made pure beaver bowlers. But generally the demand is not as big in dress hats as it is in cowboy hats."

The market for pure beaver cowboy hats isn't big either. "I might do 150 to 200 a year," Bryce allowed, "where I'll do 10,000 of the wools." Sales of beaver blends fall somewhere in between, drawing those who are willing to pay more for quality or prestige.

"A lot of times when a guy buys a hat, there's a little bit of ego involved," Bryce said, then dropped a tone and added a hint of swagger to his voice. "'Oh, I've got a 50x hat and you've only got a 10x.'"

Felting is an ancient art, and no one knows when the first felted beaver fur hats were produced. Certainly, they were already in vogue by the late 1300s, when Chaucer placed a "Flaundryssh bevere hat" (that is, one manufactured by the renowned Flemish hatters of the day) on the head of his Canterbury-bound merchant. Over the next two centuries, they became wildly popular throughout Britain and Europe, valued both as a fashionable accessory and for their outstanding ability to hold up in wet weather — a definite asset before the advent of the rain-shedding umbrella in the late 1600s.

Eventually, the insatiable demand for beaver hats exceeded the Eurasian beaver's ability to withstand the onslaught, but even before that, hunters had taken a heavy toll on the species. For much of recorded history, the most sought-after parts of these animals were their castor glands, prized for the castoreum they contained.

Hippocrates, writing between 450 and 380 B.C., was the first to recommend medicinal use of castoreum, but offered few details. Johannes Mayer Marius, the German author of a monograph on the subject published in 1685, was more forthcoming. According to Marius, the numerous ailments that could be cured or alleviated with castoreum included headaches, toothaches, pleurisy, gout, deafness, epilepsy, liver tumours, sciatica and madness. Although castoreum has gone out of fashion as a pharmaceutical, we now know it contains significant quantities of salicylic acid, the same substance that gives aspirin its potency and helps treat various skin conditions. Not coincidentally, salicylic acid is also found in the bark of the beaver's favourite food trees: willows, aspens and poplars.

One enduring myth about beavers dates back at least as far as Aesop's fable-writing in the sixth century B.C. and reappears in early European literature. It is a tribute to the historical importance of castoreum. According to this folktale, a beaver cornered by hunters would chew off his testicles and throw them to his pursuers so they would spare his life. If the beaver had already forfeited his coveted body parts during a previous confrontation, he would run to an elevated spot and lift a leg to show the huntsmen he had nothing to offer. Scholars who perpetuated this myth — including Pliny the Elder, author of the encyclopedic *Naturalis Historia* — either didn't realize or didn't care that testicles have nothing to do with castoreum, and that both the sex organs and the castor glands are tucked inside the abdomen, making it impossible for even the most motivated beaver to perform a self-amputation.

The story was further spread by medieval Christian allegorists, who saw it as a model for the salvation of human souls. "In like fashion," wrote the anonymous author of one bestiary around the middle of the thirteenth century, "everyone who reforms his life and wants to live chastely in accordance with God's commandments should cut off all vices and shameless deeds and throw them in the devil's face. Then the devil will see that that man has nothing belonging to him and will leave him, ashamed."

Besides seeking castoreum, Britons and Europeans also hunted beavers for food. This pressure intensified in the Middle Ages after church authorities classified the beaver's scaly tail as fish, making it permissible Lenten fare. The body flesh, however, was still considered mammal meat and therefore forbidden.

At the same time, there was a constant demand for the beaver's warm, water-repellent fur, which was used for everything from ordinary outerwear to regal garments: in tenth-century Wales, King Hywel Dda claimed the right "to have the worth of Beavers, Martens and Ermines in whatsoever spot they are killed," so that his robes could be trimmed with their fur.

Beaver pelts are made up of two types of hair: a soft mat of fine, wavy, two- to three-centimetre-long hairs; and an overlying layer of stiff, straight guard hairs, which are about twice the length and ten times the diameter of the base hairs. Only the underfur is used for felting, and, initially, hat-makers had only two ways to get at it. Either they removed the guard hairs one by one, plucking them with tweezers or a knife pressed against a callused thumb, and then shaved off the underfur. Or they sent their pelts to Russia, where the underfur was collected using a combing technique that remained a closely guarded national secret until the end of the seventeenth century.

The hatters' fixation on the underfur had the strange effect of making second-hand beaver pelts even more desirable than new ones during the early days of the transatlantic fur trade. When buying other types of furs, the European dealers wanted pelts in pristine condition, but they soon recognized that they were better off buying beaver pelts that had been worn for a winter or two by their First Nations suppliers. Wearing the pelts fur-side-in rubbed off the guard hairs and saved the felt-makers considerable time and expense. These castoffs — called coat beaver by the English and *castor gras* (greasy beaver) by the French — varied widely in quality. Nevertheless, until the Russian fur-combing technique spread to other countries, most buyers preferred coat beaver to the alternative, commonly known as parchment beaver or *castor sec* (dry beaver).

Once the guard hairs were removed, by whatever means, the hat-maker brushed the pelt with a solution of nitrate of mercury. This step, referred to as carroting because it turned the hair tips orange, roughened the fibres so they would bind more effectively. It also infused them with mercury, which later vapourized when exposed to heat and moisture. Day after day, as the workers handled the hot, wet felt, they inhaled the toxic fumes. And as the mercury built up in their bodies, they started to exhibit classic "Mad Hatter" symptoms: uncontrollable tremors, a lurching gait, double vision, memory loss and incoherent speech, followed by seizures, blindness and delirium and, all too often, death.

After carroting, the pelt was handed over to other labourers, often women, who shaved it and carded the loose fur, untangling the hairs with wire-toothed brushes. The fur, referred to as fluff at this point, was then transferred to a draft-free room. There it was spread out on a special slotted table and worked over with an instrument that resembled an oversized violin bow with a single string. A skilled craftsman plucked the string while repeatedly passing the bow through the fluff. The resulting vibrations dislodged loose dirt, which fell through the slots in the table, and jostled the fibres against each other, so they matted together like clothes-dryer lint.

The large, cohesive batts that came out of the bowing room were first bassoned, a procedure that used pressure, heat and moisture to further bind the fibres and start shrinking the fabric, as it was shaped into a rough cone. Then they were planked: immersed numerous times in a large kettle filled with a hot, acidic solution and agitated by hand or with wooden stirring sticks until the cone shrank to between one-third and one-half of its original size. Once sufficiently planked, the cone was removed from the kettle, stretched over a wooden block that approximated the final hat shape, dried, dyed (if desired) and treated with a stiffening agent, such as glue or shellac. After that, all that remained was to refine the shape with steam and a hot iron and add lining and trim.

It took two or three beaver pelts to make a good-quality nineteenth-century top hat, and considerably more to produce the high-crowned, wide-brimmed hats favoured by the Cavaliers and Puritans in the mid-seventeenth century, prompting some hatters to surreptitiously cut their beaver fur with lesser materials. In 1634, the Court of France responded to this practice by ordering all master hatters to state their desire to work with either unadulterated beaver or with wool and rabbit fur. Once committed, they could not stray outside the terms of their agreement and those who worked with beaver had to hallmark each hat they produced, to verify its authenticity.

In 1638, England's King Charles I instituted similar customer protection, prohibiting the use of anything other than pure "beaver wool" or "beaver stuff" in beaver hats. Charles I's royal proclamation also decreed that only English-made beaver hats could be sold in his country. Nearly a century later, British hatters were still griping about foreign competition, their chief complaint being that American hat-makers undercut them by using cheaper grades of beaver fur. In 1732, these claims led Britain's Parliament to pass the Hat Act, which curbed imports from the colonies. By then, however, colonial hatters had their own fast-growing domestic markets to serve.

Felt-making hasn't changed significantly since the birth of the beaver hat, though mercury is no longer used and the technology has been updated. Nowadays, industrial felters use mechanized blowers and rollers, boiler-fed steamers and shaping machines and pressurized dye vats. The biggest difference is that most modern hat-makers leave felt production to the specialists, a handful of commercial manufacturers scattered around the world. Smithbilt buys its fur hat-bodies from two suppliers: FEPSA (Feltros Portugueses, SA) in São João da Madeira, Portugal; and the Winchester Hat Corporation in Winchester, Tennessee, aptly located on the David Crockett Highway. Their wool hat-bodies mostly come from South America.

Once Bryce had explained the basics of the raw materials to me, we carried on to the back of the building and the heart of the Smithbilt operation. The first thing I noticed when we entered the workshop was a long wooden table covered with dozens of hats in different stages of production. The second was a row of archaic-looking machines lined up against one wall, the paint on their heavy steel bodies chipped and faded, their joints blackened with grease and their levers rubbed shiny by years of handling. Hoses snaked from the belly of each contraption to connect with copper pipes running along the wall.

"We've got a big boiler back here that produces steam all the time," Bryce said. "It gets pretty warm in the middle of summer." For the moment, however, the breeze blowing in through the open loading-bay door was keeping things comfortable. A couple of employees were shifting boxes of stock near the open door, their voices mingling with the country-and-western twang coming from a radio somewhere and intermittently drowned out by abrasive machine sounds. The only other people in sight were a grey-haired, walrus-moustached man engaged in some kind of hat-making task on the far side of the room and a younger man with a beefy build and muscular arms, who was operating one of the machines. We made our way over to the latter, and Bryce introduced him as a hat-blocker named Gerald.

Gerald's loose-fitting jeans were topped by an untucked Alexander Keith's T-shirt and a shy, gap-toothed smile. Although reluctant to talk about himself or have his last name publicized, he was happy to show me his craft. We started at the blocking machine, which resembled a pressure cooker mounted on a metal stand, with a ring of sturdy brass pincers around the inner lip of the vessel. Gerald selected a floppy white hat body, set it crown-side-up on top of the pincers and activated a foot pedal under the stand. A cloud of white vapour burst from below with a sharp hiss and enveloped the hat.

"The first thing I do is put steam on it to soften it," he explained. "Now I'm going to clamp the teeth down and then give it more steam and stretch the brim out." He tucked the edge of the felt into the shiny pincers and yanked a handle on one side of the machine. As soon as the teeth grabbed hold of the brim, he shifted his grasp to another lever and eased it down, so it pulled the brim outward as the steam billowed all around it.

Once the hat was sufficiently stretched, Gerald picked up a plum pudding–shaped chunk of wood — flat on the bottom and domed on top — and rammed it into the crown. "That's a block," he said. "For blocking the head size into the hat." Dozens of other blocks — some rounder, others flat on both ends — in a range of sizes were lined up on nearby shelves. He reached up through the steam, grabbed a long handlebar with an attached plate and hauled it down. Leaning into the bar with his whole upper body, he pressed the plate against the base of the block. Then he raised it back up, released the teeth and blasted the hat with a whoosh of cool air.

To remove the hat from the machine, he slipped his fingers into three holes drilled into the block's base. The hat stayed snugged onto the wooden form as he lifted it out and set the whole thing on the worktable. I gently laid my palm against the warm, damp crown, which still felt slightly malleable. The hat beside it, which Gerald had blocked just a few minutes earlier, was already dry and stiff — but not yet ready for the next phase of the process. Wool hats have to rest overnight after being blocked. Fur felt hats have to sit for a week, "to get a new memory."

"If we take the block off too early," Bryce commented from the sidelines, "it'll want to shrink back, and the guy will say, 'my hat's too small.'"

The hat body that Gerald had just blocked was on its way to becoming one of Smithbilt's famous white cowboy hats, which are made exclusively from rabbit fur. "I don't get any part-beavers or pure-beavers in white," Bryce said, "because no one wants to spend that much on a white hat that they won't wear very often. It's a great presentation hat, a great symbol for this city, but not that practical when you want to wear it out and about." Most beaver hats, I would later learn, are black or brown, but that's only if they're made of dyed fur. Left undyed, beaver felt is typically the colour of cooked oatmeal.

Leaving the freshly blocked hat, Gerald selected one that had already memorized its altered dimensions and carried it over to the next antique machine, a hulking green hydraulic press with a frame like a robotic praying mantis. The body of the machine held an aluminum die, which looked like a cowboy hat–shaped jelly mould. Gerald put the hat into the die and then picked up a rubber replica of the die, which he called a saddle, and fitted it inside the hat. Inside the lid of the press, he explained, was a rubber bag that would drop into the saddle and be filled with hot water from the boilers. As the bag expanded, it would sandwich the felt between the die and saddle, forcefully compacting the fibres to commit to their new shape.

"These white hats cook fast," he said. "I don't have to leave it in there very long." Less than a minute, in fact. When he lifted the lid and removed the die and saddle, the hat body had been transformed into a handsome cowboy hat with an upturned brim and a smartly creased crown.

Hydraulic presses are fast and efficient, but at Smithbilt, they're used only for shaping wool and rabbit-fur hats. The beaver hats, from 10x upward, are all hand shaped, so they can be modified to the customer's specifications. "Plus," Bryce said, "it adds to the romance."

The man in charge of that romance is company vice-president Brian Hanson, one of the partners who bought Smithbilt in 2006. Brian, who grew up on a cattle ranch just north of Calgary, had just sold his modular home–moving business and was looking for a new direction when the opportunity to work at Smithbilt came up in 2003. He liked the idea of getting involved in the venerable western hat-making trade but had no interest in just sitting in an office. He wanted to make hats himself.

Soon after he signed on with Smithbilt, Brian hired a veteran hat-maker — "an old guy who worked for Stetson for 35 years" — to come to Calgary and teach him the art of handcrafting hats. Four years later, the apprentice was ready to go it alone as Smithbilt's custom hatter — a rare breed, especially in Canada. "There's not very many people in the country who know how to do this," Brian told me. "I'd be surprised if there was 10, maybe only five."

Brian's domain is the fur room, a small corner atelier with plasterboard walls and large interior windows that look out on the main manufactory. A tall, sandy-haired man who looks made for long days out riding the range, he moved from one work station to the next with quiet self-assurance. When I entered, he was apron-clad and standing at a lathe-like machine with a black 20x hat body whirling in front of him. The hat had been blocked already, in the same way that Gerald had demonstrated; the lathe-arm gripped the block inside the crown. As the brim spun perpendicular to the floor, Brian lightly pressed it between two yellow sanding sponges. "We call this pouncing," he said, raising his voice to be heard over the strident motor.

For this first round of pouncing, he was using coarse, 200-grit sandpaper. From there, he would progress to 400 and increasingly finer grades, right up to 1,500 on a 100x hat. The higher the quality of the felt, the more sanding it gets, with as many as 10 passes for pure beaver. The machine Brian was working on — called a crown iron — had the same vintage appearance as the equipment out in the main workshop, but its fire-engine red paint was in better condition. He pointed to the actual pouncing machines at the other end of the room. "The far one is a brim pouncer and the close one is a crown pouncer. But I prefer to do 'em by hand. They're not cutting-edge technology."

After sanding with the 200-grit for several minutes, Brian motioned for me to stand back. He picked up a plastic spray-bottle filled with a clear liquid, spritzed the spinning hat and nonchalantly flicked a lighter underneath it. A corona of orange flames flared out from the black felt for a few spectacular seconds. "That burns off some of the longer hairs," he said calmly, as though flambéing a combustible object attached to a motorized machine in a closed room was a perfectly reasonable thing to do.

"Is that dangerous?" I asked.

He laughed. "I haven't started myself on fire yet. I might have lost some hair off my arms."

It struck me as a "Don't do this at home, kids" kind of trick, but as Brian continued pouncing, now with 400-grit, he appeared more concerned about the hat than his own pelt. "You have to be careful with the finer grit," he said, "because that's when it'll turn colour. So if I did this for too long, it would just be getting lighter."

With that, he set the sanding blocks aside and picked up the spray bottle again. Time for the second, and final, burning. After the brief blaze, the acrid scent of scorched fur lingered in the air. "Ever been on a cattle brand?" Brian asked. "Same smell."

"We don't burn the white ones," he added, "but the black, you can pretty well do anything to it, and black is by far our most common colour."

He did a bit more pouncing, then misted the hat with alcohol again. There were no pyrotechnics this time. Instead, he burnished the felt with his bare hands, caressing the crown and rubbing the brim between his flattened palms and outstretched fingers as the hat revolved on the lathe arm. Finally, he switched off the machine and the room fell silent. When he removed the hat, its surface was like velvet.

With the pouncing done, we proceeded to a piece of equipment that Brian called a jam blocker, out in the main workshop. "This does two things," he said. "It flattens the brim out and it maintains a consistent size." I thought the brim looked sufficiently flat, but Brian pointed out some almost imperceptible ripples caused by the pull of the teeth during the initial blocking. Five minutes compressed between the jam blocker's searing hot metal plates would erase them completely.

While we waited, we talked about the heritage of Smithbilt's hat-making equipment. Many of the machines date back to Morris Shumiatcher's time, and the oldest were built more than a century ago. There's no way of knowing the exact age of the hat blocks — unlike the machines, they aren't marked with manufacturing dates — but some of them are also as old or older than the Smithbilt name.

"The blocks have to be wood," Brian said, "because it absorbs the moisture out of the hat. Plastic wouldn't." Smooth, tight-grained poplar is best, especially for high-end beaver hats. Coarser-grained wood will impress the felt with a pattern of delicate lines that become visible when the hat is pounced.

Among the most prized blocks in the Smithbilt collection are those for making top hats, ingeniously designed to account for the fact that the uppermost portion of a top hat is wider than the middle. "They're a puzzle block," Brian explained when he showed them to me later. "The centre comes out and then you can pull it out one piece at a time, so that it maintains the shape of the hat." As he dismantled and reassembled the five inter-locking parts, it reminded me of a toddlers' toy.

A shelf labeled "Topper" held six of the slightly convex columnar forms in a range of head sizes. Below were half a dozen Prince Alberts, for making the taller-crowned style popularized by Queen Victoria's husband in the mid-1800s. Most of the blocks, whether multi-part or one-piece, were dye-blackened and patinated from their decades of use.

Once the jam blocker had ironed out the ripples, we returned to the fur room. Brian set the hat on a table and picked up a wood-and-brass brim cutter with a curved edge that fitted against the crown. Leaning over the hat and holding down the brim with his forearm, he circled the blade around the circum-ference to trim the brim to exactly 4¾ inches. Another cutting device reduced the leftover strip of felt to a neat, narrow hat-band. With a handheld detail sander, he smoothed the edge of the brim and both edges of the hatband. Then he wrapped the band loosely around the crown. For the moment, his work was done.

Traditionally, lining and trimming hats was women's work, and at Smithbilt, it still is. With the hat in hand, Brian led me into a room filled with sewing paraphernalia and introduced me to Mui Luangphasi, a young Laos-born seamstress who had been working at Smithbilt for seven years. Her jeans were fashionably ripped and distressed, and she wore a saffron T-shirt and a pink vest that matched her nail polish and lipstick. Her demeanour was as sunny as her attire.

Mui began by selecting a sweatband and placing it into an embossing machine to stamp a gold "Beaver 20x" onto the smooth black leather. Then she stitched the ends together on her Pfaff sewing machine and sewed a size tag and a small black bow onto the seam. The bow was a hat-makers' tradition. "They were originally a warning," Brian said. "It's a skull and cross-bones, because the hats used to have mercury in them."

Now that the sweatband was a closed loop, Mui had to shift to a special sewing machine to sew it into the hat. Instead of a flat stitch plate, this one had a cylindrical base, so the crown could fit over it. It was also treadle-operated, for greater control.

Brian and I watched Mui carefully rotate the hat beneath the needle. "If I jam blocked it right, the sweatband should fit perfectly," he said.

"And if not?" I asked.

"I'll have to go do it again."

It did fit, however, so she moved on to attaching the exterior band that would hide the sweatband stitching. After threading a 20x Smithbilt buckle — the future owner's bragging badge — onto the felt strip that Brian had cut from the brim, she donned her eyeglasses and sewed the hatband on by hand. Then she cut out and shaped the lining, dabbed a little glue under the sweat-band to hold it in place and popped it into the crown.

The whole time Mui was attending to the black beaver hat, about 15 minutes in all, her co-worker, an older Asian woman with tightly permed hair, sat silently at a nearby table, deftly tying narrow black ribbons around the crowns of white cowboy hats. The hats that were rapidly stacking up beside her reminded me of the ones my parents had bought for my siblings and me, as well as themselves, after we moved to Calgary from Montreal in 1972. Ours were made of white straw, but they were finished with the same long-tailed, black-ribbon flourish. As an insecure 12-year-old, new to western living, I had avoided wearing mine for fear of looking uncool. Now I found myself feeling nostalgic and wondering whether my outgrown "key to the city" was still stashed away in a closet somewhere in my parents' house.

When Mui was done with the detailing, the hat looked great, except that it was still pancake-brimmed and pudding-crowned. It was time for Brian to give it its ultimate form. His hand-shaping station, in the main workshop, was a table equipped with a tin chimney pipe that spewed steam on demand. "When a hat's open like this, I can turn it into any shape," he said. "Since I don't have a customer for this, I'm going to do the Cattleman."

Smithbilt offers six brim-shape choices on its western hats, ranging from the low-profile Roper to the radically upturned Showman. There are also eight crown options, including the Cattleman ("our most popular by far"), the Bull Rider ("a lot of the rodeo guys get that"), the flat-topped Gaucho and the classy, high-crowned Open Road. The Gus, which features a loosely creased, forward-sloping crown, is named after Robert Duvall's character in the 1989 miniseries *Lonesome Dove*. It's a sentimental favourite at Smithbilt, because they made the hats for the show, just one of the company's many TV and movie hat-making credits.

After softening the hat in a swirl of steam, Brian thumbed a deep groove into the top of the crown. Then he immersed it again in the steam and sculpted hollows on either side of the centre crease, gently plying the felt with his fingers and thumbs. When he was satisfied with the crown configuration, he steamed the hat once more and squeezed the brim between a moulded plastic plate and a matching collar to give it the rudimentary Trail Boss contours. The nuances he would create by hand.

Normally, Brian's clients come in and try on their hats at this point, so he can accommodate any anatomical quirks or personal preferences as he shapes the crown and brim. For the royal couple, whose white hats he had finished the day before, there would be no opportunity for a fitting. "Their handlers told me the size," he said. "We actually did three of them, just in case."

As Brian coaxed the brim into shape, periodically raising the hat to eye-level and appraising his efforts, Bryce and a customer wandered into the workshop. The man carried a tired-looking cowboy hat, which he hoped to wear to the upcoming Stampede.

"How old is it?" Bryce asked.

"I'm not sure," the customer replied. "Maybe 30 years?"

Earlier Bryce had told me he'd like to make nothing but beaver hats, though it would be a poor business strategy because they're so durable. "Once you get one," he declared, "you don't need another." On the positive side, owners of these hats are the most likely to take advantage of Smithbilt's refurbishing services, which range from cleaning to sweatband replacement to complete overhauls.

After they left, I asked Brian about hat longevity. "With the beaver, I can make a 10-year-old hat look like new again," he said. If it was originally hand shaped, he can even re-block it and change the shape.

He told me about his favourite beaver hat, which he "wore in the rain for years and years" before retiring it, replacing the leather sweatband twice along the way. When he showed the old Bull Rider to me later, it looked immaculate. The only reason he'd stopped wearing it, he confessed, was that country music idol George Strait had signed it for him and he didn't want to risk ruining the autograph.

When he was finished fine-tuning the black Cattleman, Brian blew it clean with pressurized air from a hose and held it up for my inspection. He didn't say anything, but his expression was one of pride and pleasure. Back in the fur room, I had asked him if he enjoyed being a hat-maker. "Yes," he had answered. "You can see what you've done at the end of the day."

From around 1780 to 1810, the number of North American beavers killed for their fur spiked, a result of the North West Company expanding aggressively into the western territories while the Hudson's Bay Company held its ground in Rupert's Land and various Spanish and American independents plundered the southwest. Then, in the following decade, beaver-pelt sales plummeted, dropping to less than half of the peak numbers and remaining low until the middle of the nineteenth century. Silk hats played a role in these trends. However, their impact was more complicated than most accounts acknowledge.

The most plausible story about the birth of the silk topper claims that in the late 1700s, a Frenchman living in China took his beaver (as top hats made of beaver-fur felt were then known) to a local hatter and asked him to replicate it in silk. When he returned to Paris, trendsetters embraced this novelty and the silk hat craze took off.

The bodies of these new hats were constructed from cotton, wrapped around a form and coated with shellac. Once the body hardened, the hatter covered it with silk plush, a finely woven velour that could be brushed to a lustre. Eye-catching, light-weight and relatively waterproof, the silk version of the top hat had much to recommend it, and once production picked up, it could be had for half the price of a beaver of equal quality. The French also had another incentive to switch from beaver to silk: Britain's North American victory over France in 1760 had left London largely in control of the world supply of beaver pelts, and these became inaccessible to French hatters after Napoleon embargoed trade with Britain in 1806.

Beaver-pelt prices fluctuated throughout the early 1800s and then bottomed out in the 1840s. Most fur traders blamed this bad news on the silk hat's ascendency. In 1843, a letter from the Governor and Committee of the Hudson's Bay Company complained about the "continually decreasing price" of their staple commodity and held out "no very cheering prospect for the future, unless the tides of fashion change, and the consumption of Beaver in the manufacture of hats become more general than it has been for some past time."

Yet for all the doom and gloom, there was still a market for beaver pelts. Hatters continued to make some of their wares from beaver felt, and clothiers used unfelted fur for coats and trim. By the 1850s, beaver trapping was on the rise again, and before long, the continent-wide take was as high as it had been through most of the 1700s. Then the momentum stalled, and beaver-pelt sales figures went into freefall. They kept on tumbling through the last decades of the 1800s, until they were almost as low as they had been at the inception of the fur trade, three centuries earlier.

Paradoxically, rather than causing this crash, silk hats had actually kept the beaver-fur trade going longer than it would have if beaver hats had prevailed. The real reason for the declining pelt sales was that there were hardly any beavers left to trap — a predicament that would have arisen sooner if consumers had stayed true to their infatuation with beaver hats. Astute observers like Hudson's Bay Company trader William Tolmie foresaw this dénouement far in advance. In 1839, concerned about the diminishing beaver harvest, Tolmie had confided to his journal that "the exterminating system of hunting . . . if not checked, will speedily eventuate in the destruction of the more valuable Fur-bearing animals." And none was more valuable than the beaver.

I don't know whether Morris Shumiatcher's original hat line included items made of beaver-fur felt, but there's a good chance it did, because beaver hats never disappeared entirely, even when silk hats ruled. During my private showing of beaver artifacts at the Canadian Museum of Civilization, I had seen the evidence. The museum's beaver hats from the 1800s ranged from a topper "manufactured expressly for" a Quebec City gentleman by the illustrious Christys' of London to a black stovepipe hat of the type once worn to church by Welsh women. The twentieth-century examples included a 1911 ceremonial bicorn that was part of the first-class civil uniform of Canada's eighth prime minister, Sir Robert Borden — its stiff, black felt body decorated with a black silk cockade, white ostrich feathers and gold bullion loop; a blue "baby doll" hat from the 1940s; and an undated, green "Genuine Beaver Soleil Coronet" that was made in Czechoslovakia for the famous Parisian Schiaparelli label, probably in the 1960s, judging by the style.

From conventional artisans to avant-garde artistes, a handful of hat-makers had kept the beaver-hat tradition going, despite the rise of the silk top hat and the decimation of beaver populations. And artisans like Brian Hanson are still turning out beaver hats for the discerning cowboy (or cowgirl).

Before I left Smithbilt, I lingered for a while in the showroom and tried on some of the inventory. The elegant dress hats seemed full of possibilities, transforming me in the mirror as I switched from bowler to Prince Albert to fedora. But the allure of the western hats, with their soft, sensuous beaver felt, was even stronger. Unlike the straw cowboy hat of my adolescence, the midnight-black 100x Cattleman I tried on sat extremely comfortably on my head. I would have cheerfully worn it out of the store, if not for the $895 price tag. Reluctantly, I set it back on its hook, said my goodbyes and set the cowbell clinking again as I departed. My hat lust would have to remain unsated.

· Six ·
FUR TRADING
ON SKYWAY AVENUE

Thanks to the beaver-hat fever that raged through Europe and Britain for so long, no other North American animal has ever been as commoditized as the beaver. It's not just that beavers were the economic engine that drove colonization or that they produced astronomical profits for enterprises like the Hudson's Bay Company and canny businessmen like John Jacob Astor, whose fur dealing helped make him a millionaire in the early 1800s. Other North American species, from Atlantic cod to plains bison, were also slaughtered in great numbers and generated fortunes. But only the beaver received the dubious honour of being widely regarded as a form of currency.

When Father Paul Le Jeune told his Jesuit superiors in 1636 that "peltry" was "the coin of the greatest value" in New France, he was referring specifically to beaver pelts. "The day-laborers . . . would rather receive the wages for their work in this money than in any other," he reported. Similarly, mapmaker David Thompson observed during his continental travels in the late 1700s and early 1800s that beavers "were the gold coin of the country, with which the necessaries of life were purchased." The sentiment was the same throughout colonial North America: beaver furs were as good as, or better than, any legal tender.

Not long after Le Jeune wrote his remarks, the Hudson's Bay Company formalized this arrangement with the introduction of a uniquely North American unit of trade, the Made Beaver, commonly abbreviated as MB.

The HBC established the Made Beaver as its standard unit of exchange shortly after the company was founded in 1670. One MB was the equivalent of one prime-quality adult beaver pelt, and until 1810, almost everything bought or sold at trading posts throughout the company empire — including lower quality beaver pelts — was priced in terms of Made Beaver. In the 1860s, the company began minting brass trade-tokens in four denominations: one, one-half, one-quarter and one-eighth MB.

The first tokens were about the size of a modern quarter. One side was stamped with the value and three sets of letters: MB (though a die-cutter's error initially rendered this as NB); HB, for Hudson's Bay Company; and EM, for East Main District, the jurisdiction in which the tokens were dispensed. The reverse displayed the company's coat of arms, with four black beavers hunkered on the shield and the motto *Pro Pelle Cutem* ("a skin for a skin") scrolled out below.

Hudson's Bay Company traders priced other furs relative to the MB and adjusted the rate according to local circumstances. In 1733, a hunter who came into Moose Factory or Fort Albany on James Bay with the skins of three martens, two otters, two deer, one wolf or one fox would receive credit for one Made Beaver. He would get two MB for a black bear, moose or lynx, and one and a half for a *queequeehatch*, as wolverines were commonly called at the time. A pound of castoreum, 10 pounds of feathers or eight pairs of moose hooves were all valued at one MB.

Goods that customers could buy with one Made Beaver included: three-quarters of a pound of coloured beads, 20 fish hooks, 12 dozen buttons, one brass kettle, two pounds of sugar, two looking glasses, six thimbles, one pair of shoes, one shirt, four spoons, one and a half ounces of vermilion, two hatchets, four egg boxes, half a yard of broad cloth, one pound of Brazilian tobacco, four fire steels, two combs, one and a half pounds of gunpowder and five pounds of shot. They paid 10 to 12 MB for a gun, six for a blanket, four for a gallon of brandy and one and a quarter for a pair of stockings.

In 1820, the rival North West Company created its own beaver token, which was slightly larger than the Hudson's Bay Company's. The dated side bore the head of a man who looked vaguely like Augustus Caesar. On the flip side, the company name framed the image of a beaver, posed much like the one on the modern Canadian nickel. Only a few of these brass or copper coins still exist. Most of them have a small hole drilled in the top, so they could be strung on a cord and worn around the bearer's neck.

The Mountain Men who operated in the Rockies in the first half of the nineteenth century called beavers, which were their most lucrative quarry, "hairy banknotes." Farther east, one major trader actually produced paper beaver-tender, at least briefly: in the late 1830s, the American Fur Company's Northern Outfit in La Pointe, Wisconsin, issued certificates known as "beaver money," which were signed by the trading post's factor and could be redeemed for merchandise.

The Hudson's Bay Company issued its last Made Beaver tokens long after the other players and their currencies had ceased circulating. Produced for the St. Lawrence-Labrador District in the early 1920s, these plain aluminum tokens lacked the coat of arms and came in denominations of one, five, 10 and 20 MB, a clear indication of how much the buying power of beaver pelts had declined in half a century.

Beaver tokens are rarities now, exchanged only by coin collectors, but the trade in beaver pelts is still going strong. Much stronger than I'd ever guessed, in fact, until I entered the North American Fur Auctions corporate headquarters on a grey March morning in 2010.

From the outside, 65 Skyway Avenue was just another low-rise office building in the centre of the commercial-industrial conglomeration that surrounds Toronto's Pearson International Airport. But there was nothing commonplace about the pungent odour that assaulted me as I stepped into the lobby. Whatever standard office smells might have been present — photocopier toner, new carpets, coffee, cologne — were completely overwhelmed by something far more potent, yet enigmatic. I recoiled instinctively, then realized it was not really so repugnant. I inhaled deeply and tried to tease apart the complex strands: kennel scent; butcher shop undertones; a whiff of musk. So this is what the fur trade smells like, I thought.

On this Friday, the opening day of the North American Fur Auctions' week-long winter sale, the building bustled with activity. At the front desk, several receptionists, including the one who had buzzed me through the locked doors and handed me a guest name-tag, were fielding phone calls. A trio of employees stood at a long counter nearby, registering new arrivals. Behind them, people scurried in and out of cubicles, clutching papers and tossing questions over their shoulders. And then there were the men milling about in the foyer, all of them wearing white lab coats with the NAFA logo stamped above the left breast pocket. I couldn't fathom what this scientific garb had to do with the auctioning of fur.

The logo consisted of the company acronym printed across an outline of North America on a blue and white globe, with the words "Since 1670" curved around the lower edge — a proud assertion of pedigree. As a direct descendent of the Hudson's Bay Company, NAFA is North America's oldest and largest fur-trading firm. Worldwide, the only larger fur auctioneer is Kopenhagen Fur, but the Danish company owes its superior position to ranched furs. No one sells more wild furs, including beaver, than NAFA.

The auction I had come for was a major international event, with 450 buyers from at least 15 countries in attendance. China, Korea and Russia were the major players. Italy, Greece, Germany, France, Spain, England, Turkey, Poland, Belarus, Dubai, United States and Canada rounded out the cosmopolitan roster. Most of the North American buyers were from Toronto, Montreal and New York City.

Although the company's fur auctions aren't open to the public, my interest in beavers had earned me a sympathetic hearing from the senior management. Alerted to my arrival by the receptionist, Oscar Carbonell, the manager with whom I had been corresponding, came out to meet me. He had warned me that auction weeks were his busiest of the year — "frenetic days" he had said in his email — but his manner was calm and solicitous. He got me a coffee, inquired about my trip and then turned me over to my tour guide for the day, a soft-spoken man named Murray Parkinson.

With his thick black-rimmed glasses and slightly grubby lab coat, its upper pocket stuffed with pens, Parkinson looked appropriately nerdy for someone whose job title was "fur technician." His specialty was grading mink, he said, but after 25 years of working on and off for NAFA, he was familiar with most parts of the operation.

I followed Parkinson down a short hallway and into the warehouse, a space that looked like an airport hangar and could have easily accommodated a pair of 747s. Ranks of fluorescent tube-lights, suspended from steel rafters, receded into the distance. Below them, long lines of waist-high tables extended towards a back wall that was too far away to see. The feral scent was stronger here, and the source was obvious. Parked between the lines of tables were hundreds, maybe thousands, of wheeled racks, their steel skeletons obscured by a burden of fur. There were more animals in this 7,000-square-metre room than I'd ever seen together in one place — and they were all dead.

Of the two or three auctions NAFA holds annually, only the winter one (usually held in February, but delayed to March that year) highlights wild fur. Up for bids this time were the pelts of three million ranch-raised mink, 15,000 ranch foxes and hundreds of thousands of wild furbearers, gathered from all across the continent. It seemed like the entire offering was spread out before us in the warehouse. Incredibly, this was only a fraction of the total: each bundle was a sample that represented a larger lot, ranging in size from a dozen or so furs to several hundred.

I couldn't spot any beaver pelts from the doorway, but there were numerous other species in view. "If it walks, crawls or looks at you funny," Parkinson said, "we've probably got it here."

We started with the mink. Parkinson had farmed these animals himself for 16 years. Now his only contact with them was handling the pelts after they had been peeled from the carcasses, scraped clean of all fat and muscle and pulled like a sock onto a long, narrow board, fur-side out, to be dried by forced air. Dry-cured like this, skins stay good for a long time, he explained, especially in cold storage, but not indefinitely. Once purchased, they have to be tanned.

The ranch mink came in an array of shades, with names straight out of *Martha Stewart Living*: sapphire, blue iris, lavender, pearl, silver blue, pastel, mahogany. "They're all just genetic mutations that are selectively bred," Parkinson said. The pelts hung from plastic straps strung through their nostrils, ten to a bundle — long, flat ribbons stripped of everything that had once defined them as living beings, except their lustrous fur. I stroked a silvery sample and imagined how sensuous it would feel against my bare arms.

I don't come from a fur-wearing family, though one of my grandmothers had a Persian lamb coat, whose tiny black curls I delighted in tugging on the rare occasions when I saw it. My own fur-wearing experience has been similarly limited. In high school, I bought myself a long wool coat with a hood edged in grey rabbit fur — largely, as I recall, because it made me feel like a romantic *Doctor Zhivago*–worthy heroine, about to cross an infinite snowy landscape in a horse-drawn sleigh. I've also owned fur-trimmed moccasins made by First Nations crafts-women. But until that moment in the warehouse, I had never had any desire to wrap myself in fur. Fine for others, if that's what they wanted, I'd always thought, but not for me. And now, to my chagrin, I found myself surrendering to the seduction of sleek guard hairs and plush underfur, admiring the way the mink shimmered and glowed, even under stark, industrial light-ing. Could I blame it on sensory overload?

In any case, I wasn't the only one fingering the goods. Scattered about the warehouse, 15 or 20 people dressed in lab coats stood at widely spaced intervals along the tables, studying pelts and making notations in thick binders. They were buyers, Parkinson told me, and their binders held catalogues that listed the lots individually, indicating the number of pelts in each lot, as well their size, grade and colour. Some of the buyers were there to purchase for themselves. Others were working

on behalf of clients, mostly garment manufacturers and fur-
riers. One individual might have as many as eight different
clients, each with a specific order to fill: so many thousand
black minks, so many violet. In preparation for the auction, the
buyers spend up to a week inspecting the lots, gauging their
value and deciding which ones to bid on. Their catalogue notes
are written in code, in case a competitor manages to peek at
the pages.

The lab coats, it turned out, were a NAFA courtesy, provided to protect the buyers' clothing. "Some fur articles are
much dirtier than others," Parkinson said, singling out raccoon
and beaver, and not all trappers wash their furs before shipping
them. "You'll see the beaver graders and their hands will be black
from the grease," he said. Over the course of my visit, I came to
understand that the white garments were like vestments, worn
by nearly all the buyers, regardless of how much time they actually spent handling fur in the warehouse. Most of them picked
up a pristine lab coat when they arrived each day and wore it
until they left.

Emerging from the racks of mink, we came to a display of bears
— polar, black and grizzly — and wolverines. Unlike most of
NAFA's offerings, these animals had been tanned and stitched
onto fabric linings, and their heads had been subjected to taxi-
dermist artistry. Splayed across a large table, their impotent paws
dangled and their heads rested on each other's shoulders. Blind
eyes stared and fake pink tongues curled behind bleached teeth.
The "raw" bear pelts that I would see later, stacked on wheeled
carts because they were too big to hang on racks, would all be
missing critical features: ears or lips or claws. They would do for
rugs, but not for trophies.

Parkinson seemed perturbed by the mounted animals, as if the grooming they had received had effaced the animal essence he related to in the dry-cured skins. We cut back through the mink racks and continued towards my main interest, the beavers, while he delivered a running commentary.

"Those are coyotes. Smells like a lot of wet dogs."

I sunk my fingers into their thick coats as we passed the racks. They felt like dogs, too.

"Kit foxes." Parkinson had already moved on down the row. "We don't get a lot of them. I think they're used mainly for linings."

"Muskrat, or musquash, whichever you want to call them. These are the hot item this year, because with the mink prices going up, the buyers want anything that has a fur similar to a mink." The muskrats had been prepared inside out. Blood stains marbled the smooth skin. Fur fringed the bottom edge.

There's a long tradition of using muskrat to impersonate other animals, Parkinson explained. "In years gone by, the Hudson's Bay Company sold in their stores what they called Hudson Seal, where they would shear these and dye it, and it was the poor man's seal. Just a muskrat coat made to look like fur seal. They had another one called Otter Fantasy, where it was dyed to look like otter." These days, I thought, they simply use synthetics made from petrochemicals.

Just past the muskrats, we finally reached the beavers: big, flat disks, furred on one side, leathery on the reverse. Parkinson heaved one of the bundles off the rack, carried it over to an inspection table and thumped it down. "These are the legs" — four slits sewed closed with coarse thread. "Ears, eyes, nose and mouth." His finger darted from hole to hole, mapping the anatomy. "The tail's been cut off."

He shuffled the pelts like a poker player sorting cards and selected examples to illustrate his points as he described the features the graders look for: size, colour, fur density, damage marks. It was hard to keep up with his high-speed delivery, but he had promised me time with a beaver specialist the next day, so I didn't worry about the details.

When we were done with the beavers, we resumed our circuit. Raccoon, wild mink, bobcat, lynx. "I hope you're not allergic to cats," Parkinson said, stopping beside the felines to highlight their differences. "Now bobcats, the part that they use is right here, the spotted belly. Clearly defined spots, nice bright white, that's what they're looking for. The lynx doesn't have as definite spots on the belly."

Later, perusing the post-auction report, I saw just how desirable those spots were. El-Ezer, a company from Pyatigorsk, Russia, had paid $800 per pelt for the premier lot of bobcat furs. That was more than double the top price paid for any of the other wild fur at this auction, aside from timber wolf, which had maxed out at $440 apiece.

After the cats, two weasel cousins: pine marten and fisher. You have to be careful grading fishers, Parkinson noted, because they eat porcupines and many of them end up with quills permanently imbedded in their bodies. His endless store of fur factoids made me feel like I had dropped into a bizarre episode of Marlin Perkins' *Wild Kingdom*.

Near the back of the warehouse, we paused to look at squirrels, the cheapest item on offer. More than 43,000 had sold that afternoon, at an average price of $1.41. The ermines hanging beside them were almost as small, but slightly more valuable. Parkinson lifted one of the slender pelts by the black tip of its long white tail. "It looks like they stretched them on tongue depressors," he quipped. I laughed with him, and then felt guilty for treating their deaths so lightly.

We carried on to the wolves. Black nose-pads pointing to the ceiling, they dangled from extra-tall racks so their bushy tails wouldn't sweep the floor. I recalled a fragment of conversation I had overheard in the cafeteria earlier. The speaker was a Russian woman named Natasha, one of the few female buyers at the auction. "I've been buying timber wolves," she said, with an accent as smooth as the finest vodka. "They're expensive, but still we buy them." Standing before these magnificent specimens, I understood the yearning in her voice. I skimmed my fingertips down one of the lifeless backs, then hurried off to catch up with Parkinson.

Our last stop was the cold storage. Floor-to-ceiling shelving stacked with large cardboard boxes filled about half of this cavernous space. The other half was crammed with furs of every type, suspended from a steel framework that looked like a giant closet organizer. Bales of beaver pelts, bound with plastic twine, were piled on shelves along one wall. Each box and bundle — collectively referred to as "the bulks" — corresponded to a sample out in the warehouse. When the auction was over, they would be shipped off to the buyers.

On our way out of the cold storage, we passed a rack of leather-side-out pelts with black-and-white-striped tails. "Skunks?" I asked.

Parkinson nodded. "They stink. Wheel them out into the warm and leave them there for about half an hour, you'll know they're there."

It was only then that I realized I had stopped noticing the warehouse reek.

That night, in my cheap airport hotel, one kilometre west of the auction house and a few hundred metres east of the blue runway lights, I slept badly. Planes kept roaring over my room, jolting me awake. Parades of dead animals blocked my attempts to reclaim sleep. What troubled me most was that I hadn't been more disturbed by what I had witnessed that afternoon. The warehouse had seemed exotic and unsettling, but not horrific. Was I just insulating myself with journalistic detachment, I wondered. Or were the souls of the deceased too distant to haunt me?

When I made those animals whole again in my imagination, restored their vitality and let them loose in the forest or on the open prairie, I did regret their deaths. And when I imagined the traps that had seized their lives, I hoped they had delivered instant oblivion, but feared that they hadn't. Yet I didn't feel qualified to sit in judgement. Except for about five years during my twenties, I've always eaten meat, and although I've killed very little of what I've consumed, I have bludgeoned fish to death after dragging them from the ocean with barbed hooks pierced through their jaws. I regularly execute slugs and insects in my vegetable garden. As an undergraduate student in biology, I dissected the requisite formaldehyde-soaked frogs and, reluctantly, one cat. I've had qualms about deaths I've inflicted or been party to, but I can't deny them.

Nor was it simply a matter of ethical consistency, because the ethics of fur are complex. The defence and prosecution kept going all night long in my head, arguing carbon footprints versus cruelty; traditional livelihoods versus evolving values; warmth and durability versus frivolous consumerism. When court adjourned at daybreak, I was no closer to a verdict than when I had started. I gave up on sleep, got out of bed and prepared for another day at the auction house.

Paddy Hall, the beaver-grading expert, was waiting for me when I arrived, and we proceeded straight to the warehouse. At least a hundred buyers were bent over the tables, scrutinizing samples. A low babble bounced off the cement floor and steel roof, muted by the acres of fur.

Hall had thinning hair, wire-framed glasses and an aging basketball-player's build. His lab coat, sleeves rolled halfway up his forearms, hung loosely from his lanky frame. A 30-year veteran of the fur-grading business, he had long ago chosen to specialize in beavers, generally an unpopular pick. "A lot of guys don't want to get their hands dirty," he explained. Or slashed and nicked by the staples and pins that some trappers use to fasten beaver pelts onto boards or hoops for drying. "You can't be putting on bandages," he said. "You have to feel the fur, so you're left with some pretty nasty little cuts."

Nevertheless, he had always liked grading beaver. When I asked why, Hall deflected the question by recalling how his first mentor — "a very, very good beaver man" — used to joke about the three qualifications for being a beaver grader. "You got to be tall. You got to be strong. The third and most important attribute: you got to be as thick as brick." He waited for my chuckle before breaking into a grin. But Hall was no dim-witted drudge. He was university educated and approached beaver grading with professorial passion and erudition. Over the next hour, he walked me through the fundamentals.

Surprisingly, the leather side of the pelts turned out to be as important to the grading process as the fur side. Hall read the black lines and blotches on the sepia- to crimson-coloured skins like a reverse fortune-teller, interpreting the past instead of predicting the future. Combat scars, signs of old infections, trap injuries, knife cuts or spoilage caused by a trapper's careless handling — it was all there in plain view if you knew the code. Only one or two percent of the pelts that pass through the warehouse are so immaculate that they qualify as Select, the top grade. The rest have varying amounts of damage, some of it the result of the trapper's poor treatment of the pelt, but much of it inflicted by other beavers in territorial conflicts.

"People have this misconception about beaver being cute and cuddly, and they're not," Hall said. Having trapped since his early teens, he's encountered plenty of beavers in the wild. "They can rip you apart if they have the opportunity," he went on. "When you see some of the damage, you wonder how these animals ever survive [their fights with each other]. Both of us, we'd be in hospital."

Once graded, the pelts, except for the most damaged, are divided into two piles — geographical sections based on a line drawn down along the Ontario-Manitoba border and straight south through the United States. This separates the more valuable eastern beavers, distinguished by their dark colouring and dense undercoats, from their generally paler and less furry western cousins. Hall took a sample of each from the racks and invited me to feel the difference between them. I slid my fingers through the faintly unctuous fur and shook my head. They seemed the same to me.

"Hard, hard," he urged. "You want to get some weight there."

I delved into the velvety depths below the coarse surface layer and decided I could perceive a slight distinction.

"A very thick underfur, that's what buyers are looking for," Hall said. "They're not overly concerned about the guard hair." Most of the beaver pelts sold at this auction would be sheared — fur-dresser's jargon for mechanically removing the guard hairs — then dyed before being turned into fashion wear. Pelts with scant underfur, from beavers trapped in the off-season or in regions with warm winters, are classed as "silky" — a cheaper grade useful only for non-sheared jackets or coats.

Like the garment-trade buyers, those purchasing beaver to be felted and made into hats — a mere five to 10 percent of the total sales — also want thick underfur, but don't otherwise care about pelt condition. The lowest grades and damaged goods suit them fine.

You have to have "fur sense" to assess undercoat density, Hall said. Sizing, in contrast, requires only a ruler to measure length and width, and enough mathematical competence to add the two numbers together. The biggest pelts, those with a combined length-plus-width measurement of more than 70 inches (graders stuck with imperial measurement when Canada went metric), are classified as triple-extra-large. A 65- to 70-inch pelt is a double-extra-large, and so on down through all the sizes: extra-large, large, large-medium, medium, small and extra-small. In the graders' vernacular, double-extra-large pelts are "blanket beavers" and extra-smalls (the product of kits) are "cubs" or "putt-putts."

"This is the article we all learn on, the little putt-putts," Hall said. "You've got this mastered, then you go to the next size up and by the time you're graduated, when you get to blanket beavers, then you're somebody." But with those blanket beavers each weighing about a kilogram and the pelts bundled in tens, a full day of handling them is a serious physical workout. After a heart attack four years earlier, Hall had been told he couldn't grade double-extra-large pelts any more, which still irked him. "It's an ego thing," he acknowledged.

The last attribute graders look at is pelt colour. Hall rummaged through the racks and pulled out sample after sample to illustrate the full spectrum, from black, often categorized as extra-dark and found mainly in the East, to the fairest of the western furs, the almost blond extra-pales, which Hall facetiously called "glow plugs." "Why these poor suckers don't get picked off by bears or timber wolves when they go out to feed at night time, I haven't a clue," he said.

By the end of the tutorial, Hall's fingertips were black. We shook hands anyway, and I went off to explore the rest of the building. Just off the warehouse was a spacious room filled with round banquet tables. Throughout the auction week, NAFA served up a lavish Chinese and Korean lunch buffet as an alternative to the more standard North American fare offered in the cafeteria. Outside of the lunch hour, the buffet room was a popular gathering place for buyers who weren't busy assessing or bidding on furs. Mostly they sat around the tables, talking and flipping idly through their catalogues or participating in boisterous games of cards or mah-jong. A few preferred to sit by the wall of interior windows that ran along one side of the hall and watch the proceedings inside the auction room. I joined these observers to see what was happening in the inner sanctum.

The room on the other side of the glass resembled a university lecture theatre, with seating for about 250 people. Fourteen tiered rows of tables and chairs faced the auctioneers' raised platform, which extended across the front of the room. A large flat-screen monitor behind the platform showed the details of each lot as it came up for bids, and the auctioneer's non-stop monologue was broadcast into the banquet room, competing with the constant clicking of mah-jong tiles. When the hammer dropped, the word "sold" and the selling price flashed onto the screen. Then it was on to the next lot, with barely enough time for the auctioneer to catch his breath.

The other social centre for off-duty buyers was a small lounge next to the cafeteria. After a few rounds of bidding, I made my way over there and claimed an empty sofa across from a Korean man who lay snoring in an armchair, with his head flung back and his shoes off, but his lab coat on. Nearby, three men with British and Scandinavian accents were making small talk while they watched a golf game on a wall-mounted TV. An American arrived and they all got up to greet him, with a familiarity that suggested long acquaintance, but little or no contact between auctions. Soon, the American man's wife joined their circle and, after a few minutes of shared gossip, she asked him for some cash so she could go shopping. "This is one mink," she said, holding up one of the $50 bills he gave her, and they all laughed. No one was talking about hairy banknotes at this sale, but the concept was still current.

On Sunday I rose early. It was the final day for wild-fur sales, and beavers were first up. In the afternoon, the auctioneers would move on to ranch-raised fox, and the last four days of the auction would be devoted to ranch mink. When I arrived at 7:30, the crowd had already started to gather. Some of the buyers stood in small clusters in the lounge, drinking coffee from cardboard cups. I joined the ones who were shuffling through the cafeteria, loading their trays with pastries, bowls of fruit, and plates of scrambled eggs, sausages and hash browns. There was nothing parsimonious about the way NAFA treated its clients (or visiting writers).

At 7:55, a female voice on the public address system skimmed across the multilingual babble, barely making a ripple. "Attention all buyers, the sale of beaver will commence in five minutes. All buyers, the sale of beaver will commence in five minutes." I stacked my dishes on a trolley and walked around to the banquet hall to find a seat with a good view of the auction.

The buyers trickled into the auction room carrying coffee cups, water bottles, catalogue binders and laptops, as well as plate-sized yellow plastic discs marked with their bidder identification numbers. They slotted the discs into metal stands and set these lollipops at their chosen places. Meanwhile, the NAFA personnel, including two women poised in front of computers, were getting into position behind the wide podium. The stars of the impending show were clearly the five men in tailored shirts and ties, who stood as if ready to run out onto a football field.

At 7:59, the most distinguished team member — tall, balding and wearing an elegant cream-and-teal-striped shirt — clipped a microphone to his matching teal tie and looked out over the 80 or so people who had now gathered. "Good morning," he said, and the chatter faded away. A moment later, at precisely eight o'clock, he launched the bidding on lot 213901 with an opening price of $60.

The numbers tumbled from his mouth: "sixty, seventy, I have eighty, two, four, six, eight, ninety, I'm bid ninety, two, four, six, eight, one hundred, one-oh-five at the back, one-ten, one-fifteen, one-seventeen." I couldn't even think that fast. "One-thirty, one-thirty-five, one-forty, one-forty-five, one-fifty, one-fifty-five, one-sixty, one-sixty." He hesitated for a split second, then slammed down his hammer. I had expected to hear "going once, going twice," but that nicety seemed to have no place in this lightning-fast contest. The blue screen behind the dais lit up with confirmation of the winning bid: $160 each for 20 select, extra-dark, double-extra-large, eastern beavers. I was still writing the price in my catalogue when he called out the next lot number and the bidding took off again at the same frenetic pace.

I couldn't always see who was bidding, but the auctioneer's eyes were as quick as his mouth. If he missed a bid, one of his four tie-wearing spotters would yelp and fling one hand into the air, as if firing a baseball at the bidder, to draw the auctioneer's attention.

The second lot was also made up of select, blanket beavers, one colour category lighter than the top lot. The auctioneer again opened the bidding at $60. This time there were no takers. Without losing a beat, he dropped the price to $50 and then hustled it up in two-dollar increments. At $57, he dropped the hammer. And on it went, lot after lot, without a pause.

After a while, I began to recognize bidding signs. Some buyers gestured with a flick of a finger. Others made more overt hand motions. At times, they used their fingers to indicate a number — a circled thumb and forefinger apparently meant 10. The signals for other numbers eluded me.

One of the most frequent bidders was a heavy-set Chinese man, seated in the third row with a few other men and a stylishly attired woman, all of them Chinese. Although they were on the far side of the room and I couldn't clearly see the man's actions, I could tell the auctioneer was keeping a close eye on him. When I learned later that Polar Deck, China's leading designer and producer of fur home-accessories — blankets, rugs, pillow slips and the like — had bought the top lot of beaver pelts, I suspected that this group had been their agents. I pictured nouveau riche Beijing couples sleeping under sheared and dyed beaver bedcovers and wondered if they ever dreamed about flat-tailed creatures swimming in sparkling northern waters.

A couple of other active contestants, including the American man I had seen in the lounge the day before, were sitting a few rows behind the keen Chinese contingent. As far as I could tell, the American kept getting outbid, but he seemed to take it all quite cheerfully, often half-smiling when he had to drop out. Afterwards, in the lobby, I heard him talking on his cell phone to someone in New York. "Beavers were selling pretty friggin' cheap," he said. Which made me wonder how serious his bidding had been.

The other buyer I recognized was a thickset, plaid-shirt-wearing woman from Moscow, Idaho, whom I'd met the previous day. Nancy Haefer, a self-described "skin dealer" with 35 years of experience in the business, purchased raw pelts, got them tanned and resold them. She bought for the novelty market, she told me, not the fashion trade. Her typical customers fell into three groups: "muzzle-loader people — the Daniel Boone and Jeremiah Jackson types who want a fur hat"; manufacturers of rustic home-décor items; and Native American creators of traditional regalia. She had come to Toronto in hopes of obtaining the kinds of pelts she couldn't easily buy in Idaho, especially wolves, wolverines and lynx. The only beavers she was interested in were the black ones, though she was willing to buy cubs in any colour if she could get a good price on a large quantity.

Haefer was sitting near the front of the auction room with her back to me. When the first lot of black pelts, a mix of triple- and double-extra-larges, came up, she jumped into the fray but was quickly left behind as the price leapt to $49, nearly $20 more than the going price for brown blanket beavers of the same quality. There were only one or two lots of black beavers in each of the smaller sizes, and they too fetched premium prices.

Aside from the blacks, however, the hammer prices were falling quickly as the auction descended through the sizes, grades and colours. Haefer had predicted that "the really nice stuff is going to do well, and the mediocre-quality stuff and the smaller sizes are going to struggle." It looked like she'd called it right.

One hour into the sale, there was a momentary pause to switch auctioneers. The first one unclipped the mike from his teal tie and handed it to a small, bearded man wearing a dark pink tie and red suspenders, and then everything kicked back into action. The new auctioneer's delivery was even faster than his colleague's and more personal. If the bidding faltered, he broke his hypersonic patter to banter briefly with the buyers, often addressing them by name. "Sorry, Jerry," he said to one who wanted to start the bidding too low. "I'd love to, but I can't." Other times he just shrugged his shoulders theatrically.

By the time the auction got to the palest of the western putt-putts, many of the buyers had left the room and the auctioneer was dropping the hammer on bids of three or four dollars. But the beaver sale wasn't over yet. The final pelts on offer were the damaged goods, with eastern and western beavers of all colours lumped together in lots based on their condition. The bidding was snappy; the prices rock-bottom. Last up were the damaged extra-smalls, which went for a pitiful dollar apiece.

As soon as they had dispensed with the final lot, the auctioneers and their assistants slipped out their private door. Everyone else headed for the coffee machines as the PA system clicked on. "Attention all buyers, the sale of otter will commence shortly. All buyers, the sale of otter will commence shortly."

It had taken only two hours and 17 minutes to sell 157,207 pelts. The average price for an eastern beaver: $19.57; for a western: $16.74. Later, when I asked Oscar Carbonell for his management perspective on the results, he seemed pleased. Despite the poor global economy, beaver prices were 25 percent higher than the year before. "China is a machine," he said.

In 1892, Henry Poland, who came from a family of British fur merchants and masters of the Skinners' Company (one of London's oldest guilds), published *Fur-bearing Animals in*

Nature and in Commerce. Poland's book summarized the state of the international fur trade and profiled more than 200 furbearers, from Abyssinian monkeys to wallaroos. Although he noted that the beaver-hat trade had almost ceased by the time he was writing, he credited beavers with "furnish[ing] one of the most important furs in the world."

After I returned from Toronto, I read Poland's description of the Hudson's Bay Company's "great fur sales in London" and was struck by how little has changed since his time. By 1892, the company no longer auctioned furs "by the light of the candle" — a practice whereby bidding closed when the auctioneer's candle burned down to a predetermined level — or held their sales in coffeehouses, as they had once done. Instead, after sorting the skins by colour and quality and laying them out for inspection in the HBC warehouse on Lime Street, they sold their wares at their College Hill Sales Rooms.

Like today's fur auctions, these affairs were "attended by buyers from nearly all parts of the world," though back then it was the Germans who were "conspicuous by their numbers." The bidding was silent — done "by movement of the head" — and fast. Poland found "the celerity with which the sale proceeds . . . most astonishing, a fresh lot being brought up the instant that one is sold." The annual fur auction schedule revolved around two major events in winter (mainly beaver and muskrat in January; all furs in March) and two smaller sales in spring and fall. Castoreum was sold at a December auction, along with "Deer-skins, Eider-down, Quills, etc."

Poland compiled a detailed record of how many North American furs the Hudson's Bay Company imported each year from 1752 to 1891, but his table only tells part of the story. The rest is filled in by a graph buried in the middle of *Wild Furbearer*

Management and Conservation in North America, the 1,150-page bible of the modern fur trade. This graph shows a conservative estimate of the average annual "harvest" of beaver pelts in North America, decade by decade from 1610 to 1984, three years before the tome was published. Despite the lack of precise data for certain periods, it's easy to track the rise and fall of the beaver's fortunes.

At the height of the colonial fur trade, from about 1780 to 1810, the number of beaver pelts sold hovered around the 300,000 mark, possibly reaching as high as 400,000 at the zenith. Other than that, the yearly take rarely broke 200,000 between 1670 (the year the Hudson's Bay Company was founded) and 1890, and it stayed below 100,000 for most of the early 1800s.

When I first looked at the harvest graph, I was astonished by the far right-hand side. In school, I had learned about the beaver-fur trade entirely in the past tense, as an era that ended when the last voyageurs hung up their paddles. Yet the bars that represented the most recent decades towered like skyscrapers over the early ones: 430,000 pelts a year in the 1950s; 590,000 in the '60s; 660,000 in the '80s. In the first year of that heady decade, trappers dispatched close to 1.1 million beavers, a record that remains unbroken.

From my few days of hanging out at 65 Skyway Avenue, I knew the fur trade wasn't as hot as it had been 30 years earlier, but the graph and Poland's statistics put this contemporary decline in a new light. Not only are beaver pelts still marketable, they're selling in far greater numbers than they did during the three centuries that nearly annihilated the species. Having seen this end of things, I was curious about where Made Beavers come from these days. Which is how I came to meet Pete Wise.

·Seven·
ONE MADE BEAVER

The beaver dangled from a chain looped around its left foreleg and thrown over a rafter. It was the first thing I noticed as I entered the workshop out behind trapper Pete Wise's house. Not the lush coyote and bobcat pelts hanging from nails on the plywood walls. Not the inside-out raccoons and otters stretched over drying boards or even the stack of cured beaver skins. They would all come into focus later and were, in any case, expected. This intact animal, on the other hand, glancing coquettishly over one shoulder through lifeless, black-bead eyes, caught me off-guard. This was the beaver I was going to skin.

NAFA's Trapper Relations Manager had suggested that Pete, a long-time trapper and experienced trapper-education instructor, would be a good person to give me a glimpse into the supply side of the modern-day fur trade. Pete had readily agreed to my request and decided that the curriculum for my visit should include a hands-on lesson in preparing beaver pelts. However, although it was January, the preferred time for catching beavers, he didn't have a fresh specimen on hand. I knew he was thawing one he had stored in his freezer the previous summer when he'd been too busy to deal with it, but I hadn't anticipated meeting it quite like this.

The week before, when Pete and I were making arrangements for him to pick me up at the airport, he had told me he would be wearing a "camo wildlife control hat, wool camo vest, grey hoodie, black pants and felt pac boots." I spotted him instantly. We collected my luggage from the carousel and walked out to his truck, a silver Toyota Tacoma with a jumble of traps and a dead calf (bait, I learned later) half-covered by snow in the back. The seat covers matched Pete's camo hat and vest. He shooed his border collie, Nunk, into the space behind the seats, tossed my bag in beside her and shifted a rifle so I could fasten my seat belt. He had already started outlining his philosophy of trapping for me. "Humaneness, in my world, is tantamount," he said.

At 62, Pete was a burly good ol' boy with blue eyes, a white horseshoe moustache and a bald head generally hidden under a ball cap. He had been trapping for 53 years, starting with muskrats in the sloughs of the Lower Fraser Valley. Originally, he had pursued his quarry with a bow and arrow, but when a local trapper showed him how to set traps and offered to buy his skins, he enthusiastically adopted a new approach. After Pete graduated from high school, he moved from job to job — bar manager one year, heavy equipment operator the next — but always trapped on the side. Eventually, it got to the point "where work interfered with trapping." Then in the late 1970s, he landed a government contract to apprehend "nuisance" beavers and realized he had found the perfect career. A few years later, he started the business that has kept him fully employed ever since. In his spare time, he runs a registered trapline.

Snakes, raccoons, coyotes, bats in attics, beavers in culverts — Wise Wildlife Control Services, which consists of Pete and a part-time assistant, does it all. Whether they exterminate the offenders or relocate them depends on the species and the situation. When it comes to beavers, Pete mostly uses lethal traps, but he'll live-trap if his client still wants him to after hearing that it will take longer and cost more. Catch-and-release inevitably involves a lot of travel, because the suitable beaver habitat around Vernon, British Columbia, where he lives, is already fully occupied.

The previous year, Pete told me, he had killed 126 beavers, the majority for paying customers and the rest out on his trapline, where he's careful to avoid overharvesting. "It's important to understand what your long-term goals are," he said. "In ADC [Animal Damage Control] work, it's just get rid of them. So, cold-hearted, merciless bastard, just get in there and take every one that you can catch. But on your trapline, you've got to set a management objective for yourself [or] you can kill 'em out."

Even when doing ADC work, he won't set killing traps around lodges in spring and early summer when the young are still dependent on their parents. Once, when he erred in calculating birth dates and orphaned a litter, he immediately rescued the three kits and bottle-fed them in his home until he could deliver them to a wildlife shelter. Another time, he spent 10 unpaid days live-trapping a beaver that he had found swimming around with a bow-hunter's arrow stuck in its back. He talked a veterinarian friend into providing free treatment and returned the wounded animal to its pond once it recovered. For Pete, there's no contradiction in such deeds.

"People say to me, 'You're a beaver trapper. What are you doing?'" He sounded offended that anyone would ask such a question. "I'm giving something back, okay?"

The biggest beaver Pete has ever trapped weighed 38 kilograms. The one he had thawed for me was only 11 kilos — a "juvie," he said. He lifted it down and placed it in my hands. It had the heft of a large sack of rice and a similar shape, aside from the tapered head and trademark tail. It was a female, but we didn't know that yet, because you can't tell the sex from the outside. I held the animal for a moment, feeling the soft, springy fur through my latex gloves. Then I laid it belly-up in the V-shaped wooden trough that trappers call a cradle.

The previous afternoon, Pete had taken me out to one of his ADC sites, a creek where he was trying to get rid of the beavers, because their dams kept flooding the adjacent pasture in summer. "The cows are literally getting milked with scuba gear on," he joked as we waded through the snow to get to the lodge, his hoot of laughter ringing across the field. Once he started working, though, his tone became more serious. He carefully explained his actions and the rationale behind them as he performed each step: sawing holes in the ice; setting the snares; stripping the bark from a fresh willow branch and wiring it to the snare pole, where its whiteness would attract a hungry beaver's attention; pulling a few sticks from the dam to entice the beavers to swim out of their lodge and through the "valley of death" that he had created. When he was done, he stood back and surveyed the scene. "What a wonderful way to make a living," he said. "You've gotta absolutely dig right in and love what you're doing."

Not only does Pete love his work, he's passionate about sharing his expertise and encouraging a high level of professionalism among trappers. He's taught British Columbia's mandatory three-day trapper licensing course for more than 18 years, and he began my beaver-skinning lesson the same way he starts all of his classes: by talking about some of the subject's most interesting anatomical features. "If you're going to trap an animal," he said, "it behooves you to understand and know what that animal is."

He pulled back the fur around the beaver's mouth to reveal the bright orange enamel on the outside of the front teeth and described how the incisors are self-sharpening, because they grow continuously and the white dentine wears more quickly than the hard enamel. Then he opened the mouth and indicated the flap of skin behind the incisors that allows a submerged beaver to gnaw on sticks without swallowing water.

Moving down the body, Pete extended one of the hind legs and showed me how the second toe of each back foot is equipped with a split claw, the basis of the Omaha Iktinike story. Beavers use these specialized claws like combs to untangle matted fur and remove dirt and mites (though they're no good for getting rid of the little louse-like parasites known as beaver beetles). During grooming sessions, beavers also use both the front and back feet to take oil from the anal glands and work it into the fur, Pete added. "That's how he waterproofs himself."

Beavers have extremely dense pelts, with 12,000 to 23,000 hairs packed into every square centimetre, and those obtained in winter, when the underfur is at its thickest, are considered prime. This beaver was summer-trapped and off-prime, but its pelt was still plushy enough to hold the impression of Pete's fingertip as he traced a line from the base of the tail to the chin, marking the route for his first cut. Some trappers open pelts with a knife. Pete prefers the precision of a small, hooked blade designed for cutting roofing shingles. He pierced the skin between the beaver's lower incisors and slid the blade down the length of the body, as if unzipping a jacket.

He picked up a handsaw next and started to amputate the feet, carving through fur, flesh and bone and tossing each severed appendage onto his workbench. The saucer-sized rear feet were flat and webbed; the front paws, small and dainty, were almost like human hands. When I looked at them again later, lying there amidst the tools, it was hard to believe both pairs came from the same animal.

"Some guys also cut the tails off," he noted. "I do not, because I like to have something to hang on to."

Above the bench, a dozen or so knives hung from a magnetic strip. Pete selected his favourite Dexter-Russell skinning knife and ran the curved, blunt-tipped blade back and forth across a sharpening steel. Then he grasped the cut edge of the pelt in one hand and started to peel it back, insinuating the blade between skin and muscle with smooth, downward strokes. The plan was that he would do one side and I'd do the other. I watched intently, trying to envision making the same moves and glad that he'd outfitted me with latex gloves and a rubberized butcher's apron like his own.

As Pete worked, blood dribbled from the beaver's mouth onto the table and the floor below. Nunk, who had been lying in a corner, crept between our feet and lapped at the red pool until he shooed her away. She loves beaver, he said, just like all the dogs he's ever owned. She steals meat scraps if she gets a chance and sometimes licks a fresh hide, but she knows better than to touch one with her teeth.

I wondered whether Nunk's nose could unravel the tangled aromas of flesh, fur and bodily fluids that filled the small shed. After an hour or so, I had ceased registering them, but their dark, primal aura still pulsated just beneath the surface of my consciousness.

When Pete was done skinning the left half of the beaver, he whetted the knife again and handed it to me. I tried to follow his instructions to "pull the hide and just run the knife down on the fat there," but it was harder than it looked, even once I'd freed the outer edge and had more pelt to grab on to. "Stretch it out and roll it over your knuckle," he directed.

As I hacked away, Pete coached from the sidelines, occasionally reclaiming the knife from me to demonstrate. Apparently, it was all in the blade angle and the tension. I couldn't get either one quite right, but he remained patient and encouraging. After all his years as an instructor, he was used to the clumsiness of novices.

Finally, I got my side of the pelt separated from the torso, relieved that I'd avoiding slicing any holes in the skin. Pete traded the Dexter-Russell for a different knife and finished up around the head, stopping short of the snout. "There's no money in lips and noses on beavers," he explained, "so we cut a lot of that off."

It had taken nearly an hour to complete the job, slow compared to Pete's usual 20 to 25 minutes for a medium to large beaver, but he reassured me that he had seen solo first attempts that took four hours. The pros, however, are almost inconceivably fast, especially when they're vying for prizes at trappers' conventions. One time, Pete had watched a competition winner skin a beaver that was three or four times the size of this one in three minutes and 10 seconds, an achievement that still astounded him. "It was just like 'Ho-o-ly!'" he said.

Stripped of its fur and footless, the object of our efforts looked debased and vulnerable. I wasn't repulsed by the blood or the glistening flesh: biology lab work had long ago cured me of any squeamishness. Yet the raw nakedness of the skinned body made me feel uneasy. I wanted to wrap the beaver back inside its fur, reverse the spell of death and set it swimming in familiar waters. There was, however, no going back for either of us. The beaver was dead, and I couldn't close my eyes to this less-than-pretty side of my country's origins. It occurred to me that in all my reading about the fur trade, I had never come across any reference to beaver carcasses.

I had seen photographs of bison skulls stacked like cordwood in piles as high as a railway boxcar and three times as long, the handiwork of voracious, nineteenth-century hide hunters. But no equivalent record of the beaver carnage. The artist Frances Anne Hopkins, who travelled by freight canoe to Hudson's Bay Company trading posts with her husband in the mid-1800s, famously rendered dreamy, rich-hued scenes with titles like "Shooting the Rapids" and "Voyageurs at Dawn." What if she had chronicled the beaver's fate, instead? With her eye for detail and sensitivity to mood, I could imagine the canvases she might have painted to commemorate what the traders left behind when they paddled off downriver in their pelt-laden canoes. Or had all those small, unclad bodies simply vanished by the time she arrived, the meat eaten and the bones slipped back into the water?

Earlier, I had tentatively broached the subject of killing with Pete and found him more than willing to respond. He told me he wished he had more time to address philosophical aspects of trapping in his courses. In the time he does have, he stresses the importance of using approved traps and setting them properly to dispatch the animal as quickly as possible. He also insists that his students treat the deceased respectfully. "You've taken it, you show proper respect for that particular animal," he tells them. Which means "you do the best job that you can, skinning, boarding and fleshing" and "there's no fun and games" in the process — no propping up your dead beaver with a can of beer for a Facebook photo, for example.

"I have great respect for the animals that I go after. I feel blessed that I'm able to catch them," Pete said near the beginning of this conversation. Later, he returned to this point and tried again to articulate his feelings. "I have this great reverence." He paused. "It's very deep. It's tough to explain."

Part of the problem, I realized, was that we were talking across a great cultural divide. I didn't doubt Pete's sincerity, but for me, skinning this beaver seemed like a desecration, as well as a privilege. I was glad to have had the opportunity — it was history made tangible, biology made intimate — but I knew I wasn't cut out to be a trapper.

Pete's philosophy of respect includes avoiding waste, and of all the species he traps, none gets utilized more completely than the beaver. He finds the meat heavy and rarely eats it now, since his wife, who does all their cooking, detests it. Instead he butchers the skinned carcasses to make bait for species like marten and bobcat, or sometimes sells them whole as food for sled dogs. (I once heard of a Yukon musher who compared beaver meat to a cold-weather energy drink for dogs.) The feet also become trap bait, except for the ones he donates to fish and game clubs for their banquets. Apparently beaver feet are a delicacy.

A friend of Pete's buys the skulls for five dollars apiece and then bleaches them and exports them to Germany. Another buyer takes the large tails, provided they are free of nicks and scars, and turns them into extremely durable leather. We were eating lunch at Friesen's Countrytyme Gardens restaurant, just down the road from Pete's place, when he told me about beaver-tail leather. He pulled out his wallet to show me how well it had held up through the many years he's carried it. It did seem to be in good shape, and the delicate beauty of the natural chain-mail pattern imprinted on its surface was striking.

As in Aesop's time, the castor glands are the most valuable beaver body part, aside from the fur, and sometimes they're worth more than the pelt. Perfumers, who prize castoreum for its refined leathery nuances, are the main purchasers. But bizarrely, this odoriferous substance is also occasionally used to flavour food products and is a key ingredient in a type of Swedish schnapps called *bäverhojt* — an acquired taste, according to those who've tried it.

Before Pete removed the castors, as trappers call them, he probed inside the pelvic cavity. The quickest way to determine a beaver's sex is to feel for the hidden penis bone, he explained. This one was a female.

Then he cut into the beaver's lower abdomen and extracted two pinkish-grey, finger-length objects that looked like crumpled balloons joined at their narrow ends. The amount of castoreum in castor glands varies seasonally, and these ones were empty, though not odourless. I leaned close and inhaled the heady, oddly pleasant fragrance. It was sweet and musky and acrid all at once, like flowers blooming between creosote-soaked railroad ties in the heat of summer.

That year, large, well-filled castors were selling for about $2.70 an ounce. Pete pointed out a pair of these "Number Ones" (the highest of NAFA's three castor-gland grades) that he'd hung on a nail to dry. "There's about four ounces there, so that set of castors is worth more than the doggone beaver is." Empty castors, also known as shells, "aren't worth a hell of a lot," so Pete just dries them, grinds them up and mixes them with poplar-bud oil and glycerine — a variation on the beaver lure recipe recorded by Virginia surveyor William Byrd II in 1728.

Looking at the Number Ones, I could see why Aesop and others in ancient Europe had equated castor glands with testicles.

I also wasn't surprised to hear that modern trappers get a kick out of playing up the resemblance. When Pete's daughter was in her teens, he kept a pair of dried castors hanging by his front door and pointed them out to her dates when they came to pick her up, with dire warnings about what had happened to the last guy who brought her home late. Apparently his philosophy of reverence didn't extend to isolated internal organs.

Having removed the castor glands, Pete opened the workshop door and pitched the carcass out onto a snow bank to deal with later. There was still lots of work to do on the pelt.

"I take great pride in my fur processing," Pete had told me earlier. "All my hides are all washed, they're all laid out properly, they're dried, they're combed. And you know what? I'm recognized for my fur handling and I win award after award after award at conventions."

Pete's furs are also regularly judged as among the best at NAFA sales. "I'll ship a bunch of fur and I'll get a letter back in the mail saying, 'Congratulations, your raccoon [or bobcat or beaver] hide in this sale was selected as being one of the premier furs.' And in recognition of your fur being in the top lot, you get hats, pins, certificates." He now has so many camo-patterned ball caps with "NAFA Top Lot Trapper" machine-embroidered on them in gold thread that he refuses these prizes, but he tucks the certificates away in a binder.

Our beaver, as I'd started to think of it, was definitely not a candidate for Top Lot honours. Still, it had to be fleshed properly or it wouldn't even be worth shipping. Any excess muscle tissue we left behind on the skin would be prone to rotting. Any lingering fat would blister and "burn" the hide and harm the fur.

The fleshing beam was a smooth plank, fastened to a heavy

wooden base and held at a steep angle by an adjustable arm. Pete laid the pelt on the beam, fur-side down with one edge draped over the upper end, and sprinkled a handful of dry sawdust over the damp skin. Then he planted both feet firmly on the base, pinned the pelt in place with his substantial stomach and started running the edge of his long-bladed, two-handled scraper down the pelt. "If you're pushing too hard and catch a burr or pinch the hide you can really do damage," he cautioned. And if that happens, "get out your needle and thread, partner."

When it was my turn, I was afraid to apply any pressure at all, but gradually my confidence increased. Shreds of red flesh and gobs of creamy fat peeled away, exposing the slick, white membrane underneath. I was getting the hang of it, but I didn't mind letting Pete complete the job. The previous night, while reading the *British Columbia Trapper Education Manual* in my motel room, I had come across an admonishment that returned to me now: "You can't turn a poor pelt into a good one, but poor handling will most certainly turn a good pelt into one of little value . . . a waste of your time and effort, and of an animal's life." I didn't want to bear that responsibility, but more to the point, I knew we'd be there until dark if the fleshing was left to me.

The last step was boarding, required because a pelt that is not held taut and flat while it dries will shrivel and wrinkle. Traditionally, trappers lashed beaver pelts onto split-willow hoops. Nowadays, they generally nail them to plywood boards marked with concentric ovals that conform to the fur industry's standard sizes. Boarding is an exacting science: if you overstretch the pelt, the fur quality suffers; if you don't stretch it enough, it will be consigned to a lower-priced size category. Even the order in which you hammer the two-inch box nails into place is important, since beaver skin has more elasticity in the tail end than around the head. Learning the sequence of the first 13 nails was part of my initiation.

Once we had worked our way all around the edge — Pete's nails as upright and evenly spaced as soldiers on parade; mine, erratic and undisciplined — he sewed up one of the leg holes to show me how it's done on high-value pelts. For the other holes, we pulled the edges together and skewered them with a few nails, so they would dry shut. Using an old-fashioned double-edge razor, Pete shaved away the last remnants of flesh. Then he sprinkled some water onto the hide to help cut the grease and wiped it down with a paper towel. My final task was to go around the pelt and ease it slightly upwards, using a piece of deer antler as a pry, so air could circulate beneath the skin as it dried. Pete checked my work and leaned the board against the wall. In four days, it would be cardboard-stiff and ready to send to the auction house.

"Hey, good job!" he said. "That's your first beaver. Pretty cool."

"How much do you think it will sell for?" I asked.

He chuckled. "Five bucks, if you're lucky. If you have a good day and the grader is kind, you're going to get five dollars."

Right. I'd forgotten that this was an off-season Animal Damage Control casualty, killed not for its pelt, but because it was in the wrong place at the wrong time.

Six months after I met Pete Wise, I travelled north to get another perspective on beaver trapping. In a way, I was also travelling back in time, to one of North America's last operational fur-trading posts.

La Ronge, Saskatchewan, sits on the southern edge of the Canadian Shield, 600 kilometres north of the province's capital city, Regina, and half that distance from Prince Albert National

Park. If you're driving from the south, you get there on a road that soon turns to gravel if you follow it through the town and up into the sparsely populated boreal forest beyond. Fewer than 3,000 people live in La Ronge today. The town was even smaller in 1967, when Alex Robertson moved there with his wife and four children and bought a grocery store.

At 42 years old, Robertson had been a Hudson's Bay Company fur buyer for nearly half his life, one of the last apprentices trained at the company fur school in Montreal. Now he would operate as an independent trader. At the time, transforming the La Ronge Grocery into the fur-focused Robertson Trading Company wasn't a major change. "Back in those days, every store in town bought fur," Alex's son Scott told me. "It wasn't unusual for someone to send their kid to the store with a mink skin and a grocery list."

By 1973, Robertson's business had outgrown its original, modest premises and he had built a new store next door. Further expansion in the 1990s produced the sprawling but unpretentious building that now occupies a half-block stretch of La Ronge Avenue. A canoe hangs over the front porch, and plain block-lettered signs in the window advertise some of the wares for sale inside: rain suits and work boots, antler carvings and locally made moccasins, groceries, ice, fishing tackle, souvenir T-shirts. They barely hint at the incredible variety of items found within.

Robertson Trading is still a grocery store and fur-buying post. It's also a hardware store, a clothing store, an outfitter for those who work and play in the surrounding wilderness, a gallery and a museum. Merchandise, artifacts, photographs, paintings, pelts and taxidermied trophies crowd the shelves, swing from the ceiling, adorn the walls and perch on high ledges — a colourful and eclectic mix of the mass-produced and the handmade.

At a checkout till, a box of doughnut-sized rolls of rabbit wire is flanked by bingo blotters and chewing gum. Birch bark berry baskets rest atop a stack of Pepsi 12-packs. Fox pelts and moose-hide purses hang down the side of the dairy cooler, while painted wooden model floatplanes glide above the milk and eggs. The gut-webbed snowshoes and chainsaw oil are one aisle over from the breakfast cereal.

The piquant scent of smoke-tanned moose, caribou and deer hides permeates the whole place. "The smell of the North," Scott calls it. It's also the smell of authenticity. Local Cree and Dene artisans make all of the fur-trimmed and beaded leatherwork sold in the store, using traditional materials, methods and designs. They can also buy their supplies here, selecting from rainbow strings of Czech glass beads and sorting through the whole hides and furs that spill from huge cardboard boxes sitting on the red-and-white checkerboard linoleum at the back of the store.

The senior Robertson was a keen collector of First Nations arts and crafts, initially because he appreciated their particular blend of beauty and functionality, and later because he wanted to preserve exceptional examples and help sustain these traditions. He enjoyed displaying his acquisitions in the store, though he sometimes had a tough time convincing customers they were off limits. The "Definitely Not For Sale!" sign in the middle of a parade of moccasins pinned to an overhead beam attests to the persistence of the covetous. On another beam, steel clothes hangers square the shoulders of buckskin jackets and vests decorated with the exquisite floral and geometric beadwork patterns characteristic of the region, and hold them well out of reach of those who might ignore the "Sorry, this item is NOT FOR SALE" tags.

"This wasn't done to attract tourists," Scott said emphatically. We were standing at the back of the store by the "trading desk" — the counter where fur-buying transactions take place — looking towards the forbidden treasures. But his sweeping gesture took in everything from the Number Ones hanging from a plaque that read "Our Policy on N.S.F. cheques" (that old castor joke again) to the stuffed wolverine glaring down at us from above the Budweiser barbecue sauce. "My father spent his lifetime in the fur business, so he surrounded himself with the stuff he liked and found attractive and was comfortable with. Fur was such a big thing in my father's life, we actually buried him on a black beaver skin."

Scott was nine when his family moved to La Ronge, and he played an active role in the trading company from the very beginning. "Even as kids, we would bale beaver and stuff wolves into sacks and all that kind of thing," he said. After high school, he left the North for just long enough to earn a commerce degree at the University of Saskatchewan, and then returned to continue working with his father. Eventually, he was the one running Robertson Trading, though Alex remained involved right up to his death in 2010, a year and a half before my visit.

When Scott smiles, his clean-shaven face looks almost boyish, despite the salt-and-pepper colouring of his cropped hair. But he doesn't smile often when he's talking about the fur side of the business, which has become "a shadow of what it was." When he was a kid, he told me, there were four major fur buyers in town and "it was a dogfight for every parcel." In the 1980s, when fur prices were rocketing and the fur warehouse at the back of the store was chock-full in winter, Scott and his brother used to take turns sleeping there to guard against break-ins. The would-be thieves, who did manage one successful heist, were after pelts, not cash, for as Scott is fond of saying, "fur is a currency."

These days, Robertson Trading is the only fur buyer in La Ronge, the warehouse never overflows and the Made Beaver is a distinctly devalued currency. "Back when the fur business was healthy, my father and I would probably bale up five or six thousand beaver skins every year," Scott said. "I don't know if I bought 200 beaver last year."

There were no auction-bound furs in the warehouse when I visited, but that wasn't unusual for July. It would be early October before the next lot started coming in, and the smart trappers would hold off until the cold weather brought their quarry into prime condition. "The real meat and potatoes" of the winter buying happens between mid-November and the end of December, Scott said. "Then you have a very short window, a week or so, to get that stuff baled and shipped or you miss the February sale." In the case of beaver, baling means packing the oval pelts "50 to a bag, fur to fur, skin to skin. And then you wrestle these things with rope to tie them as tight as you can. Sometimes you have someone standing on it while you're baling it."

Robertson Trading usually gets a small number of pelts tanned and sells them in the store, mostly to local artisans. The rest they send to NAFA for the annual wild-fur auction. "We live or die by that February sale," Scott said, recalling how he and his father used to spend every Boxing Day baling fur.

There are many reasons why the fur business has waned since the 1980s glory days. A shortage of beavers isn't one of them. "This country is polluted with beaver today," Scott said. And yet, even with the beaver population "higher than we've ever seen in our history here," he had bought fewer beaver pelts the previous year than ever before.

He places some of the blame on the anti-fur movement and doesn't hide his disdain for animal rights advocates who "condemn the harvest of a flat-tailed, web-toed water rat," especially if the objectors happen to be wearing leather. "That beaver is going to die an ugly death no matter what," he responds. "When he can no longer outrun, outwit or outfight the predator that's after him — and there is always somebody after him — he is going to be turned belly-up and eaten alive. So if he dies in a trap or in a snare or by a bullet, what's the difference?"

He also argues that trapping is environmentally friendly, comparing it to berry-picking: "So long as you don't pull that blueberry plant up by the roots or a forest fire doesn't go through and destroy that berry patch, you can pick berries in the same place your great-great-grandmother did. You can pull beaver, marten, mink, muskrats out of the same lake that your great-great-grandmother did."

But the defence that seems closest to Scott's heart is that trapping is an integral part of First Nations identity. "With the demise of the fur business, we've seen the demise of aboriginal languages and culture, the beadwork and all that kind of stuff." There was both sadness and frustration in his voice. "The skins that come in today aren't as well prepared as their father's and mother's and grandmother's were. The average aboriginal kid now knows more about his cell phone than he does about his language, his culture, his parents' and grandparents' trapline."

"So, is trapping still important to La Ronge?" I asked.

"From an aboriginal cultural perspective, I would say of course it is," Scott replied, "but as an economic activity, it's minute. In 1948, beaver prices averaged $44. Last year they averaged $16 and change. The year before that, $12 and change."

Near the end of our conversation, Scott mentioned that one of the most active trappers in the area was Vern Studer. "An interesting guy to talk to if you have time," he said. "He's 86 years old and still trapping." How could I resist?

A quick phone call and an hour later, Vern was at the store, more than happy to accept a cup of coffee from the machine in the staff room ("It's the best coffee in town," he confided) and tell me about his experiences. He struck me as the kind of man the word spry was invented for, full of sinewy vigour and bright-eyed behind his aviator sunglasses.

Born in 1925, Vern Studer was 11 when his family moved from west-central Saskatchewan to homestead by a remote lake about 50 kilometres north of La Ronge. His father prospected for gold in the summer and trapped in the winter. Within a few years, Vern was working alongside him, and by 15, he had his own trapline. From then on, he was out tending traps almost every day from fall through spring, travelling his 25- to 35-kilometre routes on foot or snowshoes, because the terrain was too rugged for dogsled travel. His father was adamant that they take a day off every weekend. Often they devoted this ostensible rest day to catching up on pelt prep.

In his twenties, Vern sought out more lucrative opportunities in northern Saskatchewan's booming resource extraction sector and discovered his love of flying. For more than five decades, he mostly made his living as a bush pilot, working on contract for mining and mineral exploration companies, but he always trapped at least a bit each winter. "There's something about it," he said. "Trapping gets in your blood. We used to joke that if you have a good summer in the exploration business, you can afford to go trapping in the winter — though it's not funny when you're raising a family of eight children, which we did, but

I certainly never did it on trapping alone."

Vern laments the fact that "trappers are becoming scarce," yet acknowledges that there's little incentive for young people to follow in his footsteps. When he goes into schools to talk about trapping, the first thing the students ask him is always how much money they can make. "I tell them, I don't want to discourage you, but if you think it's a picnic out there, you've got another thought coming. It's hard work and if you don't work hard, you're not going to get anything." His bottom-line advice is, "get all your schooling and then if you want to, maybe on a weekend you can go out with your grandfather." However, he also tells them, "it's a wonderful lifestyle, a healthy lifestyle."

Seventy years on, Vern is still trapping in the same area where he began as a teenager — still one of the district's most active trappers, according to Scott — and regularly walking his trapline when it's too early in the season to get around by snow machine. "It keeps me in shape," he said with a grin. He's also still flying his beloved two-seater Taylorcraft F-19.

The best way to assess beaver numbers is to monitor their food caches, he explained, and the easiest way to do that is from the air. "Every fall, I fly my trapline. You can see the feed beds, and I can tell right away by the feed bed how many beaver are in that lodge, within a few. Sometimes you see a lodge and a little bit of mud on it; they've just starting mudding it up: it's a pair of beaver, that's all, one pair. And it's a young pair, so you don't want to trap those. You want to let them multiply, see. But all of sudden you see a lodge with a whole bunch of feed out there — oh my God, you know — and it's all mudded up: you know there's probably 15, 20 beaver in there. You got to hit that beaver house hard. If you don't, you know they're going to disappear, they're going to move out." It's a matter of balance, he concluded. "If you do trap right, you'll always have fur there."

This was no casual platitude. Vern has seen the alternative firsthand. When the Studers first arrived, there were no beavers in the vicinity, but there was plenty of evidence of their recent presence, most notably, "dead houses that were cut wide open." It had been common practice, Vern explained, for hunters to break into lodges and plug the entrances once the occupants fled into the water. Trapped beneath the ice, the beavers eventually returned, only to find the hunter waiting at a hole he had chopped into the ice above the blocked run, armed with a long pole with an iron hook on the end. "They'd clean 'em right out," he said.

Around the time Vern began trapping, the provincial government started bringing in beavers from other regions and "planting them around the North." No one was allowed to touch these animals or their offspring until the early 1940s, and even then, trapping was tightly controlled.

"When they opened the beaver season, we were allowed only one beaver per live lodge," Vern recalled. "We had to bring in a survey every year to show where our lodges were and they actually went out and checked. Some people put in dead lodges, figuring they'd get an extra beaver, but you can tell right away from the air if a beaver lodge is alive." Trappers received a metal tag for each beaver they were allocated and faced serious penalties if they brought in an untagged pelt. Vern doesn't remember when the quota system ended, but he knows it worked. "They rebounded very fast."

While the 1930s were the dustbowl years in southern Saskatchewan, the drought had different consequences up in the boreal forest. "When we come up here in '36," Vern said, "the whole North was on fire." As beavers returned, things changed, and not coincidentally, in his opinion. "The beaver would dam up muskegs, they would dam up lakes, and if you've got a high water level, then you've got less danger of fires spreading." As a trapper, he was also keenly aware of how wildlife reacted to the beaver revival: "Mink, muskrat, otter, they all came back." Ducks and moose, too, he added.

Driving south from La Ronge, I considered all the knowledge that trappers like Vern Studer and Pete Wise hold. The ability to discern demographic information from the amount of mud on a lodge or the size of a food cache, for example. Or to brush the snow from a creek's frozen surface and find a beaver's under-water trail, as Pete did after he showed me how to set snares. When ice-bound beavers leave their lodge to get food from their winter larder or to check their dams, he explained, the water's cold embrace squeezes the insulating air from their fur. Bubbles stream out behind them and rise to become trapped beneath the ice — pale circles, as indelible as tracks imprinted on wet cement.

·Eight·
THE MIGHTY BEAVER

For centuries, fur traders dictated the beaver's value. Then, in the same decade that beaver trapping peaked in North America, biologists began redefining what makes beavers important. In 1981, the year that trappers sold more beaver pelts than ever before or since, the beaver's standard name tag still read "fur-bearer." Five years later, *Castor canadensis* was declared a quint-essential keystone species.

In a stone arch, the keystone is the topmost element, a wedge-shaped block that locks all of the other pieces into place: remove the keystone and the structure collapses. Similarly, a keystone species is central to how a particular ecological community functions. By definition, the species' effect on other animals and plants is disproportionately large, relative to its own abundance. Some keystone species, such as sea otters and wolves, hold sway by preying on their neighbours. Others, from prairie dogs to elephants, are keystone habitat modifiers, also known as ecosystem engineers. The trio of biologists that coined the latter term in 1994, cited the beaver as the archetype.

Scientists weren't the first to note that beavers punch well above their weight in terms of ecosystem influence. People like Lala, Lillian Collier's Tsilhqot'in grandmother, comprehended

171

their clout long ago. So did observant trappers. But scientific validation has increased respect for the critical role beavers play and inspired additional research. Three decades after the keystone title was bestowed, biologists are still discovering new ways that beavers embody this name.

The tidal marshes of the Skagit River Delta — broad silt flats covered with scrubby vegetation and inscribed with shallow channels that are swamped by salt water twice a day — are one of the last places I would have expected to encounter beavers. Biologist Greg Hood wasn't expecting to find beavers there either. So when he started coming across dams and lodges in this unlikely environment in 2005, his curiosity kicked in and he had to find out what the builders were up to. The short answer was: creating superlative salmon-rearing habitat, though not intentionally.

The Skagit River pours out of the Cascade Mountains in northwestern Washington State and empties into Puget Sound about 90 kilometres north of Seattle. The 327-square-kilometre delta at the mouth of the river is one of the largest in the region, but ecologically, it barely resembles its original condition. Since the 1870s, more than 90 percent of the great fan of low-lying land has been diked and isolated from the exuberant river flows and surging tides that shaped it over the preceding millennia. The delta is mostly bountiful farmland now, famed for its tulips and vegetable crops. As a senior research scientist with the Skagit River System Cooperative, Dr. Hood is more interested in what lies on the uncultivated, seaward side of the dikes.

To get to his beaver study site, we launched a flat-bottomed skiff from a slip off a quiet rural road, motored up Tom Moore Slough, one of the delta's main arteries, and turned right at

Steamboat Slough. Greg, bundled up in a fleece jacket zipped right up to his rust-coloured beard, steered from a standing position in the stern, scanning the jade-tinted water for shoals and driftwood. On this late April morning, the dense shrubbery that crowded the shores was greening up and the air held a hint of spring warmth, despite the partly overcast sky and steady breeze. A bald eagle cruised above us for a while, then veered off to the north.

A short distance up Steamboat Slough, Greg nosed the boat up to a muddy bank, switched off the engine and hopped out. Seeing his hip-waders sink calf-deep into the muck, I disembarked cautiously from the bow and was grateful when my rubber boots set down on relatively solid ground.

A narrow gully snaked inland from our landing point, one of the countless capillaries of the delta's intricate circulatory system. If we had come six hours later, this channel would have been full to the top of its banks, armpit high for me. Now, at low tide, the water was only ankle-deep. With Greg in the lead, we began sloshing upstream, our view limited to the eye-level vegetation on either side.

The tidal marsh plants of the Skagit Delta, I learned as we walked, have distinct real estate preferences. Grass-like Lyngbye's sedge and spiky cattails dominate the emergent zone closest to sea level. Thickets of willow, black twinberry and wild rose blanket the high ground, which they share with the odd towering Sitka spruce and widely scattered alders and cottonwoods. Sweet gale, a bushy shrub with a moderate tolerance for tidal flooding, claims the critical mid-elevation territory in between.

The beavers that inhabit these tidal wetlands build their dams and lodges in the sweet-gale sector and the adjacent willow–twinberry–wild rose zone, the same parts of the delta that attracted the vanguard of European colonists. Because the settlers found this land easier to clear than the more heavily forested inland areas and easier to drain than the emergent zone, it was the first place they claimed. Today, only five percent of the Skagit Delta's original tidal shrublands are left. Most of the region's other major river deltas retain even less.

We had landed in the middle of the scrub-shrub zone. A few hundred metres up the gully, we came to our first beaver dam of the day. If Greg hadn't pointed it out to me, I would have dismissed it as a random pile of sticks and kept right on walking. Admittedly, the dam was in disrepair, but even the well-maintained examples we saw later challenged my preconceived ideas of beaver engineering. On average, the tidal marsh dams are only 1.9 metres wide, slightly more than the span of my outstretched arms, and 41 centimetres tall, just less than knee-height. The narrowest dam Greg measured during his research was 30 centimetres wide and the shortest was 20 centimetres tall. I've seen cat doors bigger than that.

But as Greg pointed out, the size of the dams is simply a response to the local environment: they're smaller than most beaver dams in freshwater streams, because the channels themselves are smaller. Despite their dimensions, they create about the same head (the difference in water depth on either side of the dam) as a typical freshwater dam.

The truly unusual thing about Skagit Delta beaver dams is that they get completely submerged every time the tide comes in. They're redundant when covered by a metre or more of water at high tide. However, when the tide ebbs, leaving only a dribble of water in all but the largest undammed channels, they're indispensable to the beaver's existence here. At low tide, the water held by the dams gives the beavers safe swimming routes to foraging areas and keeps their lodge entrances immersed. The salinity, about 10 times higher than freshwater, doesn't seem to bother them.

If Greg had done nothing more than determine that beavers can reside in salty tidal marshes (documenting a fact that once would have been common knowledge among people who lived nearby), this would have been a worthy scientific contribution. But he wasn't content to stop there. What he really wanted to know was what this meant for fish, especially the threatened Chinook salmon that hatch upriver and swim down to the delta to spend anywhere from a few weeks to a few months maturing before they head out to sea.

He began his quest for answers by mapping and measuring the length, width and depth of low-tide pools — those created by beaver dams, as well as depressions formed by bank slumps or driftwood — along 13 kilometres of tidal channels in the shrub zone. Then he blocked off channel segments, both dammed and unimpeded, and carefully netted, recorded and released all of the fish occupying them at low tide. When he crunched the numbers generated by his field research, the results were striking: the presence of beaver dams quadrupled the amount of low-tide pool habitat in the channels, and the pools held 12 times more juvenile Chinook salmon than the shallows. Other guppy-sized fish, such as three-spine sticklebacks and prickly sculpins, were also more abundant in the beaver-dam pools. "What the beaver are doing is providing a low-tide refuge for these fish," Greg explained to me.

Riding out low tides in bathtub-sized beaver ponds is a good strategy for tiny swimmers on several counts. For one thing, when heavy winter rainfall or spring snowmelt up in the mountains increases the river flow, small fish that have the misfortune of being in the undammed shallows tend to get swept into the bigger channels, where larger fish and diving birds such as mergansers and kingfishers can easily pick them off. Furthermore, if they get flushed right out of the delta and into the bay, they're vulnerable to salinity stress.

The ponds also offer protection against the depredations of great blue herons, whose saucer-sized tracks are stamped all across the delta mud at low tide. "Typically, a pool that's 30 to 40 centimetres deep or deeper is way too deep for a great blue heron," Greg said.

But depth isn't all that keeps the herons from terrorizing the little fish. Beaver pools are also safe havens, because they're hemmed in by bushy battlements. Greg gestured to the serried ranks of sweet gale that overhung the channel we were walking up. "I doubt if a great blue heron would even land in here," he said. "It's too awkward to manoeuvre."

This unassuming shrub is everything to the Skagit Delta beavers. They not only find protection beneath its canopy, but they build their lodges in sweet gale thickets, they use the stems for dam construction and they eat the leaves and twigs.

After Greg discovered there were beavers living in the salty wetlands at the mouth of the Skagit River, he began combing the scientific literature for more information. He was amazed to find no written record of beavers inhabiting this kind of habitat in Puget Sound — or anywhere else. Most locals were completely unaware of the delta's dam-builders. And no one, scientist or citizen, had connected the dots to understand the importance of the tidal marshes and their resident beavers to juvenile salmon. Greg calls this loss of knowledge "ecological amnesia."

Historically, scrub-shrub tidal marshes were common in large river deltas on the West Coast and so, presumably, were intertidal beavers. As European settlers moved in, most of these flat, fertile lands were converted first to farm fields and then to towns and cities: Seattle rose from the Duwamish River Delta and Vancouver appropriated the mouth of the Fraser, to name only the two biggest examples. With the habitat under siege, it didn't take long for trappers to clear out all of the beavers. Soon, it was as if they had never even been there.

Greg's concept of ecological amnesia goes well beyond not knowing what we've got 'til it's gone. It's a more serious matter of completely forgetting what we had and why it mattered. Take the juvenile Chinooks hiding in deep beaver-dam pools beneath the sweet gale's sheltering branches, for instance. Fisheries managers concerned about the perilous state of salmon stocks have spent a fortune on habitat recovery efforts all along the West Coast, from Alaska to California, without realizing, until now, that beavers might have something to contribute to these efforts.

There's no doubt that beavers are ecologically essential, but because they have been mostly absent since scientists began taking notes on natural phenomena, we're still figuring out the extent of their contributions. Greg Hood's revelations are one of the latest additions to the beaver's keystone species resumé. There may be more to come as beaver populations recover.

A few years ago, on a warm June evening, I was sitting on the shores of Amikeus Lake in Ontario's Algonquin Provincial Park, watching water bugs trace ephemeral lines on the glassy surface while I waited for a visitation. A numbered post nearby identified the spot as Stop 5 on the Beaver Pond Trail. I don't know how many Beaver Pond Trails or similarly named routes there are in North America, but I had hiked quite a few and this was one of the best yet.

In front of me, a long dam curved around the narrow end of the pond, barely clearing the water, which lapped at the top of the barrier and trickled over in one place. On the downstream side, the structure stood nearly two metres high, a thick, angled rampart of sticks, grouted with mud and adorned with sprouting greenery.

Within ten minutes of my arrival, one of the trail's luminaries appeared. At first glance I thought it was just a chunk of wood. Then I noticed the V-shaped wake. As the swimmer neared, its features became evident — first the knobby ears, then the obsidian eyes and water-slicked mahogany fur. When it got close enough that I could see its flaring nostrils, I expected a startled dive. Instead, it approached to within a metre of the shore and cruised back and forth in front of me for several minutes. Peering into the tea-coloured water, I observed the ruddering action of its tail and the way it propelled itself with slow, alternating kicks of its webbed hind feet, while keeping its front paws tucked tight against its chest. The beaver examined me in turn and intermittently emitted a low rumble that sounded like a cross between a growl and a purr. Finally, it swam over to the dam and clambered out of the water.

At that point, I thought I might be treated to a dam-repair demonstration — there was, after all, the matter of that trickling water to attend to — but all the beaver did was browse on a bush that was growing out of the dam. Then it belly-flopped back into the pond and paddled away, apparently satisfied that Amikeus Lake was in no danger of emptying any time soon.

On the far side of the pond, my new acquaintance emerged from the water again and spent the next 10 minutes on ablutions.

Sitting upright like a fat Buddha, its tail folded under its haunches, it began with downward strokes of its front paws, pressing water from the fur on its chest, belly and sides. Occasionally, it grasped folds of skin and leaned down to nibble at the fur. Then squeezing gave way to scrubbing, as it worked the waterproofing oils from its anal glands into its coat. The beaver's skinny little front legs seemed too short to reach all the desired body parts, but it twisted and turned with remarkable flexibility for such a chubby animal. It also scratched vigorously at its head and torso with its hind feet, lying down at one point to get at its back. I was too far away, and the light was fading too fast, for me to see the split nail on either hind foot, even with my binoculars. Otherwise it was a fine and rather comical display of grooming. I didn't mind that the beaver had skipped the dam maintenance.

Dam-building, the beaver's most notable engineering feat, is an endeavour unmatched in the animal world. In most environments, the basic design is the same, but beavers are artists as much as they are technicians. Every project is a response to local conditions, which dictate the height, width, curvature and materials.

When wood is available, beavers choose it as their main building material, with a decided preference for small-diameter branches and stems. They anchor the first pieces into the channel bottom and banks and weave in others as they go, packing in sediment dredged up from underwater to fill the gaps. They often reinforce dams with stones and typically seal them with mud on the upstream side. Sometimes before incorporating sticks into a dam, they strip off the bark and eat it. If their favourite food-trees are in short supply, they save the good stuff for sustenance and use less palatable types of wood for construction.

When they lack wood, beavers make do with whatever's at hand: aquatic plants, sagebrush, cornstalks and corncobs, all kinds of human rubbish — plastic, metal or otherwise. In the Yukon, biologists found one dam that was built almost entirely out of boulders the size of soccer balls — some weighing four or five kilograms — with a few sticks jammed in here and there. Gold miners had previously stripped away most of the forest alongside the creek, leaving a moonscape of cobbles and gravel. Regenerating willows, alders and poplars had drawn beavers back to the area. A couple of years after the resourceful stone-masons erected their unorthodox dam, which measured nearly three metres wide and a metre high, it was still functioning, despite having been damaged by a passing grizzly bear.

Beavers aren't intentional altruists. When they impound water, it's for their own purposes. But they earn their keystone credentials by creating vital wetland ecosystems and sharing them, whether they want to or not, with a multitude of other species.

Converting a narrow, racing stream into an expansive pond dramatically increases local biodiversity, as well as the number of organisms occupying that area. The warmer, more tranquil pond-water teems with plankton and insects, and a complex food web spins out from this nutritional hub: kingfishers plunge deep in pursuit of trout; jewel-toned dragonflies dart after mosquitoes; and raccoons scoop wriggling tadpoles from the shallows. While moose wade in deep to feast on succulent aquatic plants, the well-watered shoreline plants offer a smorgasbord of grazing opportunities for everything from voles to deer. Even flood-killed trees at the pond edge are an asset — a scarce and valuable resource in the natural world, these snags are exploited first by woodpeckers and later by other birds and mammals that claim the woodpeckers' abandoned holes. For cavity-nesting ducks like buffleheads, goldeneyes, mergansers and wood ducks, such waterfront homes are crucial to breeding success.

Besides granting immediate benefits to wetland dwellers, beavers also create habitat legacies. An adult beaver can chew through as much as a ton of wood each year, just for sustenance. Add to that the wood needed for dams and lodges and it's easy to see why beaver colonies regularly exhaust their supplies and are forced to relocate. Even fast-growing trees, such as aspen, poplar and birch, and rapid regenerators like willow, can't always keep up with the demand. When resident beavers depart, their dams slowly disintegrate and their ponds dry up, becoming marshes and then wet meadows. Shrubs and trees gradually fill the opening and eventually new beavers move in and start all over again. A full cycle of damming, abandonment and reoccupation can take decades or even centuries.

A natural beaver landscape, operating without human interference, is geographically dynamic — a patchwork quilt that is constantly being picked apart and reassembled in new patterns. No one knows quite what that quilt looked like spread out across the continent before our predecessors ripped it away, only that it featured a profusion of blue, with scraps of cyan, azure and turquoise scattered in every direction.

Water, however, is not the only element beavers influence with their engineering. They are also significant geomorphic agents or landscape shapers. In the animal world, only humans have a greater ability to influence large-scale topography.

The first scientists to seriously consider the beaver's geomorphic influence were American geologists Rudolf Ruedemann and Walter J. Schoonmaker. While working in the Catskill Mountains in the 1930s, the pair realized that geological processes alone could not account for the shape of the region's river valleys. There had to have been another force at work during the 25,000 years following the retreat of the last glaciers. And that force, they reckoned, was *Castor canadensis*. According to their widely accepted hypothesis, countless generations of beavers and their dams built up the valley bottoms layer by layer and eventually transformed the formerly steep-sided Vs into broad, gently graded alluvial plains.

Subsequent measurements of the fine-grained, nutrient-rich sediments and organic matter that get trapped behind beaver dams have confirmed that the quantities can be substantial. Biologists who studied boreal forest beaver ponds in northern Quebec in the 1980s found that a small dam (with a volume of four to 18 cubic metres) could retain 2,000 to 6,500 cubic metres of sediment. In other words, taking the upper end of this calculation, a beaver family working with just five cords of wood could amass enough material to fill 1,700 single-axle dump trucks.

More recently, a research team led by ecohydrologist Cherie Westbrook discovered another way that beavers sculpt landscapes. Studying one beaver dam complex on the Colorado River in Rocky Mountain National Park over a six-year period, they found that beaver-induced flooding altered natural patterns of scouring and sediment deposition as prodigiously as if the beavers had been driving around on bulldozers. Large amounts of silt and clay ended up on terraces high above the floodplain, in places that regular flooding, caused by rain or snowmelt, would reach only once every 200 years. After a spring torrent breached the main dam, the beavers moved elsewhere, but the transported muck stayed behind, creating fertile new growing sites for colonizing plants, including willow, the local beavers' main food and building material.

Westbrook's research showed that beaver landscaping isn't always the slow process that Ruedemann and Schoonmaker envisioned. It took less than a decade for a single beaver colony living along one short stretch of the Colorado River to redistribute enough sediment to fill nearly 200 single-axle dump trucks. No wonder she and her colleagues concluded that "abundant beaver in the past may have strongly influenced the formation of the Colorado River valley."

By the time I met Cherie Westbrook in the summer of 2013, I almost felt like we were old friends. I had read her journal articles, checked out her academic web page, talked with her at length on the phone and corresponded with her by email. I knew she had done her PhD at Colorado State University and then moved to Saskatoon to launch the University of Saskatchewan's wetland ecohydrology research program; that she's passionate about peatlands, those ancient ecosystems built on thick layers of soggy, dead, slowly decaying plant material (she's the only person I've ever heard describe peat as "exciting"); and that she has a laugh that bubbles up like a spring.

We rendezvoused at one of Cherie's study sites in Kananaskis Country, a multi-use recreation area at the edge of the Rocky Mountains about halfway between Calgary and Banff. In person, she looked just like her photos: strawberry-blonde, fresh-faced and fit. I had a feeling she would be hard to keep up with when she was in full field-research mode, but I didn't have to worry about being put to the test. Since we both had busy schedules, our plan was to do a quick tour of a few beaver ponds, while continuing the conversation we had started at a distance. I tossed my daypack and rubber boots into the back of her pickup truck, slung my binoculars around my neck and climbed into the cab.

One of the things we talked about that morning was Cherie's work in the Colorado River valley. I'd been hearing a lot about rapidly rebounding beaver populations and all the problems they were causing, but in Rocky Mountain National Park, the species is struggling. In the 1940s, the park was home to an estimated 600 beavers, a marked improvement from the previous century. Then they started disappearing, for no obvious reason. By the early 2000s, only about 30 remained. Biologists now attribute this crash to a "predator-driven trophic cascade." Predator numbers are down, elk populations are flourishing and willow stands are taking a beating from excessive elk browsing, leaving the beavers on short rations.

Without beaver dams to periodically shift sediment onto the terraces, the topography and vegetation in these areas will inevitably change. At the same time, without beaver dams to slow the river flow, erosion will increase, deepening the channel. And as a river channel becomes more incised, the water table in the adjacent area drops.

"In places like Rocky Mountain National Park where there's no beaver, the channels are super-incised and the water tables are much lower than they were historically, and so the whole system is drying up," Cherie said. "It just fundamentally changes state from a wetland system to a dryland system, and it's very difficult to get it back to a wetland system with beaver."

"Can't you just bring in more beavers?" I asked.

She shook her head. "The problem is, you can't let the river get too incised, because then they have to put in really tall dams and tall dams are not structurally sound. There's kind of a limit there, where you flip the switch on the system, changing it from one stable state to another. There's a tipping point when the effects no longer are reversible. You can't loop back to where you were by restoration."

In certain parts of the American Rockies, where beaver populations never recovered from the havoc wreaked by the mountain men, the switch has been flipped already. "Yellowstone, in some places, has gone past the tipping point," Cherie said. "Rocky is quickly going towards it." Managers in both parks are working on multiple fronts to revive beaver populations, she added, but success is by no means guaranteed.

I hadn't realized that disengaging the beaver's geomorphic influence could have such dire consequences, and my face must have reflected my dismay. Cherie gave a rueful laugh. "I try to avoid talking doom and gloom," she said apologetically.

Cherie's return to Canada in 2005 was also a return to her first scientific love. "My interest has always been wetlands," she told me the first time we talked. "I got sidetracked a little bit with rivers, but wetlands have always been near and dear to my heart." As have beavers.

Growing up in the 1970s and '80s in southern Ontario, where "you couldn't really be a kid without running across beaver dams," she developed a great curiosity about the animals that built these structures. It was only when she got out in the field as an undergrad that she discovered the dam-builders weren't particularly popular with hydrologists. "We had beaver everywhere," she recalled with a chuckle, "and they're always screwing up your hydrology studies."

The standard response at that time was to blow up dams and remove any beavers that got in the researchers' way. Cherie chose to take the opposite approach and learn more about how beavers influence hydrology, a question she considers both understudied and undervalued.

"I feel it's a really important topic and I see my niche there," she said. "Almost all of the research that's done on hydrology — surface water, groundwater — is done in the absence of beaver, so we really don't understand the kinds of wide-scale watershed effects that beaver may have had and how beaver coming back into the system might potentially alter the system." Although she didn't use the phrase "ecological amnesia," I heard echoes of Greg Hood in her words.

One example of almost-forgotten knowledge that Cherie cites comes from *The Romance of the Beaver*, a book written by naturalist, photographer and artist Arthur Radclyffe Dugmore and published in 1914. Dugmore's meticulous sketches are the book's greatest strength. The most fascinating one is a map that shows how beavers working in an area of low-relief terrain in northern Ontario diverted a stream over a watershed divide and into a different basin.

"They actually pushed water over the drainage divide by ponding it up high enough," Cherie said. "That's really interesting and it's completely unstudied." She wonders about both the hydrological and geochemical consequences, especially in light of ongoing industrial development in the boreal forest region.

"I'm thinking Fort Mac here," she went on, referring to Alberta's Fort McMurray and the surrounding oil sands. "You expect the [hydrological] system to drain a certain way, but once you put beaver in that system, it might drain in an entirely different way and your watershed divide might not work out for you anymore, so you really have to understand the complicating factor of beaver there. The whole goal of the oil sands is to return those systems back to nature, and people have this sense of how the systems are going to operate, but what I don't think they've thought very much about yet is how beaver moving back into these areas is going to affect the reclamation efforts." (In fact, Cherie wasn't alone in these concerns. The same week we met, the University of Alberta's Oil Sands Research and Information Network published a report entitled *Potential Impacts of Beaver on Oil Sands Reclamation Success*, which warned of the paucity of relevant beaver research.)

For the most part, the surface-water effects of beaver engineering are obvious, from sprawling swamps to ponds strung like pearls along narrow creeks. But we can't see groundwater, at least not directly. That's where the hydrologists, with their monitoring wells, pressure transducers and other scientific devices, come in. Although this equipment looks mundane, it's turning up some very interesting data.

Like most of the places Cherie works these days, the Bateman Creek valley is a peat-based wetland, built on a metres-thick body of decomposing plant matter. (In contrast, alluvial river systems, like the one she studied in Colorado, have a foundation of mineral soil.) Located in the foothills on the eastern edge of Kananaskis Country, Bateman Creek flows through a gently undulating landscape of treed ridges and open leas, with the smoky blue peaks of the Rockies looming to the west.

In front of us as we set off, sedge meadows and willow thickets spread out across the long, flat-bottomed valley, completely obscuring the narrow, meandering creek and creating the impression of solid ground — a deception quickly dispelled by my first squelching steps along the vague trail that she and her students had trampled through the sedges on their way back and forth over the past six years. Cherie had told me that the beaver ponds influence the entire valley's hydrology. The water threatening to pour over the tops of my boots reinforced this point.

The fact that beaver dams raise the groundwater table around beaver ponds is well documented and clearly signalled by lush bordering vegetation. "But we really hadn't understood how large an area a dam could affect in terms of hydrology," Cherie said. "It's considerably larger than we thought back in the '80s. It could be a couple of square kilometres if you're talking about a large dam and the valley bottom is really wide." The Bateman Creek valley — about half a kilometre from side to side and more than a kilometre long — is a prime example.

In addition to elevating the water table, beaver dams also stabilize groundwater levels, which normally decline over the summer, when plants are at their thirstiest. "Feel the evapotranspiration?" Cherie asked, as we moved away from the aspen- and pine-clad slopes and into the centre of the valley, the wet ground sucking at our feet with every step. Once she mentioned it, I did notice that the air was moister.

"In areas like this," she continued, "the water table drops somewhere between a metre and a metre and a half a year, unless there are beaver dams present. Then it only drops about five centimetres over the summer, so it would be higher and basically the same all year round." At her Colorado River study site, the water table dropped about two metres in summer when unimpeded by beaver dams and barely at all when dammed.

And then there are the downstream effects. Whereas surface water is only stored upstream, behind the dam, groundwater storage occurs both above and below the dam. "In a beaver-dominated system, the groundwater starts to move very slowly back towards the stream somewhere downstream," Cherie had explained during our first phone conversation. "It might be a kilometre, it might be three, it might be 200 metres." But regardless of the distance, the outcome is the same: "Once the water gets into the groundwater system, it moves a lot slower than if it's stored right on the surface, and so in the periods between rain storms, the water is really slowly released back to the stream along these groundwater flow paths. What you're doing is increasing the amount of low flows, and that's going to drought-proof the whole system."

Increasing the low flows is especially important in areas that are expected to become drier with climate change, she said, because "where you have a system tending towards a drier state, you're going to lose the low flows. You might still get the peak flows, but the low flows will become even smaller."

Our talk of low flows seemed a little ironic, considering that less than two months earlier, southern Alberta had experienced its most intense peak flow scenario in recorded history. On the other hand, the highs and lows were really two sides of the same coin: climate change models for the region predict both a drying trend and more frequent extreme rainfall events. The June 2013 storm, which had dumped 200-plus millimetres of rain in two days, definitely met the definition of extreme. The ensuing flooding, the costliest natural disaster in Canadian history to that point, inundated thousands of homes in Calgary and other communities, forced the evacuation of more than 100,000 people and shut down several highways for days. It also blew out a 10-metre section of Bateman Creek's biggest beaver dam.

Well before we reached the ravaged structure, I started catching glimpses of a broad, half-empty channel bordered by sedges and willows. Then we turned and started walking along the top of what turned out to be the dam, and a vast mudflat came into view. We were overlooking the exposed bottom of what had been an immense beaver pond, dubbed "The Pacific" by Cherie and her crew. "This is very cool," she said. "It's always been underwater since I've been working here."

The dam stood more than a metre high above the drained pond, a massive dark brown bulwark of compacted peat with a fringe of sedges running along the top, like a green Mohawk haircut. Beaver-gnawed sticks, as white as bones, protruded from the bare slope of the upstream wall and lay strewn about on its surface. The shorter downstream wall was nearly vertical and obscured by vegetation. The whole edifice stretched about 200 metres across the valley — except for the gap in the middle, where it looked like a tank had punched through it.

According to the earliest air photos of the area, the dam was at least 70 years old, which isn't exceptional in a peatland environment. Cherie suspects peatland dams can stick around for thousands of years in a relatively undisturbed state. "That doesn't happen on river channels," she said. "There, you get a high flow every 50 years or whatever that will blow the dam. You don't see those high flows in peatlands." Not normally, anyway.

While this dam had succumbed to the June 2013 deluge, most of the others along Bateman Creek had held fast and slowed the floodwaters as they surged down the valley, demonstrating the capacity for beaver dams and ponds in any kind of terrain to mitigate flood damage up to a certain point. Unfortunately, if the volume and speed of the flow exceeds a dam's ability to resist it, the downstream consequences can be severe.

There was no sign of any attempt to rebuild the dam and no one had spotted any beavers in the neighbourhood since the flood. Perhaps they had been swept away or maybe the hole was just too big to fill. In any case, the pond now sat essentially empty. I knew in theory that the bottom of a beaver pond isn't as flat and featureless as a swimming pool, but I had never actually seen the complex topography. Here, the reality was laid out for me like a relief map: mounds covered with a green stubble of new growth; puddle-filled hollows connected by a network of channels, including a deep trough running along the base of the dam.

In both popular culture and scientific circles, the beaver's ability to build with wood overshadows the species' other construction skill — digging. Admittedly this isn't a unique talent within the animal world. Nor do modern castorids produce anything as nifty as the spiral tunnels excavated by their long-dead distant relative, little *Paleocastor*. They do, however, dig some pretty impressive canals when the conditions are right. These waterways can extend up to several hundred metres in length and are often more than a metre wide and equally deep. Their usual purpose is to provide safe, navigable routes between ponds and foraging sites, so the beavers can avoid the dangers of overland travel. Less frequently, beavers use them to redirect a stream into their home pond.

Like canals, the channels revealed on the floor of the drained "Pacific" would have been excavated one muddy paw-full at a time. Beavers make these underwater pathways to create extra depth, so they can swim more easily under winter ice or when the water level drops in summer. In peatlands, pond-bottom digging may also be an essential part of pond construction.

An hour or so earlier, in the nearby Bow Valley, Cherie and I had been standing precariously on the narrow crest of another peatland dam, this one intact, discussing how beavers operate in these environments. The large, amorphous sheet of water at our feet reflected the dull sky, the nearby mountains and the grey skeletons of drowned spruce trees. Here and there beneath these ethereal images, I could see the bottom. The pond seemed implausibly shallow, and the dam itself was extremely modest, just an easy step up from the wet sedge meadow on the downstream side.

Although peatlands cover huge swathes of the beaver's range, especially in the North, where population densities are highest, research on beavers in these ecosystems has been limited. "Very few people in the world are looking at beaver and peatlands," Cherie said. "We don't really even know that much about how they build dams in peatlands." But she's working on figuring it out and her years of investigation suggest it involves a whole lot of excavating.

"What I think the beaver are doing is actually digging out some of the peat and building it up." She pointed to the water directly in front of us. "On the upstream side of the dam here, there's a lot more depth, because they're pulling out the sediment and piling it on top of the dam." The sponginess beneath my boots corroborated what she was saying, even though the dam was so carpeted with plants that it was impossible to tell what they were growing on. There would be sticks in there somewhere, according to Cherie's observations of other peat dams, but they weren't the main building-material.

Because peatland dams are designed to contain groundwater seepage in an almost level landscape, they don't need to be very high, but they do tend to keep getting longer as the beavers work to prevent the water from flowing around the ends. "The Wood Buffalo dam would look very similar to this one," Cherie said, referring to Jean Thie's contender for the world's longest dam, up in Wood Buffalo National Park.

It makes sense that beavers would build dams out of quarried peat: when building with wood, they typically scoop up mud and plaster it onto the upstream side of the dam to make it more watertight. However, the excavation work performed by peatland-dwelling beavers appears to go far beyond that. Cherie suspects they also dig out entire ponds, because in such flat terrain, damming alone isn't enough to create the amount and depth of open water they need. "I don't think that they're building a little dam and then flooding the area," she said. "This doesn't look like flooding to me in the same kind of way that you would see flooding in a river system."

She does know for sure that when beavers move into peatlands, they significantly increase the amount of open water — a change that might be of merely academic interest if peatlands weren't so globally important for their long-term carbon storage capacity.

On our way back to the truck from the Bow Valley dam, Cherie paused for a moment and bounced up and down a few times on the waterlogged ground. Bubbles broke from the dark peat and rose through the shallow layer of water. "That's methane," she said, trapped CH_4 bubbling up to the surface in a process called ebullition. Trampolining on peat adds infinitesimally to greenhouse gas emissions through methane ebullition. Creating large areas of open water in peatlands, as beavers do, dramatically increases CH_4 release.

However, this doesn't mean we should be trying to get rid of peatland beavers. In Cherie's opinion, the beavers are actually critical to "having the peatlands continue to be peatlands," especially as the climate becomes less favourable to such ecosystems. "To make peat you have to have high water-tables," she explained, "lots of water and not lots of oxygen," so when the plants die, they can't decompose. By keeping water tables high, beavers "actually help promote peat development." What's more, she and other scientists are starting to think that many North American peatlands may owe their origins to beavers.

By the time Cherie began her studies, beavers had bounced back from the devastation of the fur-trade era, but the hydrological, geomorphological and ecological consequences of removing this keystone species from the landscape are always in the back of her mind as she works. As she once said to me, "We're talking about beaver in every headwater stream across North America prior to European colonization." By this she meant the approximately 85 percent of all streams that are classified as first-, second- or third-order streams and are therefore small enough to be dammed by beavers. "If you imagine beaver building dams and storing sediment and water in all of these different headwater systems," she said, "then you can start to imagine how the water flows and the sediment flows through the large river systems would be fundamentally changed by that."

When I asked about her assessment of the continent-wide effects of the beaver's near-annihilation, her answer was simple: "I think it fundamentally changed the way watersheds operate."

Another scientist who has been paying close attention to the relationship between beavers and water is Glynnis Hood (no relation to Greg Hood), an associate professor of environmental studies at the University of Alberta. Fittingly, she lives and works in the Beaver Hills, just east of Edmonton, a rolling, hillocky area, pocked with shallow sloughs and pothole lakes.

The Beaver Hills lost their namesake in the mid-1800s and remained without beavers until a few were reintroduced to Elk Island National Park in 1941. Half a century later, Hood and a colleague, Suzanne Bayley, examined the impact of their return by studying aerial photographs, beaver census figures and climate data. Their analysis showed that beavers had had "an overwhelming influence on wetland creation and maintenance" in the park, with an incredible ninefold increase in the water surface area of the recolonized wetlands. Even in dry years, ponds with beavers were considerably fuller than those without.

In 2002, the final year of their study and the region's driest since the notorious 1930s, the beaverless wetlands were visibly more parched than the occupied sites, and some were reduced to mudflats. That summer, the beavers' key concern was water management, but building bigger dams wasn't much use when there was so little surface water available. Instead, they focused on digging channels in and around their ponds to maintain as much water depth as possible, especially around the food caches they were building in front of their lodges. Some of the beavers made it through the following winter with as little as 70 centimetres of water in which to swim back and forth to their pantries. The unlucky ones, those whose ponds froze solid, either starved to death inside their homes or fled in search of food, only to be killed by predators.

Hood and Bayley didn't specifically track the keystone dividends generated by the beavers' engineering investment, but other scholars are adding annually to the growing body of writing on the subject. Recently, Hood and one of her students, Chantal Bromley, published a journal article that describes how beavers affect the melting of pond ice in spring. Over the course of one winter, they had studied more than 60 beaver ponds in a provincial park in the Beaver Hills, about half of them "active" (these had obvious food caches and lodge-top air vents rimmed with frost) and the other half vacant. Come spring, patches of water appeared about 10 days earlier in the ponds with resident beavers than in those without. The thawing nearly always began near the cache or the lodge's main entrance, possibly because the beavers stirred up the water in these areas as they swam beneath the ice, mixing it with warmer water from just below the living platform inside the lodge. No one had ever documented this mode of habitat creation before.

Hastening pond melt may not sound like much of a keystone contribution, but a patch of open water in an otherwise-frozen landscape is an oasis for early-migrating waterfowl. It can also give early-nesters like Canada geese a head start and make all the difference in their breeding success. Similarly, stragglers flying south in late fall stand to benefit when beavers delay freeze-up by slapping their tails next to forming ice or pulling at the edge of the ice to break it — activities that biologists have occasionally witnessed but not yet studied.

From Greg Hood's discovery of salmon-friendly beavers in Pacific coast tidal marshes to Chantal Bromley's patient survey-ing of snow-covered ponds, none of this research could have been done during the beaver's lost years. And all of it helps us reconstruct a complete picture of how ecological communities and hydrological systems function when beavers are in their rightful place.

The eminent conservationist Aldo Leopold once observed, "To keep every cog and wheel is the first precaution of intelligent tinkering." If we had carelessly lost the cog called beaver, noth-ing could have replaced it.

·Nine·
DÉTENTE

North America may never truly be Beaverland again, but we haven't passed the tipping point in most places, and populations are thriving in many parts of the beaver's historic range. Depending on your perspective, that's either a blessing or a curse. On one hand, there's a growing understanding that beavers are an important part of our world. On the other, coexistence isn't always easy. That certainly seemed to be what the beaver glowering at me from inside the live-trap at the edge of the lake was thinking.

Except for an occasional ear twitch, the animal hunkered down inside the wire mesh enclosure was motionless. After a night of confinement, it had every reason to be displeased and no way of knowing how lucky it was to be alive and physically unharmed. The price beavers pay for trying to modify habitats claimed by humans is often death. This one had been granted a conditional amnesty. Shawn Dalman, the sole proprietor of Shawn Dalman's Critter Removal, leaned down and peered back at his prisoner. Confident that all was well, he then began undoing the wire with which he'd fastened the cage to a shoreline willow to keep the beaver from accidentally drowning itself.

A lake in name only, the beaver's abode wasn't much bigger than a couple of Olympic-sized swimming pools laid end to end. Head-high native willows crowded the perimeter, backed by a forest of Douglas fir and red cedar, except where the trees had been cleared to accommodate three waterfront lots — a little piece of southern Vancouver Island paradise within easy commuting distance of Victoria. But all was not well in paradise. Beavers had built a dam, and the enlarged lake was encroaching on the human domain. The year before, when the water had risen more than a metre and threatened to swamp the septic fields, the homeowners had hired Shawn to solve their problem. Now, a new pair of beavers had moved in, and he was back for round two.

According to James A. Serpell, the director of the University of Pennsylvania's Center for the Interaction of Animals and Society, our attitudes towards different species are determined by the interplay between two factors: "affect" (our emotional reaction to the species, from cherished to despised) and "utility" (how beneficial we find the species, from very to not at all). If you analyze these two determinants in graph form, with affect on the vertical axis and utility on the horizontal, you get a four-quadrant grid and four attitudinal categories: cherished and useful; cherished but useless; despised yet useful; and despised and useless, or even detrimental. I'm not sure where Shawn's clients would have placed their relationship with beavers on this graph, but they definitely wanted these ones gone.

They did not, however, want them dead, so Shawn had deployed a Hancock trap. Also known as clamshell trap, it looked like an oversized suitcase made out of chain-link fencing strung onto an aluminum frame. Two springs the size of jumbo soup cans powered the hinge. Later, when he showed me how he sets this contraption, he called the springs "brutal" and I stayed well clear of the action. He pinned the frame to the ground with his boot and prised the two halves apart with his gloved hands, then dropped to his knees and used the full strength of his well-muscled arms and the weight of his body to force the upper half completely open. As he sprawled across the trap to engage the safety catch, his ruddy complexion flushed another shade redder.

"That looks like a dangerous manoeuvre," I commented. Shawn grunted his agreement.

When he had set the Hancock trap the previous evening, he had carefully positioned it in shallow water, so a captured beaver would stay wet enough to avoid overheating, yet could easily keep its head above water to breathe. For a lure, he had swizzled a stick in a jar of toffee-coloured, castoreum-scented paste and laid it on the bank. Any beaver drawn to investigate this provocative odour would have to walk across the trap. And the instant one foot touched the trigger in the centre of the hinge, the two halves would snap together, locking the hapless animal inside the cage with just enough room to adjust its position now and then. After a night crouched in such close quarters, this beaver looked justifiably sullen.

Shawn gently lifted the trap from the water, carried it up the bank and set it on the grassy slope. The beaver huffed and rumbled softly, then squirted a stream of yellow liquid from between its hind legs. A familiar, sweetly acrid scent wafted up from the ground.

"Castoreum?" I asked.

"Yup," Shawn said. "They do that when they're mad."

Once the beaver stopped protesting, Shawn strapped the cage onto a backpack frame, slung the load over one shoulder and strode away up the hill. I wasn't carrying 20-plus kilograms like he was, yet I had to trot to keep up. When he reached his pickup truck, he slid the trap into the back and covered it with blankets to keep the beaver cool and damp and as calm as possible during the next stage of its ordeal.

Nearly two hours and about 100 kilometres later, we turned off the logging road we had been following for the last 15 minutes, bumped down a short track and stopped beside a tributary of the San Juan River. We had arrived at Shawn's favourite beaver-release site, which also happens to be one of the few places where he's allowed to let beavers go. His other government-approved emancipation sites are just as remote, which makes live-trapping and relocation an expensive option. The bill for dealing with this one animal would top $600.

Shawn hefted the beaver suitcase out of the truck and placed it in the water at the edge of a slow-moving side channel, then flicked up the hooks on either side of the frame and started pulling the two halves apart. The beaver didn't wait for the trap to open all the way. The instant its feet were free, it somehow extruded its rotund body through a gap that looked no wider than the span of my hand and started paddling. A moment later, it ducked beneath the surface, hurtling through water so clear that for a moment the swimmer seemed to be soaring through the air. It came up again at the main channel, swung out into the current and began rocketing downstream. One more dive and it was gone.

Standing side by side on the shore, Shawn and I stared at the river as if we could track the beaver's underwater progress. I silently wondered how long it would be until this exile found a new home and how it would fare in the meantime. Based on its size, Shawn had appraised it as "last year's kick-out" — a two-year-old that had left its birth lodge the previous fall. Its first attempt to settle obviously hadn't worked out well and a reunion with its mate seemed doubtful, even though Shawn would be setting the clamshell trap again that night, aiming to catch the second beaver.

As we drove back to town, I quizzed Shawn about his work. Mostly he deals with raccoons, river otters, cougars and bears, he told me. Only about 10 percent of his business involves trapping beavers, typically 12 to 20 of them a year. If the customer doesn't choose live-trapping, he sets a rotating-jaw trap that slams down on the victim's neck and is designed to kill instantly. Submersion traps that hold the beaver underwater until it is rendered unconscious because the oxygen supply in its bloodstream has been depleted and replaced by carbon dioxide (a death that can take more than five minutes) are legal, but he doesn't use them.

When he does use lethal traps on beavers, Shawn sends their pelts to the NAFA auction house along with furs from his registered trapline, where he mainly targets martens. The beaver pelts are never big money-makers, but he figures selling them is better than throwing them away. Mostly, though, he'd prefer not to have dead beavers to deal with.

"I'd much rather release them than knock 'em off," he replied, when I asked how he felt about the beaver liberation he'd just performed. "You can only do so much killing."

From an accounting perspective, the resurrection of *Castor canadensis* is undeniably one of North America's greatest conservation success stories. Beaver numbers have climbed steadily since they bottomed out in the low hundred thousands (if not lower) at the beginning of the twentieth century, and the species has now returned to all of the states and provinces from which it went missing. In 1988, the continent's beaver population was

pegged at six to 12 million by Robert J. Naiman, the director of the Center for Streamside Studies at the University of
Washington, and two other scientists. More recently and with
greater scientific rigour, a team led by Cherie Westbrook's colleague, Colin J. Whitfield, estimated that there are now between
9.6 and 50 million beavers living in North America. Both the
high- and low-end figures for this year-2000 estimate represent
exponential growth from the study's starting point one century
earlier. And the numbers are still climbing.

As Shawn Dalman, Pete Wise and others in the nuisance
animal control business well know, not everyone is pleased by
this turn of events. All across North America, our relationship
with beavers has followed the same pattern, with concerns about
extinction rapidly giving way to complaints of overabundance as
our positions on Serpell's affect/utility graph shift. The Prince
Albert National Park experience offers a textbook example of
this change of heart.

When Grey Owl brought Jelly Roll, Rawhide and their four
kits to Ajawaan Lake in 1931, there were no other beavers in the
northern half of the park and only a small, though uncounted,
remnant population in the southern half. In 1935, a survey determined that the park had approximately 500 resident beavers.
Twenty years later, there were at least 15,000 and official discon-
tent with their presence was at an all-time high.

Problems had started to surface soon after Prince Albert
National Park superintendent James Wood welcomed Grey
Owl to Ajawaan and endorsed his beaver conservation goals.
In 1932, the park service's chief engineer, J.M. Wardle, had
recommended the removal of beaver dams that were imped-
ing the Spruce River in the southern half of the park. On the
record, Wardle hoped that "the colony could be persuaded to go

elsewhere in the Park." Privately, he probably favoured extermination. In Kootenay, Banff, Waterton and Jasper national parks, he warned, beaver damage to roads, waterworks and trails had already become "quite an item of expense."

Within 10 years, Wood's successor was dealing with all of the problems that Wardle had predicted, as well as some unforeseen ones. No one, for example, expected a beaver to seek shade under a parked car in the Waskesiu campground, especially not the driver who inadvertently ran over it. Throughout the 1940s, Prince Albert National Park staff live-trapped and relocated numerous problem beavers within the park. They also sent dozens of "surplus" animals to Riding Mountain and Wood Buffalo national parks and gave hundreds more to the Saskatchewan government to restock beaverless areas around the province. *Holiday at Waskesiu*, a National Film Board documentary made in the late '40s, captured the action as a pair of wardens grabbed a penned beaver by the tail and wrestled the thrashing beast into a burlap sack for shipping.

Less film-worthy was the park's testing of a new beaver deterrent (Repellent 96A-modified) formulated by the U.S. Department of the Interior's Wildlife Research Laboratory. In 1948, following the lab's instructions, Prince Albert employees optimistically painted the substance onto tree trunks along the lakeshore near Waskesiu, where a high level of beaver activity was "spoiling the scenery." The beavers ignored it and carried on with their logging.

The next decade brought harsher measures. From 1952 to 1955, the park dynamited countless dams and lodges and hired trappers to kill thousands of beavers in the park. The managers sold the pelts through the Hudson's Bay Company and distributed some of the meat to destitute First Nations families. They also donated the preserved heads of two adult beavers to the School of Dental Surgery in Birmingham, England, for scientific study.

In 1955, the peak year of the assault, the eradication quota was set at 10,000 beavers. Although only about 2,500 were trapped in the end, the victims included 43 from Ajawaan Lake. That fact was not mentioned in replies to the late Grey Owl's fans, whose letters continued to flow in from across North America and from as far away as France, Denmark and Malaya.

After Prince Albert National Park's beaver reduction program ended in 1956, the wardens went back to dealing with problem beavers by live-trapping whenever possible. When I spoke with the park's wildlife ecologist, Seth Cherry, in 2011, he told me they rarely have trouble with beavers these days, except in unusually wet years, which that year happened to be. A few weeks before our conversation, the park staff had dispatched a couple of beavers whose dams had flooded a campground access road.

"We couldn't relocate them," Cherry said regretfully. "We have beavers everywhere, and beavers are territorial. Sometimes I think killing is the most humane way to deal with them."

It was hard to believe that only 80 years earlier, reinstating beavers to this trapped-out region had seemed like a pipe dream.

Compared to many rodents, beavers aren't prolific. They can reach sexual maturity as yearlings, but most don't mate until they are two or three years old, and when they do, it's as monogamous pairs that stay together for life and raise only one family a year. Litter sizes can range from one to nine, but families typically consist of just two to four kits. Such moderate fecundity stands in stark contrast to that of animals like Norway rats, which start breeding about two months after they're born and produce litters of six to 22 young, three to 12 times a year. So how did a breeder as restrained as the beaver manage such a rapid comeback?

Part of the answer is natural dispersal — an instinct for spreading out across the land. Grey Owl hailed the beaver as "the Imperialist of the animal world" and described its strategy in terms befitting his own British colonial roots: "He maintains a home and hearth, and from it he sends out every year a pair of emigrants who search far and wide for new fields to conquer; who explore, discover, occupy, and improve, to the benefit of all concerned."

The metaphor may be heavy-handed, but it's conceptually sound. At some point, usually around age two, all beavers leave home to search for their own domain. The itinerant lifestyle is dangerous — Pete Wise calls transient juveniles "wandering fools" — so the searchers stop as soon as they find a promising situation. If necessary, however, they can cover a lot of ground. Recaptures of tagged beavers indicate that they're willing and able to travel at least 50 kilometres to reach an acceptable new address, if you measure the distance between the start and finish straight across the map; or 80 kilometres if you assume an all-water route, which is more likely. Terrestrial travel is generally a last resort for beavers, though one rambler was found almost 12 kilometres from the nearest water body.

Eradication campaigns waged against the beaver's leading four-footed enemy, the timber wolf, and secondary predators such as coyotes, mountain lions and bears, also accelerated the beaver's resurgence. Again, Prince Albert National Park offers a telling example. With the superintendent's blessing, so many wolves were shot, snared and poisoned there in the late 1940s and early '50s that one warden later recalled wolf pelts "stacked like cordwood" in a park warehouse. At the same time, the superintendent was battling the beaver boom, apparently oblivious to the effects of his wolf purge.

Humans have also contributed to the recovery by reducing our own predation on beavers — leaving some to reproduce, instead of killing every one in sight — and by expediting dispersal, rather than waiting for young wandering fools to fill in the blank spaces on the historical range map one generation at a time. Grey Owl's reintroduction scheme remains the most famous of these undertakings. A program carried out in Idaho in 1948 takes the prize as the most innovative.

The Idaho Fish and Game Department began transplanting delinquent beavers from settled areas of the state to unoccupied wilderness locations in the 1940s, and soon discovered that the rugged terrain and lack of roads made it an arduous and expensive process. The smelly, fidgeting beavers spooked the pack horses and mules that carried their crates, and the hot, jolting trips took a heavy toll on the reluctant passengers. The best solution, someone suggested, would be to fly the beavers to their destination and parachute them to the ground. Research and experiments commenced.

The beaver-dropping box that the department's Scotty Heter designed for the operation was so ingenious that it earned a place in the August 1950 issue of *Modern Mechanix*. Built out of common-grade lumber, with ventilation holes drilled through the walls, the valise-like container was big enough to accommodate two adult beavers. Cleverly positioned sling ropes kept the box closed as long as there was tension on the parachute lines. When the canopy collapsed upon landing, the ropes fell away and the box opened.

Heter conducted numerous trial flights with an old male beaver, fondly known as Geronimo, who soon became so accustomed to the routine that he would stoically crawl back into the crate as soon as his handlers approached. Once the system was perfected, Geronimo's reward was a one-way trip to the backcountry, accompanied by three young female beavers. After this last touchdown, he remained in his travelling case for a long time, perhaps skeptical that his flying days were over. Finally, however, he ventured forth and carried on with the business of establishing a colony.

Altogether, the Idaho Fish and Game Department delivered 76 live beavers to targeted meadows in the fall of 1948, all launched from an altitude of 150 to 250 metres. The only mishap occurred when an improperly lashed sling rope loosened early, and one beaver managed to crawl out in mid-descent. Perched on the top of the box, this Houdini had almost made it to safety when it jumped or slipped about 20 metres above the ground, with fatal results. The rest of Heter's paratroopers all took to their new homes, and by the following year, they had constructed dams and lodges at all of the drop sites.

The most remarkable manifestation of the beaver renaissance has been the species' return to major urban centres, including the largest city within its historic range. New York, originally known as New Amsterdam, was founded on the fur trade, and beavers were once so commercially important to the city's existence that a pair of the animals grace its official seal. But long after beavers began to rebound elsewhere, the garbage-clogged, polluted Bronx — New York City's only freshwater river — remained utterly uninviting. Even when efforts to undo the damage finally got underway in the 1990s, no one was thinking much about beavers, so the sudden appearance of a member of the species in 2007 astonished everyone. It was the first time a wild beaver had been seen within the municipal limits in more than 200 years. The ecstatic restoration team named the new resident after congressman José E. Serrano, a driving force behind the $15-million clean-up.

The castorid José, who likely swam downriver from semi-rural Westchester County, settled on the banks of the Bronx River and built his (or her — no one knew for sure) lodge right next door to the Bronx Zoo. Three years later, a second trail-blazer joined José and was dubbed Justin Beaver by an online poll, though its sex was also unknown. As of fall 2014, the two were still cohabiting, but hadn't produced any offspring.

In Canada's largest city, Toronto, beavers are more common, but still rare enough to attract attention. One pair, spotted scouting out the trendy Queen's Quay neighbourhood along the harbourfront in 2011, drew crowds of camera-wielding viewers.

Even in smaller cities, beavers often receive celebrity treat-ment. In 2009, two Members of Parliament made the national news after encountering a beaver on a busy downtown Ottawa street as they walked back to their apartment late one night. Seeing cars braking and swerving to avoid the animal, the men decided to intervene. First they called 911. Sorry, not our prob-lem, the dispatcher responded. So, they took matters into their own hands and became beaver wranglers. While one controlled traffic, the other nudged the beaver along with his gym bag. Their fitful and erratic journey to the river, which was only three or four blocks away, took nearly an hour, but when they finally reached their destination, the beaver needed no more coaxing. It plunged into the water and swam away, and the politicians went home to bed.

While urban pioneers like José and Justin are acclaimed as indicators of restored ecosystem health and warmly welcomed, their descendants may get a more hostile reception. Once the novelty wears off, humans tend to be unenthusiastic about having beavers as neighbours.

Whether they settle in cities or out in the country, the list of grievances against beavers is long. They flood roads and railways (because to their eyes, a culverted roadbed across a stream is a ready-made dam that only needs a little work to block that irksome hole). They fell trees that we value as scenery or fruit producers or future timber. They submerge waterfront real estate and farmland. They transmit *Giardia*, a water-borne parasite that causes the intestinal misery known as "beaver fever." They move in under cottage docks and treat them like pre-fab lodges. Occasionally, they even kill dogs.

One recent and well-publicized dog-killing incident occurred in Red Deer, Alberta, where a rescued beaver named Mickey once drew thousands of tourists, and a bronze statue of little Doris Forbes cradling her illustrious pet graces the city's Coronation Park. But Mickey's fame came in the 1940s, when beavers were still rare in most of North America.

The event that put Red Deer's beavers back in the spotlight occurred just a few kilometres away from the statue of Doris and Mickey, in the Three Mile Bend Recreation Area. For 20 years, this suburban, off-leash park's network of ponds had been home to beavers, usually one or two families, without any reported problems. In 2010, however, the beavers got fed up with dogs chasing them in the water and started fighting back. Although they inflicted some wounds that required stitches, the canine harassment continued, until one of the beavers finally slashed its tormentor, a full-grown husky, with its razor-sharp teeth and the dog died of blood loss. National media responded with a flurry of stories. "No more Mr. Nice Rodent," declared the photo caption in one newspaper.

A week later, while the authorities debated how to deal with the situation, an anonymous vigilante shot one of the beavers and left its lifeless body floating in the water. The confrontations stopped after that, though there is no way of knowing whether the dead beaver had been the sole defender. It was equally likely that heightened awareness had made local dog-owners more cautious and responsible.

When I stopped by Three Mile Bend the year after the "No more Mr. Nice Rodent" incident, I found the walking paths well posted with signs that read: "Wildlife and pets don't mix. Keep your pets under control." As I strolled around the ponds, looking in vain for their infamous inhabitants, I wondered about the bigger question that this episode raised: Can beavers and humans successfully mix? In 2012, this line of inquiry took me to Gatineau Park, North America's longest running large-scale experiment in making our interspecies relationship work.

Gatineau Park, a 361-square-kilometre conservation area on the Quebec side of the Ottawa River, lies just north of the city of Ottawa. With more than 50 lakes nestled among its rolling, forested hills, as well as countless streams, bogs, marshes and swamps, this little slice of the Canadian Shield is an ideal environment for beavers. Roughly 1,200 of them live here, distributed between about 300 colonies. On the human side, Gatineau receives close to three million visitors a year, including the Prime Minister, whose official summer residence sits on the shores of Lac Mousseau (also known as Harrington Lake) in the middle of the park.

My guide to Gatineau and its beaver-management strategies was National Capital Commission conservation officer Richard Moore, the man who "takes care of the beavers at Mr. Harper's place," as he jokingly boasted. He's also responsible for ensuring that the rest of the park-dwelling beavers don't create problems for the general public, a job he's been doing since 1988.

Richard sported a grey crew cut, a white uniform shirt with button-flap pockets and epaulettes and a wide belt rigged to carry a radio, a fistful of keys, pens and a notebook. A beaver held pride of place in the centre of each of his conservation officer shoulder patches. However, his employers' attitude towards beavers has not always been so positive.

Back in 1931, when the Quebec government outlawed beaver trapping throughout the province, hardly any members of the species remained in the Gatineau Hills. By the time the ban was lifted in 1941, Gatineau Park had been created, putting the furbearers living within its boundaries permanently off-limits to pelt-seekers. The beaver population burgeoned over the next few decades and so did management headaches, as park staff struggled to keep culverts clear and repair roads washed out by breached dams. They exterminated hundreds of beavers annually, but as fast as they emptied out lodges and dismantled dams, newcomers moved in to rebuild and repopulate.

In the late 1970s, with the help of trapper Michel LeClair, the park started experimenting with alternatives to lethal control. The solution LeClair came up with transformed the dynamic. Instead of trying to oust beavers and constantly fighting with them about water levels, he devised a way to surreptitiously thwart their dam-building objectives. Three decades on, LeClair's beaver bafflers, both the original model and later editions, control pond levels at about 75 locations around

Gatineau Park. They have also inspired similar efforts all over North America.

"I think we're pretty much up in front of anything you can see in beaver control devices," Richard said as we headed out to look at some examples. "Everybody comes to Gatineau Park to see what we do."

Our first stop, a short drive from the visitor centre, was an enormous pond by the Gatineau Parkway/Meech Lake Road intersection. It was so big that several hockey teams could have played concurrent games on its frozen surface in winter, though they would have had to stickhandle their way around at least two beaver lodges and numerous cattail tussocks. Now, under a clear blue summer sky, the pond stretched languidly out from the roadside to the forested shoreline half a kilometre away. Lily pads plastered the still waters like patches of tarnish on an old looking-glass and their bulbous golden flowers glowed neon bright.

"The beavers eat the lily roots," Richard said. "Just like a big carrot: *tk, tk, tk, tk*." His droll rendition of the chewing sound had to have been learned firsthand.

"You like watching beavers?" I asked.

"Oh yeah," he said enthusiastically. Even after all these years.

It was the wrong time of day for beaver viewing, but fresh mud piled up along the edge of an otherwise inconspicuous dam informed us they were nearby. The dam cut across a corner of the pond near where we were standing on the roadside. Just beyond it, a wire structure stuck up out of the water. At first I thought it was a rusty shopping cart. In fact, it was an integral part of the system that protected the culvert beneath our feet.

LeClair's stroke of brilliance was finding a way to modify beaver dams so they continue to meet their builders' needs, if not their loftiest ambitions, while regulating water levels to satisfy human requirements. He did this by inserting a long pipe through the base of the dam and enclosing the upstream end in a wire cage to prevent the beavers from plugging the opening. With the intake placed at the desired maximum water height, the pipe drains the pond until it drops to the chosen level and leaves the rest for the beavers. Any time the water rises above the intake, the siphoning resumes. LeClair's pond leveler system has been refined over the years and modified to fit different situations, but the basic principle remains unchanged.

The stream that passed under the Gatineau Parkway emptied into a much smaller pond on the far side and then flowed towards Meech Lake Road. We crossed the parkway and clambered down the bank for a closer look at a dam just above the Meech Lake Road culvert. A length of large-diameter, flexible black plastic pipe snaked through the dam, with a triangular cage around the intake. There wasn't much to see, really, but this deceptively simple setup had been doing its job for at least a decade. The weathered state of the few sticks that were twined through the wide-gauge steel mesh showed that the beavers had long ago ceased trying to seal this perplexing leak.

Richard pointed to a second dam farther upstream. "They try, they try, they try and then they said 'Just leave it. We'll go up there,' and they built a new one." Between the control device we were looking at and the one on the other side of the parkway, there had been no need for him to tamper with the upstream dam.

Altogether, it was a textbook example of Gatineau's coexistence philosophy, which Richard had described to me earlier: "They're living there and we put our water control device in, we control the water level and everybody's happy. The beavers live in their pond. We live with them."

Or mostly live with them. Occasionally, in situations where other measures won't work, the park still resorts to trapping. Now, however, they kill only about 20 beavers a year, a far cry from earlier days, when the annual death toll sometimes approached 1,000. Relocating beavers that are in the wrong place at the wrong time is rarely an option. There's no vacant habitat anywhere in the park, which seems to have reached its carrying capacity. During Richard's quarter-century tenure, the population size has remained virtually unchanged.

For the next couple of hours, we drove around looking at beaver ponds and flow control devices and talking about the challenges and pleasures of trying to live with an ecosystem engineer whose blueprints are often antithetical to our own. We passed the site where Richard, then a student on a summer job placement, had helped LeClair install Gatineau's first beaver baffler in 1980. In another lake, a shiny new cage glinted in the sun.

At one point, we pulled over and hiked a short way through the forest to see the park's latest advance in pond leveller design, which substitutes a plastic barrel for the wire cage. As we skirted the pond edge, birdsong ricocheted through the leafy canopy and frogs leapt from the tall grass and plopped into the water ahead of us. "There's a lot of them in here," Richard observed, referring to the frogs. It was indeed a rich ecosystem, thanks in large part to the beavers. Although it had been a dry, hot spring, the ground was soft and damp, sinking beneath my feet with every step, while emerald-green grasses and ferns brushed against my knees.

Driving along Fortune Lake Parkway on the way back to the visitor centre, we crossed a 30-metre-long section of patched pavement. In the 1980s, a severe rainstorm had ruptured an unmanaged beaver dam on one side of the road and swept away a few car-lengths worth of asphalt. Wash-outs like this are rare now and to minimize them even further, the park recently started stabilizing high-risk dams by staking T-posts at half-metre intervals along the whole length. "If ever it goes," Richard explained, "it's going to go in between two posts at the most."

Although establishing, monitoring and maintaining all of these systems takes time and money, it's more efficient and less expensive than the old way of doing things. "When you only trap, you have to go back year after year to the same place," Richard said. It was the same message that Shawn Dalman had told me he tries to impress on potential clients before they commit to trapping and removal. "If you've got beavers now," he warns them, "next year there's going to be more right behind them."

Probably few people notice the patched pavement on Fortune Lake Parkway or recognize it as a reminder of the damage beaver activities can inflict on human infrastructure, but many see and appreciate the beavers themselves. Education is part of the park's mandate, conveyed in part through the Eager Beaver campfire program, in which a nature interpreter dresses up a volunteer from the audience in items that correspond to parts of the beaver's specialized anatomy: goggles for the transparent eyelid-like membranes that allow beavers to see underwater; a nose pincher and ear muffs representing the flaps that automatically seal a beaver's nostrils and ears when it dives; a wool blanket topped by a rain poncho to symbolize the insulating underfur and overlying layer of waterproofed guard hairs. In the visitor centre, park visitors can also view a cross-sectional model of a managed pond, complete with pond leveler.

"This is a conservation park, and I think we're helping people understand what we're trying to do," Richard said. To his knowledge, there aren't many places where people can stop on the side of the road and watch beavers in a pond as big as the one by the Gatineau Parkway/Meech Lake Road intersection. "People really do enjoy that," he added, clearly pleased to be part of their experience.

If I had been staying overnight, I would have taken Richard's advice and returned that evening to parking lot P8, from which a short walk would have almost guaranteed me some first-rate beaver viewing.

Gatineau Park has not been alone in developing technology for managing beaver-caused flooding. In the U.S., Vermont-based Skip Lisle led the way with his Beaver Deceiver, a trademarked trapezoidal fence system that foils attempted culvert damming. Lisle perfected his original product, as well as his Castor Master pipe-and-filter system, in the 1990s, while working on a contract to beaver-proof roads across the 500-square-kilometre Penobscot Indian Nation lands in Maine.

Around the same time, researchers at South Carolina's Clemson University came up with the Clemson Pond Leveler, which works on the same principle as the Gatineau devices, but uses solid PVC pipe with numerous intake holes drilled into it, instead of flexible polyethylene pipe with a single opening. Other refinements and inventions have included diversion dams that deflect resident beavers' attention away from culvert fences; culvert protectors designed to frustrate damming efforts without blockading fish; and turtle doors equipped with sharply angled wings that keep beavers from pushing sticks through the openings.

Remedies for tree-felling, the other behaviour that frequently gets beavers blacklisted, are more straightforward, but not infallible. The most effective solutions are to wrap the trunks with galvanized wire mesh or to fence off the trees, individually or in groups. Brushing a mixture of sand and paint onto trunks sometimes works, because beavers don't like to gnaw through grit. Whatever the deterrent, it needs to be applied high enough up the trunk that the beavers can't chew above it, keeping in mind that snow will raise their working platform.

Unfortunately, it's rarely feasible to safeguard every tree and shrub within reach of a colony. Though beavers prefer to stay within 15 metres of the water's edge, they'll travel up to 60 metres on land to reach sources of food and building materials if necessary. And while they generally target trees with diameters of less than 40 centimetres, the largest beaver-cut stump on record measured just over one metre in diameter; sawed off flat, it would have made a table big enough to seat four people for dinner. Sometimes, beaver consultants say, the best way to take the pressure off prized trees is to offer substitute rations in the form of arborists' trimmings. If you can't beat 'em, feed 'em.

Ultimately, the most important component of any system aimed at facilitating coexistence is the one that can't be seen: a thorough understanding of how beavers think and operate. Like Richard Moore, the best beaver managers put in plenty of time watching, learning and appreciating.

Whereas some people struggle to coexist with beavers, or even clamour for their expulsion, others champion the opposite position. Merely tolerating beavers isn't enough, they maintain. We should deliberately encourage their presence and capitalize on their natural tendencies. It's not an entirely new message. After all, as far back as 1892, *Castorologia* author Horace T. Martin was warning that "we must not overlook [the beaver's] service in preserving a water supply." And appreciation of the species' ecological contributions continued to develop over the following decades. What distinguishes current beaver conservation efforts from those of the early- to mid-1900s is a sense of urgency, fueled by unprecedented levels of habitat degradation and biodiversity loss. Escalating concerns about the consequences of climate change have also upped the ante, especially in the arid West.

These days, many of the beaver's most ardent supporters live in places that have a significant beaver deficit combined with pressing concerns about drought. In the late 1970s, biologists Bruce Smith, Larry Apple and Dick McCuistion kicked off the modern era of beaver-assisted restoration in just such a place. When the trio began their project, streambank erosion and a diminished water table had destroyed more than 80 percent of the riparian habitat on Bureau of Land Management holdings in southwestern Wyoming. The willows and herbaceous plants that once grew beside the streams had withered away, drought-tolerant sagebrush and greasewood had taken over and the animals that relied on the formerly verdant waterside corridors had disappeared. Streamflow changes also threatened two rare subspecies of cutthroat trout.

Conventional bank stabilization techniques weren't working, so Smith, Apple and McCuistion decided to try bringing beavers back into the picture. One of the worst sites they tackled was Sage Creek. Eighty years earlier, local ranchers had easily forded this modest watercourse on foot or horseback. Now, it had widened to 25 metres and become an 18-metre-deep gorge in places. At all of their reintroduction sites, the biologists provided their beaver crews with a starter kit of pre-cut aspen trunks and branches. But at Sage Creek, the spring runoff was so powerful it kept washing away the new dams. As a last resort,

Smith and company offered their workers some old truck tires to supplement the conventional building materials. The beavers happily accepted and their tire-enhanced dams held.

Within three years, all of the ravaged creeks where the beavers had re-established a presence showed significant signs of healing: reduced erosion, higher water tables, more willow and more wildlife. On one badly damaged creek, the silt load decreased by 90 percent, from 33 tons a day to four. Best of all, the effects of the beaver engineering were enduring.

I first heard about the Wyoming experiment from Hilary Cooke, a biologist who studied streamside bird communities in the same region two decades later. She and her co-researcher, Steve Zack, found that the more beaver dams there were along a stretch of stream, the greater the diversity and abundance of birds, drawn to these areas by the wide, lush riparian borders.

As sediment accumulated behind the beaver dams, Cooke explained to me, the stream channel was elevated back to a level where water once again flowed laterally into the groundwater system and recharged the water table. More groundwater meant more leafy trees and shrubs, and more birds.

"The beavers were reconnecting the stream with its historical floodplain," she said. "That was the part that we just got so excited about. One hundred years of cattle grazing wiped out the riparian habitat in these sagebrush areas and there's an opportunity to use beaver to restore it."

In 2010, a group of researchers from the University of Connecticut and Kansas State University published a study on the beaver's potential role in revitalizing North American waterways. By their calculations, the continent once had at least 25 million beaver dams and the loss of this infrastructure during the colonial fur-trade era significantly messed things up. "A lot of rivers are in trouble and need work and restoration," said one of the co-authors, fluvial geomorphologist Melinda Daniels, after the study was released. "Our argument is that the restoration target for streams with forested riparian zones has got to acknowledge the diversity brought to river systems by active beaver populations."

Like the findings of Hilary Cooke and Steve Zack, as well as Cherie Westbrook, Glynnis Hood, Greg Hood and other researchers, this study provides a solid scientific foundation for the beaver-supported ecosystem restoration and water conservation initiatives that have been gaining momentum during the past decade.

These include the Seventh Generation Institute's "Building Riparian Resilience through Beaver Restoration" project in New Mexico, where the beaver population remains perilously low — or, in scientific terms, far below "the threshold of ecologically effective density." Next door, in Utah, The Grand Canyon Trust is training volunteers to identify potential reintroduction sites in three national forests and to keep an eye on existing colonies. It's old-fashioned fieldwork with a twenty-first-century twist, care of Utah State University's Joe Wheaton. He and associates in the Department of Watershed Sciences have developed a beaver-monitoring app with which anyone who comes across signs of beaver activity can submit GPS coordinates and photos to the project database. Such citizen science is an equally important facet of Alberta's collaborative Leave It to Beavers watershed stewardship project, which involves ranchers, other private landowners and public land managers, and in a reintroduction scheme in eastern Washington, where the Methow Conservancy is "Increasing Stream Complexity One Beaver at a Time."

The most ambitious of these undertakings is also based in

Washington. In 2009, state authorities proposed to construct major reservoir dams on several Columbia River tributaries to compensate for decreasing snowpack and rainfall. The Lands Council, a non-profit conservation organization, countered with what they called "The Beaver Solution." Commissioning beavers to build dams, the council reasoned, would be more economical and environmentally friendly than building concrete dams and would achieve the same goal of holding early spring runoff for gradual release during summer. A study they conducted conservatively estimated that beaver dams could store 2.5 trillion litres of water in eastern Washington alone.

Backed by the state, The Beaver Solution team is now investigating suitable reintroduction sites, planting trees by the thousands to support future beaver colonies and mediating disputes between disgruntled landowners and beavers, where these water-keepers are already on the job.

With North America facing a multifaceted water crisis — flash floods here, multi-year droughts there, growing uncertainty everywhere — we, and many other species, need beavers as a moderating force more than ever. While not a miracle cure, beaver engineering can help in significant ways: diverting rainfall and snowmelt into the groundwater system, where it will recharge aquifers and slowly move downstream; tempering storm torrents; and increasing the amount of surface water on the land, to the benefit of all kinds of wildlife and ourselves.

The idea of intentionally increasing beaver abundance may seem ludicrous to people who live in places with an apparent surfeit of these animals, yet today's continent-wide beaver numbers still fall far short of the pre-colonial zenith and many populations remain below natural densities.

The problem is not that there are too many beavers. It's that while they were absent, we humans took over a large portion of their habitat. Much of this appropriated territory is now drained, paved, built upon or otherwise rendered unfit for beaver use. And where it is still habitable for beavers, we're frequently at odds with them about how it should be managed, a difference of opinion that arises partly from our sense of species superiority and partly from historical circumstances. It's been so long since beavers were present in full strength that our view of the North American landscape is radically skewed. More often than not, we see returning beavers as interlopers, instead of recognizing them as an integral part of how our hydrological and ecological systems work — or should work. We need to cure our amnesia, rethink our relationship and acknowledge how much we stand to gain by engaging beavers as keystone partners and climate-change allies.

As I discovered during my travels through Beaverland, *Castor canadensis* is one of the world's most extraordinary animals: dam builder, landscape shaper, habitat creator and history maker. Intriguing. Endearing. Frustrating at times, it's true, but well worth the bother. Never mind being faster than a speeding bullet, more powerful than a locomotive or able to leap tall buildings in a single bound. The Mighty Beaver is a superhero in its own inimitable way.

SOURCES

General

Horace T. Martin's *Castorologia, or The History and Traditions of the Canadian Beaver* (Wm. Drysdale & Co., 1892) was the first major work devoted to *Castor canadensis* and lives up to its subtitle: "An Exhaustive Monograph, Popularly Written and Fully Illustrated." Although much of Martin's information is antiquated, his perspective on beavers at what turned out to be the species' low point offers many useful insights. *The Canadian Beaver Book: Fact, Fiction and Fantasy* by Jim Cameron (General Store Publishing House, 1991) also pointed me in interesting directions during the early days of my research.

The most comprehensive recent compilation of scientific information about beavers is Bruce W. Baker and Edward P. Hill's "Beaver" chapter in the second edition of *Wild Mammals of North America* (edited by George A. Feldhamer, Bruce C. Thompson and Joseph A. Chapman; Johns Hopkins University Press, 2003); it provided me with a solid biological overview and numerous valuable details. I also frequently consulted Stephen H. Jenkins and Peter E. Busher's "*Castor canadensis*" Mammalian Species monograph (American Society of Mammalogists, 1979) and Milan Novak's "Beaver" chapter in *Wild Furbearer*

Management and Conservation in North America (edited by Milan Novak, James A. Baker, Martyn E. Obbard and Bruce Malloch; Ontario Trappers Association, 1987).

The Beaver: Natural History of a Wetlands Engineer by Dietland Müller-Schwarze and Lixing Sun (Cornell University Press, 2003) and *The Beaver Manifesto* by Glynnis Hood (Rocky Mountain Books, 2011) also helped ground my biological research.

Novak et al.'s colossal *Wild Furbearer Management and Conservation in North America* provided me with a wealth of information about beaver trapping and hunting, as well as the fur trade, both historical and contemporary. Other sources that proved essential to my understanding of the colonial fur trade were: Harold A. Innis' *The Fur Trade in Canada: An Introduction to Canadian Economic History* (Yale University Press, 1962); Richard Mackie's *Trading Beyond the Mountains: The British Fur Trade on the Pacific, 1793-1843* (UBC Press, 1997); and Eric Jay Dolin's *Fur, Fortune, and Empire: The Epic History of the Fur Trade in America* (W.W. Norton & Co., 2010). *Beavers in Britain's Past* by Bryony Coles (Oxbow Books and WARP, 2006) opened my eyes to the early European beaver-human relationships that set the stage for the transatlantic fur trade.

Introduction

Canadian etymologist Bill Casselman discusses the origins of the word "beaver," including when the vulgar usage first appeared in print, on his website (billcasselman.com).

I learned about the The Three-Pence Beaver stamp on the Canada Post website (canadapost.ca/cpo/mc/personal/collecting/stamps/archives/2001/2001_apr_150_years.jsf). Based on a sketch by Sir Sandford Fleming, it was the world's first official postage stamp to feature an animal, and until 1939, it remained the only one that depicted a rodent. Thomas Mulvey's quote is from Cameron's *The Canadian Beaver Book*.

Information about Bill C-373 is from Cameron's *The Canadian Beaver Book* and the Parliament of Canada website (parl.gc.ca/parlinfo/compilations/houseofcommons/legislation/privatememberspublicbills.aspx).

The full text of Senator Nicole Eaton's speech is posted on her website (nicoleeaton.sencanada.ca/en/p102483). I also learned about Eaton's campaign from Anne Kingston's article, "Beaver Be Dammed" (*Maclean's*, November 4, 2011).

Information about the beaver beetle is from "Distribution and Biology of the Ectoparasitic Beaver Beetle *Platypsyllus castoris* Ritsema in North America (Coleoptera: Leiodidae: Platypsyllinae)" by Stewart B. Peck (*Insecta Mundi*, 2006).

Sources for other information in the Introduction are listed under the relevant chapters.

1. Into the Heart of Beaverland
I drew on a wide variety of sources for biographical information about the explorers mentioned in this chapter (John Cabot, David Thompson, Henry Kelsey, Jacques Cartier), usually beginning with *The Canadian Encyclopedia* in print (Hurtig Publishers, 1988) or online (thecanadianencyclopedia.ca).

The beaver's historical range is described in Baker and Hill's "Beaver" chapter.

Thomas J. Farnham commented on beaver abundance in the lower Sacramento Valley in his *Travels in the Californias, and Scenes in the Pacific Ocean* (Saxton and Miles, 1844). I found his quote in Mackie's *Trading Beyond the Mountains*.

All of David Thompson's quotes in this chapter are from

David Thompson's Narrative of His Explorations in Western America: 1784-1812 (I used the Greenwood Press, 1968, facsimile edition). Additional information about Thompson came from various sources, including *The Canadian Encyclopedia* and Parks Canada's "Persons of National Historic Significance" website (pc.gc.ca/docs/v-g/pm-mp/lhn-nhs/phn-pns/index_e.asp).

Jean Thie's satellite-assisted beaver research is documented on his EcoInformatics website (geostrategis.com), with pages on both the Beaver Capital of Canada and the World's Longest Beaver Dam. When I went to Pakwaw Lake, I had not yet spoken to Jean or had the pleasure of meeting him in person. That opportunity came a couple of years later, when I was researching an article for *Canadian Geographic*, "Rethinking the Beaver," which ran in the December 2012 issue.

Pierre-François-Xavier de Charlevoix's quote is from Volume 1 of his *Journal of a Voyage to North America*, published in 1761 (available as part of the American Libraries collection at archive.org).

Horace T. Martin's quotes are from his book, *Castorologia*.

The comment that beaver lodges were designed with "the genius of a clever architect" was made by M. de Bacqueville de La Potherie, whose letters were published in 1753 and reprinted in J. B. Tyrrell's *Documents Relating to the Early History of Hudson Bay* (Champlain Society, 1931). Cameron's *The Canadian Beaver Book* contains an entertaining collection of artistic renderings and quotes reflecting early perceptions of beaver engineering, including La Potherie's and Charlevoix's.

The original report of the 652-metre-long beaver dam appeared in Enos A. Mills' *In Beaver World* (Houghton Mifflin Company, 1913). Although I doubted it would be still standing a century later, I contacted Donnie Sexton of the Montana

Department of Tourism to find out its current status. She took my question to a local Fish, Wildlife and Parks administrative assistant, who assured her that this former record-holder no longer exists.

Wood Buffalo National Park's external relations manager, Mike Keizer, helped me picture the world's longest beaver dam and the surrounding landscape. He also (thankfully) convinced me that the challenges of getting there on foot were more than I wanted to take on. I viewed photographs and video footage from his flyover on the park website (pc.gc.ca/eng/pn-np/nt /woodbuffalo/ne.aspx). In July 2014, American adventurer Rob Mark became the first person to reach the dam since Thie's discovery. Mark chose a less expensive route than the one Keizer described to me — a 16-kilometre slog that took three days each way. Adrian Lee reported on Mark's journey in "Meet the First Person to Explore the World's Largest Beaver Dam" (*Maclean's*, September 28, 2014).

Information about beaver dam lengths is primarily from David R. Butler's *Zoogeomorphology: Animals as Geomorphic Agents* (Cambridge University Press, 1995) and my discussions with Jean Thie. Müller-Schwarze and Sun's *The Beaver* states that dams may be as long as several hundred metres and as high as three metres. In "Beaver Assisted River Valley Formation" (*River Research and Applications*, 2011), C.J. Westbrook, D.J. Cooper and B.W. Baker note that the maximum height of a beaver dam is structurally limited to 2.5 metres. Reports of higher dams may reflect differences in how height is measured.

I found beaver toponyms for Canadian locations through the federal government's Canadian Geographical Names Data Base (rncan.gc.ca/search-place-names/search?lang=en) and for American locations through the U.S. Board on Geographic

Names website (geonames.usgs.gov).

The Dunne-za/Tsattine name for the river now known as the Peace River is from *A Traveller's Guide to Aboriginal B.C.* by Cheryl Coull (Whitecap Books, 1996). The Mi'kmaq translation of Beaver Harbour, Nova Scotia, is from *Place-names of the Province of Nova Scotia* by Thomas J. Brown (Royal Print & Litho., 1922).

Information about Hochelaga is from the online Quebec History Encyclopedia (faculty.marianopolis.edu/c.belanger/quebechistory/encyclopedia/index.htm) and the online Canadian Encyclopedia, which also offers "big rapids" as a possible translation.

2. Ancient Antecedents

Natalia Rybczynski showed me around the Canadian Museum of Nature's research collections in June 2012 and patiently answered subsequent questions that I posed by email. I also learned about the Castoridae lineage and beaver woodcutting from two of her scientific papers: "Castorid Phylogenetics: Implications for the Evolution of Swimming and Tree-Exploitation in Beavers" (*Journal of Mammalian Evolution*, 2007); and "Woodcutting Behavior in Beavers (Castoridae, Rodentia): Estimating Ecological Performance in a Modern and a Fossil Taxon" (*Paleobiology*, 2008).

Information about the Ellesmere Island Beaver Pond site is from the two Rybczynski articles and "An Arctic Mammal Fauna from the Early Pliocene of North America" by Richard H. Tedford and C. Richard Harington (*Nature*, September 2003).

For information about food caches, lodges and bank dens, I primarily relied on Baker and Hill's "Beaver" chapter and Müller-Schwarze and Sun's *The Beaver*.

My discussion of Bryony Coles' work is largely drawn from *Beavers in Britain's Past* and all of her quotes are from this deeply researched and engagingly written book. She elucidated a few points for me by email.

The population estimate and range information for *Castor fiber* at the end of the 1800s are from the species listing on the IUCN Red List of Threatened Species (iucnredlist.org).

Most published information about giant beavers refers to the most widespread species, *Castoroides ohioensis*. Fossils of *Castoroides leiseyorum* have been found only in Florida and South Carolina (see the Paleobiology Database at fossilworks.org). I learned about giant beavers from several sources, most notably: Rybczynski's "Castorid Phylogenetics" paper; C. Richard Harington's "Giant Beaver, *Castoroides ohioensis*, Remains in Canada and an Overlooked Report from Ontario" (*The Canadian Field-Naturalist*, 2007); and H. Gregory McDonald and Robert C. Glotzhober's "New Radiocarbon Dates for the Giant Beaver, *Castoroides ohioensis* (Rodentia, Castoridae), from Ohio and Its Extinction" (*Unlocking the Unknown: Papers Honoring Dr. Richard J. Zakrzewski*, edited by Greg H. Farley and Jerry R. Choate; Fort Hays State University, 2008).

Length and weight information for *Castor canadensis* is from Baker and Hill's "Beaver" chapter.

Giant beavers are often referred to as having been the size of modern black bears. P.S. Reynolds disputes this comparison in "How Big Is a Giant? The Importance of Method in Estimating Body Size of Extinct Mammals" (*Journal of Mammalogy*, 2002) and counters with a body mass estimate of 60 to 100 kilograms. In "Giant Beaver, *Castoroides ohioensis*, Remains in Canada and an Overlooked Report from Ontario," Harington argues that giant beavers weighed up to 200 kilograms and notes that

Reynolds' estimates fall within the wide range documented for black bears. The dog breed weights I used for comparative purposes are from the dog weight chart at askavetquestion.com.

I read about Catherine Yansa and Peter M. Jacobs' radiocarbon dating study of a giant beaver tooth in the abstract of Yansa's presentation to the Geological Society of America's 2009 annual meeting (Paper No. 94-4: "Pleistocene-age Giant Beaver [*Castoroides ohioensis*] and Extant Beaver [*Castor canadensis*] Environments of Southern Wisconsin") and Sid Perkins' *Science News* article, "Ancient, Giant Beavers Didn't Have a Taste for Wood" (originally posted on news.discovery.com on October 23, 2009). I also corresponded with Yansa about the study by email. Yansa's quote about giant beavers having been like little hippos is from Perkins' article. Richard Harington's write-up on giant beavers on the Yukon Beringia Interpretive Centre's website alludes to the debate about whether these animals were woodcutters (beringia.com/research/beaver.html).

The other researchers working with Rybczynski when they found the Pleistocene-age *Castor* dam on the Old Crow River were Yukon government paleontologist Paul Matheus and Keith Rispin, a student assistant from Vuntut Gwich'in First Nation. I learned about their discovery from a "Your Yukon" column by Claire Eamer (taiga.net, February 2006).

Larry D. Martin wrote about *Paleocastor* in "The Devil's Corkscrew" (*Natural History*, 1994) and, with co-author Debra K. Bennett, in "The Burrows of the Miocene Beaver *Palaeocastor*, Western Nebraska, U.S.A." (*Palaeogeography, Palaeoclimatology, Palaeoecology*, 1977). I also read about these fossils in "The Origin of Daemonelix" by A.L. Lugn (*The Journal of Geology*, 1941). The Lakota legend explaining the origin of *Ca'pa el ti* and information about indigenous peoples using giant beaver incisors as carving tools and amulets are from Adrienne Mayor's fascinating *Fossil Legends of the First Americans* (Princeton University Press, 2005).

I found First Nations stories about giant beavers in the following publications: Yamoría's slaying of the giant beavers that lived in Sahtú is from George Blondin's *When the World Was New* (Outcrop, The Northern Publishers, 1990); the Dene story of human-eating giant beavers is from George Blondin's *Yamoria the Lawmaker: Stories of the Dene* (NeWest Press, 1997); Robin Ridington wrote about predatory giant beavers in Dunne-Za culture in *Little Bit Know Something: Stories in a Language of Anthropology* (University of Iowa Press, 1990); the Maliseet Gluskap story is from "The Giant Beaver: A Prehistoric Memory?" by Jane C. Beck (*Ethnohistory*, 1972); and the Kootenai story of the Flathead River's creation is from Ella E. Clark's *Indian Legends from the Northern Rockies* (University of Oklahoma Press, 1966).

Jane C. Beck's quote about fossil memory is from "The Giant Beaver." The possibility of ancestral memory of Pleistocene animals is also discussed in Mayor's *Fossil Legends of the First Americans* and Vine Deloria Jr.'s *Red Earth, White Lies: Native Americans and the Myth of Scientific Fact* (Scribner, 1995).

3. The Hunter and the Hunted

Much of the information on specific First Nations discussed in this chapter is from Barry M. Pritzker's *A Native American Encyclopedia: History, Culture, and Peoples* (Oxford University Press, 2000). Robert J. Muckle's *Indigenous Peoples of North America* (University of Toronto Press, 2012) and Duane Champagne's *The Native North American Almanac: A Reference Work on Native North Americans in the United States and Canada* (Gale Research, 2001) provided a useful cultural overview.

I gained insights into aboriginal relationships to the non-human world, and to prey animals in particular, from Champagne's *The Native North American Almanac*; Shepard Krech III's *The Ecological Indian: Myth and History* (W.W. Norton & Company, 1999); *Native Americans and the Environment: Perspectives on the Ecological Indian*, edited by Michael E. Harkin and David Rich Lewis (University of Nebraska Press, 2007); Calvin Martin's *Keepers of the Game: Indian-Animal Relationships and the Fur Trade* (University of California Press, 1978); and *Indians, Animals, and the Fur Trade: A Critique of Keepers of the Game*, edited by Shepard Krech III (University of Georgia Press, 1981). "Symbolic Orientations and Systematic Turmoil: Centering on the Kaska Symbol of Dene" by Roger F. McDonnell (*Canadian Journal of Anthropology*, 1984), in which the author describes an experience of watching a beaver with a Kaska man, deepened my understanding, while reminding me how far I am from truly grasping these cultural concepts.

I found the Omaha story about Ictinike in *Literature of the American Indian* by Thomas E. Sanders and Walter W. Peek (Glencoe Press, 1973). The Anishinaabe story is from "The Woman Who Married a Beaver: Trade Patterns and Gender Roles in the Ojibwa Fur Trade" by Bruce M. White (*Ethnohistory*, 1999).

I recorded Ida Calmegane's quotes and stories while visiting her at her home in Tagish in May 2012. Catherine McClellan's *My Old People Say: An Ethnographic Survey of Southern Yukon, Parts 1 and 2* (National Museums of Canada, 1975) and Julie Cruikshank's *Life Lived Like a Story* (UBC Press, 1992) provided additional context; these books were particularly useful because both of these anthropologists had worked extensively with Ida's mother, Angela Sidney. Some information about the gold-rush period is from my own book, *Women of the Klondike* (Whitecap Books, 1995).

I used the clan name spellings given on the Carcross-Tagish First Nation website (ctfn.ca/origin-clans); alternatives that appear elsewhere reflect ever-changing linguistic conventions.

The spelling of the Tlingit word for beaver is from the *Interior Tlingit Noun Dictionary* compiled by Jeff Leer, Doug Hitch and John Ritter (Yukon Native Language Center, 2001).

My private viewing of Canadian Museum of Civilization beaver artifacts, organized by Nathalie Guénette, occurred in June 2012. My artifact descriptions are based on the museum's catalogue information and my own observations.

Additional information about traditional First Nations beaver hunting techniques is from A.W. Schorger's "The Beaver in Early Wisconsin" (*Transactions of the Wisconsin Academy of Sciences, Arts and Letters*, 1965) and Milan Novak's "Traps and Trap Research" (in Novak et al.'s *Wild Furbearer Management and Conservation in North America*).

Ancient evidence of beaver hunting is discussed in J.V. Wright's "Archaeological Evidence For the Use of Furbearers in North America" (in Novak et al.'s *Wild Furbearer Management and Conservation in North America*) and "Chronology of Sites at Killarney, Canada" by E.F. Greenman (*American Antiquity*, 1966). Kenneth E. Kidd's "The Excavation and Historical Identification of a Huron Ossuary" (*American Antiquity*, 1953) describes fragments of beaver pelt preserved through contact with a copper kettle.

Information about the caloric value of beaver meat is from J.V. Wright's "Archaeological Evidence For the Use of Furbearers in North America."

"The Fur Trade in North America: An Overview from a

Historical Geographical Perspective" by Arthur J. Ray (in Novak et al.'s *Wild Furbearer Management and Conservation in North America*) offers an excellent historical summary of the North American fur trade from the late 1400s to the mid-twentieth century. Dolin's *Fur, Fortune, and Empire* was also an important source. Additional information is from the online Canadian Encyclopedia and Innis' *The Fur Trade in Canada*.

For a complete history of the Hudson's Bay Company, there's no better place to start than Peter C. Newman's *Company of Adventurers* (I used the 2005, Penguin edition). The text of the royal charter is available on the company's history website (hbcheritage.ca/hbcheritage/collections/archival/charter/).

Father Paul Le Jeune quotes his Innu acquaintance in *The Jesuit Relations and Allied Documents: Travels and Explorations of the Jesuit Missionaries in New France, 1610–1791, Volume VI*, edited by Reuben Gold Thwaites (Burrows Brothers, 1898).

The old Cree man's lament about the destruction of the beaver is from *David Thompson's Narrative of His Explorations in Western America: 1784–1812*, as is Thompson's quote about castoreum.

Information about beaver scent-marking is primarily from the comprehensive chapter on this subject in Müller-Schwarze and Sun's *The Beaver*.

"Castoreum and Steel Traps in Eastern North America" (*American Anthropologist*, 1972) by Robin F. Wells describes the early use of this deadly combination, including William Byrd II's instructions for creating a castoreum-based beaver lure.

I learned about Sewell Newhouse from Novak's "Traps and Trap Research" chapter and Tom Parr's "Antique Traps: Newhouse Bear Traps" article on the Fur-Fish-Game website (furfishgame.com/featured_articles/Archived/2012-09/antique_traps_09-2012.php).

The estimated number of indigenous languages spoken in North America when Europeans arrived is from Muckle's *Indigenous Peoples of North America.*

The Vuntut Gwich'in words for beaver (and other translations in this chapter, unless indicated otherwise) are from First Voices, an online language archives (firstvoices.com).

The story of Yamoría's time living with beavers is from Blondin's *When the World Was New.*

Ernest Thompson Seton's estimate that there were 60 to 400 million beavers in North America prior to European contact was published in his *Lives of Game Animals* (Doubleday, 1929) and is still commonly cited by biologists. So far, no one has published a more precise estimate.

I gleaned beaver extirpation dates for different jurisdictions from several sources, including *Changes in the Land: Indians, Colonists, and the Ecology of New England* by William Cronon (Hill and Wang, 1983), Krech's *The Ecological Indian: Myth and History* and Müller-Schwarze and Sun's *The Beaver.*

John James Audubon's failed attempts to obtain a beaver specimen during his Missouri River expedition are chronicled in his *Selected Journals and Other Writings* (I used the 1996 Penguin Books edition, edited by Ben Forkner). Bob Arnebeck's blog post, "Audubon and the Beaver That Got Away" (bobarnebeck-fur.blogspot.ca, March 24, 2011) alerted me to this story.

The scientific literature is frustratingly devoid of estimates of the North American beaver population at its low point. In 2004, I came across an article on the American Humane Society's website that placed it at 100,000 in 1900. Although that web page has long since disappeared, this figure continues to appear here and there on the internet, without reference to the source. Whether or not the continental population hit that exact number,

I believe it's entirely plausible that it bottomed out in the low hundred thousands, given the widespread extirpation of beavers that had occurred by that time.

4. Back From the Brink

Thoreau's quote is from *The Journal of Henry David Thoreau* (Houghton Mifflin Co., 1906).

My most important sources for understanding Archibald Stansfeld Belaney were Donald B. Smith's excellent biography, *From the Land of Shadows: The Making of Grey Owl* (Western Producer Prairie Books, 1990) — from which most of the biographical details in this chapter are drawn — and Belaney's own writings: *The Men of the Last Frontier*, *Pilgrims of the Wild* and *Sajo and the Beaver People* (which I read combined in a single volume as *The Collected Works of Grey Owl*, Key Porter Books, 2004); and his articles in *Canadian Forest and Outdoors* (1931–34). Anahareo's *Devil in Deerskins: My Life with Grey Owl* (New Press, 1972) was also enlightening.

My research at Prince Albert National Park in July 2011 included my trek to Beaver Lodge, a day combing through the park archives and a visit to the Friends of PANP's Grey Owl exhibit (housed in the Waskesiu Heritage Museum). I also drew on W.A. Waiser's informative *Saskatchewan's Playground: A History of Prince Albert National Park* (Fifth House, 1989).

Grey Owl's first film, *The Beaver People*, can be viewed on the National Film Board website (nfb.ca/film/beaver_people). The accompanying synopsis erroneously gives the production date as 1928, instead of 1930.

A number of quotes in this chapter are from letters that I found in the park archives: James Woods on the potential for beavers to provide water for fire fighting (August 20, 1931); J.C.

Campbell on Grey Owl's publicity value (November 7, 1931); the Gordons expressing concern about Jelly Roll and Rawhide (April 17, 1938); Roy Hubel reporting on the condition of the two beavers (August 29, 1938); Gertrude Bernard requesting permission to visit Beaver Lodge (January 9, 1939); Superintendent Herbert Knight's assurances that Rawhide and Jelly Roll were still living at Ajawaan Lake (June 25, 1941). Many other letters and documents from the archives provided useful details and background information.

All of Grey Owl's quotes in this chapter are from his books. The get-rich-quick-vandals comments are from *The Men of the Last Frontier*. The quotes about Jelly Roll's mischievous proclivities and the need she filled in his life, and Grey Owl's declaration about beavers and wilderness are from *Pilgrims of the Wild*.

My imagined scene of visiting Grey Owl at Beaver Lodge in the 1930s was inspired by the film "Grey Owl's Strange Guests" (viewable on YouTube) in which "a party of young campers" calls on him. The phrase "Little Brethren of the Wilderness" appears in Grey Owl's *Canadian Forest and Outdoors* article, "King of the Beaver People" (1931).

The Lakota story, "Double-Face Tricks a Girl," is from *Voices From Four Directions: Contemporary Translations of the Native Literatures of North America*, edited by Brian Swann (University of Nebraska Press, 2004). Other sources that mention pet beavers in a traditional First Nations context include Blondin's *Yamoria the Lawmaker* and McClellan's *My Old People Say, Part 1*.

Samuel Hearne's account of pet beavers is from his *A Journey to the Northern Ocean* (TouchWood Editions, 2007; originally published in 1795 under the title, *A Journey from Prince of Wales's Fort in Hudson's Bay to the Northern Ocean in the Years 1769, 1770, 1771, 1772*). I read about the beaver that liked to lie in front of the fireplace in Martin's *Castorologia*. Information about Lady Dufferin's short-lived pet is from *My Canadian Journal, 1872-8: Extracts from My Letters Home Written While Lord Dufferin was Governor-General* by Harriot Georgina Blackwood, Marchioness of Dufferin and Ava (I used the 1971 Coles edition).

I learned about Dorothy Richards from "Beavers in Her Basement" by Aline A. Newman (*Highlights for Children*, 1994) and the Beavers: Wetlands & Wildlife website (beaversww .org/about-us/history). Audrey Tournay's memoir, *Beaver Tales* (Boston Mills Press, 2003), describes her years of living with and advocating for beavers.

The longevity record for wild beavers is from Joseph S. Larson's "Age Structure and Sexual Maturity within a Western Maryland Beaver (*Castor canadensis*) Population" (*Journal of Mammalogy*, 1967).

Information about George Simpson's beaver policies is from Ray's "The Fur Trade in North America," Mackie's *Trading Beyond the Mountains* (which also provided Simpson's quotes) and Dolin's *Fur, Fortune, and Empire*.

The story of the Watts and the creation of the Rupert House Beaver Preserve is primarily from William Ashley Anderson's *Angel of Hudson Bay: The True Story of Maud Watt* (Clarke, Irwin & Company, 1961), with supplementary details from the Hudson's Bay Company website (hbcheritage.ca/hbcheritage/ history/people/associates/jameswatt) and Brian A. Back's website (ottertooth.com/Hudson_Bay/angels.htm). I gained insight into the Cree community's involvement in this conservation initiative from the Crees of Waskaganish First Nation website (waskaganish.ca/beaver-reserves) and Harvey A. Feit's "Myths of the Ecological Whitemen: Histories, Science, and Rights in North American-Native American Relations" (in Harkin and Lewis'

Native Americans and the Environment). Information about the Beaver Preserve token is from the Coins and Canada website (coinsandcanada.com/coins-articles.php?article=currency-museum-of-the-bank-of-canada&id=290).

In addition to visiting the Colliers' homestead in July 2011, I learned about Eric Collier from his memoir, *Three Against the Wilderness* (I used the 2007 TouchWood Editions reissue); James Stewart's fine website (ericcollier.wordpress.com), which includes video clips of his interviews with Veasy Collier; and the ABC Bookworld author bank (abcbookworld.com/index.php).

Henry Wansy's quote is from *Changes in the Land: Indians, Colonists, and the Ecology of New England* by William Cronon (Hill and Wang, 1983).

The characterization of beavers as "choosy generalists" and information about their diet are from Baker and Hill's "Beaver" chapter.

5. Hats

In addition to my informative tour of the Smithbilt Hats factory, I learned about the art of turning beaver pelts into hats, including the felting process, from: Martin's *Castorologia*; felt-maker Suzanne Pufpaff's website (yurtboutique.com/beaver.htm); the White Oak Society (whiteoakhistoricalsociety.org/historical-library/fur-trade/the-beaver-fur-hat); and a virtual tour of one of the factories that supplies felt hat-bodies to Smithbilt (fepsa.pt/company/a-fabrica).

Biographical information about Morris Shumiatcher is from a plaque placed at the site of the original Smithbilt factory in Calgary (at 1208 – 1 Street SW) by the Jewish Historical Society of Southern Alberta in 2012.

Information about Chaucer's "Flaundryssh bevere hat" is

from *The General Prologue: Critical Commentary* by Malcolm Andrew (University of Oklahoma Press, 1993).

My primary sources of information about biological and chemical aspects of castoreum were Müller-Schwarze and Sun's *The Beaver* and Baker and Hill's "Beaver" chapter. Martin's *Castorologia* introduced me to the writings of Hippocrates and Johannes Mayer Marius on the medicinal use of castoreum.

I read about Aesop's fable of "The Beaver and His Testicles" in Dolin's *Fur, Fortune, and Empire* and obtained Pliny's version from Volume III of H. Rackham's English translation of Pliny's *Natural History* (Harvard University Press, 1956). Coles' *Beavers in Britain's Past* provided later versions of this story, as well as information about beaver tails being considered fish and King Hywel Dda's robes. The bestiary quote is from Richard W. Barber's *Bestiary: Being an English Version of the Bodleian Library, Oxford, M.S. Bodley 764 with all the Original Miniatures Reproduced in Facsimile* (Boydell Press, 1999).

The two types of beaver hair are described in Baker and Hill's "Beaver" chapter.

I drew on several sources to calculate the number of pelts required to make a top hat. According to Suzanne Pufpaff's website, four pounds of pelts produced one pound of fur (meaning that each pelt produced about four ounces of fur), and the best hats were made with nine to 12 ounces of fur. Schorger's "The Beaver in Early Wisconsin" provided an estimate of 3.3 ounces of fur per one pound of pelts, and seven to 12 ounces of fur per hat. From Arthur Dobbs' *An Account of the Countries Adjoining to Hudson's Bay* (J. Robinson, 1744), I learned that pelts typically weighed about 1.5 pounds.

Information about the hats worn by Cavaliers and Puritans is from Julia V. Emberley's *The Cultural Politics of Fur*

(McGill-Queen's University Press, 1997). French and British laws concerning beaver hats are discussed in Innis' *The Fur Trade in Canada* and Dolin's *Fur, Fortune, and Empire*.

I gained insights into the nineteenth-century beaver-hat trade from James A. Hanson's "The Myth of the Silk Hat and the End of the Rendezvous" (*Rethinking the Fur Trade: Cultures of Exchange in an Atlantic World*, edited by Susan Sleeper-Smith; University of Nebraska Press, 2009). Mackie's *Trading Beyond the Mountains* provided additional information, as well as the quotes from the Governor and Committee of the Hudson's Bay Company and William Tolmie. I also read about silk hats at silktophats.eu/historytophat.html.

For beaver-pelt sales statistics and historical context, I relied on "Furbearer Harvests in North America" by Martyn E. Obbard et al., an extremely informative chapter in Novak et al.'s *Wild Furbearer Management and Conservation in North America*.

6. Fur Trading on Skyway Avenue

Father Paul Le Jeune's quote is from *The Jesuit Relations and Allied Documents: Travels and Explorations of the Jesuit Missionaries in New France, 1610–1791, Volume IX*, edited by Reuben Gold Thwaites (Burrows Brothers, 1898). David Thompson's quote is from *David Thompson's Narrative of his Explorations in Western America: 1784–1812*.

Information about beaver tokens is from the Hudson's Bay Company Archives website (gov.mb.ca/chc/archives/hbca/info_sheets/index.html) and the Coins and Canada website (coinsandcanada.com/coins-articles.php?article=currency-museum-of-the-bank-of-canada&id=290).

The 1733 Made Beaver exchange rates for furs and trade

goods are from *An Account of the Countries Adjoining to Hudson's Bay of America* by Arthur Dobbs.

I read about "hairy banknotes" in Dolin's *Fur, Fortune, and Empire*. Information about the American Fur Company's beaver money is from Schorger's "The Beaver in Early Wisconsin."

The NAFA section of this chapter is mostly based on my March 2010 visit to the company's Toronto headquarters. I supplemented my hands-on tutorials by reading "Fur Grading and Pelt Identification" by Martyn E. Obbard (in Novak et al.'s *Wild Furbearer Management and Conservation in North America*). I obtained additional information about NAFA and sales figures from the company website (nafa.ca).

The Agreement on International Humane Trapping Standards was signed by Canada, the European Union and Russia in 1997, and began regulating the traps that Canadian trappers can legally use in 2007. The United States and the EU have a separate but similar agreement. The text of the AIHTS is available on the Fur Institute of Canada's website (fur.ca). For beavers, the maximum allowable time to irreversible unconsciousness, measured by "loss of corneal and palpebral [eyelid] reflexes," is 300 seconds (five minutes); however, AIHTS standards apply only to commercially manufactured traps, not to trapper-constructed traps, such as the under-ice snares and foothold-on-slide-wire sets that are used for trapping beavers underwater. (Article 7 of the agreement states that "such traps [must] comply with designs approved by the relevant competent authority.") Several trappers I spoke with told me that AIHTS-certified rotating-jaw traps (often called Conibears, after their Canadian inventor, Frank Conibear) are so effective that they kill beavers almost instantly.

All of Henry Poland's quotes are from his book, *Fur-Bearing*

Animals in Nature and in Commerce (Gurney & Jackson, 1892). Biographical information about Poland is from *Eighteenth-Century Naturalists of Hudson Bay* by C. Stuart Houston (McGill-Queen's University Press, 2003).

I found the graph showing average annual beaver pelt harvest in Obbard et al.'s "Furbearer Harvests in North America" chapter. The authors of that chapter note that their harvest estimates are conservative: because various historical sources often report different pelt numbers for the same year, the numbers shown on the graph represent the lowest figure reported for any given year. I also consulted the raw data for the graph, which are compiled separately in *Furbearer Harvests in North America, 1600-1984* by Milan Novak, Martyn E. Obbard, et al. (Ontario Trappers Association, 1987).

7. One Made Beaver

The first half of this chapter is largely based on my visit with Pete Wise in January 2011. I also learned about trapping beavers and preparing pelts from Hatler and Beal's *British Columbia Trapper Education Manual*; and "Pelt Preparation" by G. Edward Hall and Martyn E. Obbard (in Novak et al.'s *Wild Furbearer Management and Conservation in North America*). When I read the author bios at the end of the "Pelt Preparation" chapter, I discovered that G. Edward Hall was the man I knew as NAFA beaver grader Paddy Hall.

Facts about the anatomical details Wise showed me are from: Baker and Hill's "Beaver" chapter in *Wild Mammals of North America*; Novak's "Beaver" chapter in *Wild Furbearer Management and Conservation in North America*; and Müller-Schwarze and Sun's *The Beaver*.

Biographical information about Frances Anne Hopkins (née

Beechey) is from the online Dictionary of Canadian Biography (biographi.ca/en/index.php). Her profile on this website includes thumbnails of her paintings "Shooting the Rapids" and "Voyageurs at Dawn."

The Yukon musher who compared beaver meat to an energy drink for sled dogs was Brian Wilmhurst, quoted by Patrick White in "Dogsled Race Set to Be Soggiest on Record" (*Globe and Mail*, January 24, 2014).

I read about the use of castoreum in food products on numerous websites, some of which greatly exaggerated the situation. The rumour-busting website, Snopes.com, offers the most solid information on this subject (snopes.com/food/ingredient/castoreum.asp). For information about *bäverhojt*, including a recipe for making your own, see the November 13, 2011, Weaving Monk blog entry (weavingmonk.com/blog/2011/11/baversnaps-unusual-swedish-liqueur.html).

I visited La Ronge and interviewed Scott Robertson and Vern Studer in July 2011. For additional information about the Robertson Trading Company and Alex Robertson, I drew on the company website (robertsontradingltd.ca) and biographical notes on the Saskatchewan Craft Council website (page no longer available) related to the council's 2010 Robertson Trading Post Collection exhibition.

8. *The Mighty Beaver*

The term "keystone species" was coined by R.T. Paine and introduced to the world in his "Note on Trophic Complexity and Community Stability" (*American Naturalist*, 1969). Since then, the concept has been widely discussed in scientific books and articles. "The Keystone-species Concept in Ecology and Conservation" by L. Scott Mills, Michael E. Soulé and Daniel F.

Doak (*BioScience*, 1993) is an excellent starting point for anyone wanting to know more.

Beavers were first identified as ecosystem engineers in the paper that launched this term: "Organisms as Ecosystem Engineers" by Clive G. Jones, John H. Lawton and Moshe Shachak (*Oikos*, 1994).

I first heard Greg Hood talk about the Skagit Delta beavers during a field trip organized by the Institute for Journalism and Natural Resources in July 2009. I returned in April 2011 for an exclusive tour of his research site. My understanding of his research was also informed by our email correspondence and his articles (published under his full name, W. Gregory Hood): "Beaver in Tidal Marshes: Dam Effects on Low-Tide Channel Pools and Fish Use of Estuarine Habitat" (*Wetlands*, 2012); "Large Woody Debris Influences Vegetation Zonation in an Oligohaline Tidal Marsh" (*Estuaries and Coasts*, 2007); and "Sweetgale, Beaver, Salmon, and Large Woody Debris in the Skagit River Tidal Marshes: An Overlooked Ecological Web" (*Skagit River Tidings*, 2002).

Algonquin Provincial Park, which I visited in June 2012, proved to be an ideal location for researching beavers. Besides walking the Beaver Pond Trail numerous times, I observed beavers and their habitat on other hiking trails and at roadside pullouts, spent a couple of rewarding afternoons in the park archives and enjoyed the beaver exhibit in the visitor centre.

Information about dam construction is primarily from Baker and Hill's "Beaver" chapter and the Hinterland Who's Who species profile (hww.ca/en/species/mammals/beaver.html). I learned about the dam made of boulders from Thomas S. Jung and Jennifer A. Staniforth's "Unusual Beaver, *Castor canadensis*, Dams in Central Yukon" (*Canadian Field-Naturalist*, 2010).

In "A Beaver's Food Requirement" (*Journal of Mammalogy*, 1940), Edward R. Warren reported on free-living beavers that were fed by a Forest Service contractor in Colorado during the 1920s; each animal consumed approximately one ton of aspen per year. In "Boundary Dynamics at the Aquatic-terrestrial Interface: The Influence of Beaver and Geomorphology" (*Landscape Ecology*, 1987), Carol A. Johnston and Robert J. Naiman note that "An individual beaver cuts about a metric ton of wood for growth and maintenance annually."

The beaver cycle of dam-building, pond abandonment and reoccupation is described in numerous sources, including Ronald L. Ives' classic paper, "The Beaver-Meadow Complex" (*Journal of Geomorphology*, 1942).

The concept of animals as geomorphic agents is comprehensively examined in Butler's *Zoogeomorphology*. Rudolf Ruedemann and Walter J. Schoonmaker's article, "Beaver-dams as Geologic Agents" appeared in *Science* (1938).

The number of cubic metres of sediment stored behind beaver dams is from "Ecosystem Alteration of Boreal Forest Streams by Beaver (*Castor canadensis*)" by Robert J. Naiman, Jerry M. Melillo and John E. Hobbie (*Ecology*, 1986). The study of the beaver dam complex on the Colorado River in Rocky Mountain National Park is described in Westbrook, Cooper and Baker's "Beaver Assisted River Valley Formation." I did the conversions to dump-truck loads. (According to earthhaulers.com, small single-axle dump trucks typically carry about 3.8 cubic metres of material.)

I first interviewed Cherie Westbrook in July 2012 while researching my *Canadian Geographic* article, "Rethinking the Beaver." We met in person in August 2013. This section draws on both interviews, as well as our email correspondence and my reading of several of her publications: "Beaver and Overbank Floods Influence Groundwater-surface Water Interactions in a Rocky Mountain Riparian Area" by Cherie J. Westbrook, David J. Cooper and Bruce W. Baker (*Water Resources Research*, 2006); "Changes in Riparian Area Structure, Channel Hydraulics, and Sediment Yield Following Loss of Beaver Dams" by Kim C. Green and Cherie J. Westbrook (*B.C. Journal of Ecosystems and Management*, 2009); and "Beaver Hydrology and Geomorphology" by C.J. Westbrook, D.J. Cooper and D.R. Butler (*Treatise on Geomorphology, Volume 12: Ecogeomorphology*, Elsevier, 2013).

Information on beaver populations in Rocky Mountain National Park is from Westbrook, Cooper and Baker's "Beaver Assisted River Valley Formation." The predator-driven trophic cascade hypothesis is explained in "Declining Beaver Populations in Rocky Mountain National Park" by Bruce Baker (fort.usgs.gov/science-tasks/2213).

The map showing where beavers pushed water over a drainage divide is in *The Romance of the Beaver: Being the History of the Beaver in the Western Hemisphere* by Arthur Radclyffe Dugmore (Lippincott, 1914). I learned more about Dugmore from the Luminous-Lint website (luminous-lint.com/app/photographer/A_Radclyffe__Dugmore/A).

Existing research on how beavers may affect oil sands rehabilitation is synthesized in *Potential Impacts of Beaver on Oil Sands Reclamation Success: An Analysis of Available Literature* by B. Eaton, et al. (Oil Sands Research and Information Network, University of Alberta, 2013).

Alberta Construction Magazine described the impact of the June 2013 deluge in an online infographic, "The Flood: 6 Months Later" (albertaconstructionmagazine.com/theflood).

Information about beaver canals is primarily from Baker and

Hill's "Beaver" chapter and the Hinterland Who's Who online species profile.

When I met with Westbrook, she and her post-doctoral colleague, Colin Whitfield, were completing a study on beavers and methane emissions. Their findings were subsequently published in "Beaver-mediated Methane Emission: The Effects of Population Growth in Eurasia and the Americas" by Colin J. Whitfield, et al. (*AMBIO*, 2014).

While beavers increase methane release when they create ponds in peatlands, their activities can also contribute to carbon storage, an effect discussed in Ellen Wohl's "Landscape-scale Carbon Storage Associated with Beaver Dams" (*Geophysical Research Letters*, 2013).

I met Glynnis Hood in August 2009, while researching an article, "Leave it to Beavers," (*British Columbia Magazine*, 2013). We spent a pleasant morning exploring beaver territories in Miquelon Lake Provincial Park, near her home, and talking about her research. Hood's Elk Island National Park study is described in her book, *The Beaver Manifesto*, and in "Beaver (*Castor canadensis*) Mitigate the Effects of Climate on the Area of Open Water in Boreal Wetlands in Western Canada" by Glynnis A. Hood and Suzanne E. Bayley (*Biological Conservation*, 2008). I also consulted Duncan Thorne's *Edmonton Journal* article, "Nature's Engineers Prove Vital for Wetland Preservation" (February 18, 2008).

Information about the pond-ice study is from "Beavers (*Castor canadensis*) Facilitate Early Access by Canada Geese (*Branta canadensis*) to Nesting Habitat and Areas of Open Water in Canada's Boreal Wetlands" by Chantal K. Bromley and Glynnis A. Hood (*Mammalian Biology*, 2013).

Aldo Leopold's quote is from his essay, "Conservation," in *Round River* (Oxford University Press, 1953).

9. *Détente*

I interviewed Shawn Dalman while accompanying him on a beaver live-trapping call in May 2011.

I read about James A. Serpell's affect/utility four-quadrant grid in Hal Herzog's *Some We Love, Some We Hate, Some We Eat: Why It's So Hard to Think Straight About Animals* (HarperCollins, 2010). Herzog's thought-provoking book also helped me sort through my ambivalent feelings about beaver trapping. "Those of us in the troubled middle live in a complex moral universe," Herzog writes in his introduction. "We middlers see the world in shades of gray rather than in the clear blacks and whites of committed animal activists and their equally vociferous opponents. Some argue that we are fence-sitters, moral wimps. I believe, however, that the troubled middle makes perfect sense because moral quagmires are inevitable in a species with a huge brain and a big heart. They come with the territory."

Although many trappers use the term "drowning set" to describe traps or snares that kill beavers by holding them underwater, others consider this is a misnomer. The *British Columbia Trapper Education Manual* by Hatler and Beal states that beavers "are naturally 'programmed' to avoid trying to breathe underwater (which would result in drowning). Instead, they are rendered unconscious as the oxygen supply in their blood is depleted and replaced by carbon dioxide [which] is much less stressful than drowning." Novak's "Traps and Trap Research" chapter (in Novak et al.'s *Wild Furbearer Management and Conservation in North America*) refers to this process as "carbon dioxide–induced narcosis (submersion asphyxia or anoxia)" and notes that "sensory perception may [be] absent 5-7 min[utes] post-submersion." In "The Diving Habits of the Beaver" (*Science*, 1935), Laurence Irving and M.D. Orr reported observations of unrestrained beavers that voluntarily remained submerged for at least 15 minutes with no apparent ill effects.

The 1988 estimate of the North American beaver population is from "Alteration of North American Streams by Beaver" by Robert J. Naiman, Carol A. Johnston and James C. Kelley (*BioScience*, 1988). The year-2000 estimate is from Whitfield et al.'s "Beaver-mediated Methane Emission." (Another modern estimate appears in Müller-Schwarze and Sun's *The Beaver*; they place the population at approximately 20 million but do not explain how they determined this number.)

I learned about the 1930s to 1950s proliferation of beavers in Prince Albert National Park and the attempts to deal with the problems they caused from Waiser's *Saskatchewan's Playground* and documents I found in the park archives, including *Beaver Study in Prince Albert National Park* by Andrew Radvanyi (unpublished report, 1956) and numerous letters. Park interpreter Brad Muir kindly provided me with a copy of the film *Holiday at Waskesiu*. I interviewed Seth Cherry during my July 2011 visit to Prince Albert National Park.

Information about beaver breeding biology is from Baker and Hill's "Beaver" chapter.

Grey Owl's quotes about the beaver's Imperialist tendencies are from his book, *The Men of the Last Frontier*.

The 50- and 80-kilometre journeys by beavers are reported in James R. Beer's "Movements of Tagged Beaver" (*Journal of Wildlife Management*, 1955). I read about the beaver found nearly 12 kilometres from water in Novak's "Beaver" chapter.

Information about the wolf eradication program in Prince Albert National Park is from Waiser's *Saskatchewan's Playground*.

The story of the Idaho Fish and Game Department's beaver air-drop is told by Elmo W. [Scotty] Heter in "Transplanting Beavers by Airplane and Parachute" (*Journal of Wildlife Management*, 1950). The *Modern Mechanix* article is titled "Airborne Beavers Fight Floods."

The return of beavers to the Bronx River has received wide coverage, including in Peter Miller's fascinating article, "Before New York" (*National Geographic*, 2009). I got updates from the Calendar & News section of the Bronx River Alliance website ("José and Justin Beaver Still Hard at Work Along the Bronx River," February 19, 2014) and email correspondence with the Alliance's executive director, Linda R. Cox.

I read about the Toronto beavers in "Beavers Scout for a Home in Queen's Quay Condo Corridor" by Antonia Zerbisias (thestar.com, July 17, 2011). Jane Taber told the story of the two beaver-wrangling Members of Parliament in a *Globe and Mail* column (April 4, 2009).

Information about Mickey and Doris Forbes is from an undated City of Red Deer brochure, *Explore Red Deer's Public Art*. I read several accounts of the conflict between beavers and dogs at Three Mile Bend, the most informative of which were two articles on the CBC website (cbc.ca/news/canada/calgary/beavers-attack-dogs-in-red-deer-park-1.910750 and cbc.ca/news/canada/calgary/beaver-shot-to-death-in-red-deer-park-1.894954). The "No More Mr. Nice Rodent," photo caption appeared in the *Victoria Times Colonist* (July 15, 2010).

I visited Gatineau Park in June 2012 and learned about the park's beaver management program through a joint interview with conservation officer Richard Moore and senior biologist Jocelyne Jacob, as well as the guided tour with Moore. Gatineau's Eager Beaver interpretation program is described on the park website (ncc-ccn.gc.ca/places-to-visit/gatineau-park/article/2013-08-09/parks-engineer).

Information about Skip Lisle is from several sources, including Madeline Bodin's "Leave it to Beavers" (*Woodland*, 2013). A 1994 Clemson University Extension Services publication, "The Clemson Beaver Pond Leveler," explained this device to me. The Beavers: Wetlands & Wildlife website (beaversww.org/solving-problems) and the Worth a Dam website (martinezbeavers.org/wordpress) offer a wealth of information about coexisting with beavers and inspiration to pursue non-lethal solutions to conflict situations.

Overland distances travelled by beavers to obtain food and building materials are from the Beavers: Wetlands & Wildlife website.

In *The Romance of the Beaver*, Dugmore wrote about a beaver-cut stump with a diameter of 107 centimetres, found along the Jefferson River in Montana; Dugmore guessed that it was a cottonwood, which seems a reasonable assumption.

D. Scott Brayton described Smith, Apple and McCuistion's beaver reintroduction project in "The Beaver and the Stream" (*Journal of Soil and Water Conservation*, 1984).

Hilary Cooke's quote is from a conversation we had in May 2012. I also learned about her research from a paper she co-authored with Steve Zack: "Influence of Beaver Dam Density on Riparian Areas and Riparian Birds in Shrubsteppe of Wyoming" (*Western North American Naturalist*, 2008).

The University of Connecticut and Kansas State University study is described in "The River Discontinuum: Applying Beaver Modifications to Baseline Conditions for Restoration of Forested Headwaters" by Denise Burchsted, et al. (*BioScience*, 2010). Melinda Daniels' quote is from a Kansas State University press release, "The Ecosystem Engineer: Research Looks at Beavers' Role in River Restoration" (January 3, 2011).

I learned about the beaver restoration projects in New Mexico, Utah, Alberta and Washington State from the websites of the Seventh Generation Institute (seventh-generation.org/new-page-2), The Grand Canyon Trust (grandcanyontrust.org), the Leave it to Beavers Water Stewardship program (rockies.ca/beavers/index.php), the Methow Stream Conservancy (methowconservancy.org/beaver_project.html) and The Lands Council (landscouncil.org/beaversolution), as well as *Beaver as a Climate Change Adaptation Tool: Concepts and Priority Sites in New Mexico* by Cathryn Wild (Seventh Generation Institute, 2011). Joe Wheaton's beaver monitoring app is described on the Utah Water Watch website (extension.usu.edu/utahwaterwatch/htm/beaver-monitoring-app/how-to-monitor).

IMAGE NOTES

Page vi: istock photo © shaunl.

Page 2: Vignette from a map of the British colonies in North America. "A view of ye industry of ye beavers of Canada . . . the cataract of Niagara" by H. Moll. 1715 i.e. 1731.

Page 16: Ellen Jo Roberts.

Page 40: Hunting scene from the North Red River area, probably near old Fort Douglas, now Winnipeg. Wisconsin Historical Society, Peter Rindisbacher, *Indian Spearing Beaver*, ca. 1821 Image ID: 3884.

Page 64: Grey Owl feeding a beaver kit. Lovat Dickson Collection / Library and Archives Canada / PA-147582. Ca. 1936.

Page 98: Scenes of mid-nineteenth-century beaver-fur hat manufacturing, from Charles Knight's *Pictorial Gallery of the Arts*. Science, Industry and Business Library: General Collection, The New York Public Library Digital Collections. 1858-.

Page 122: Hudson's Bay Company brass Made Beaver fur trade tokens, showing obverse and reverse sides. National Currency Collection, Currency Museum, Bank of Canada.

Page 146: Susan McBride with beaver pelts, Alberta, 1967. McBride family photo, courtesy of Susan Conners, née McBride.

Page 170: Canadian National Railways / Library and Archives Canada / PA.

Page 198: Idaho conservation officers preparing for a beaver parachute drop, ca. 1948. Idaho Fish and Game Department.

Page 226: Beavers sacrificing their castor glands to avoid being killed by hunters. Salisbury Bestiary, 13th century.

ACKNOWLEDGEMENTS

Researching this book was a fascinating and fun endeavour, made all the more so by the people I met along the way. I am especially grateful to the following individuals who allowed me to enter into their lives and work and generously shared their beaver knowledge: Natalia Rybczynski; Ida Calmegane; Bryce Nimmo, Brian Hanson, Mui Luangphasi and Gerald; Oscar Carbonell, Murray Parkinson and Paddy Hall; Nancy Haefer; Pete Wise; Scott Robertson; Vern Studer; Greg Hood; Cherie Westbrook; Glynnis Hood; Shawn Dalman; and Richard Moore.

I would also like to express my appreciation to others who furthered my research in various valuable ways: EcoInformatics president Jean Thie; retired University of Calgary historian Donald B. Smith; Karen Hill of Saskatchewan Tourism; Wood Buffalo National Park's Mike Keizer; paleontologist Grant Zazula; paleoecologist Catherine Yansa; archaeologist Bryony Coles; University of Victoria historian Wendy Wickwire; Nathalie Guénette at the Canadian Museum of Civilization; Prince Albert National Park communications officer Shannon Bond, whose enthusiasm and assistance enriched my Saskatchewan research trip; Brad Muir, Marcia Klein and Seth Cherry, also of Prince Albert National Park; Ria vander Klis and Tegan Heard of the Chilcotin Lodge in Riske Creek; Eric Collier–fan James Stewart; NAFA's Bob McQuay and Vittorio Villacis; Michelle Hiltz of Alberta Innovates; Rory Eckenswiller, Patrick Moldowan, Jennifer Hoare, Brad Steinberg and Ron Tozer, who collectively ensured that my time in Algonquin Provincial Park was enjoyable and productive;

Bronx River Alliance executive director Linda Cox; Gatineau Park biologist Jocelyne Jacob; Dan Buffett and Darryl Kroeker of Ducks Unlimited Canada; Hilary Cooke and Don Reid in the Wildlife Conservation Society's Yukon office; Amanda Parrish of The Lands Council; biologist Kathryn Martell; John Olson and Brenda Kelly of the Wisconsin Department of Natural Resources; USDA biologist Jason Suckow; and CRD Regional Parks biologist Marilyn Fuchs. The Institute for Journalism and Natural Resources made a pivotal contribution by introducing me to Greg Hood and his beaver research.

My research and writing for this book were assisted by much-appreciated grants from the British Columbia Arts Council and the Canada Council for the Arts.

A number of people read early drafts of portions of the book and gave me helpful feedback and encouragement. Thank you to author J.B. MacKinnon and my University of Victoria associates: Lynne Van Luven, who was excited about this project from the very beginning and has celebrated each step along the way, while providing welcome writerly advice; David Leach, who nudged me into new territory and offered astute insights that helped me negotiate the unfamiliar terrain; and the ever-dynamic W416 Gang. I am also much obliged to anthropologist Julie Cruikshank for her indispensable assistance and comments.

As always, my literary agent Carolyn Swayze deserves plaudits for her role in keeping my career on track. I am happy to count both Carolyn and her husband and business partner, Barry Jones, as friends as well as professional associates.

In these difficult days of publishing, I am most fortunate to have landed with ECW Press, where every member of the team is a pleasure to work with. Special thanks to Jack David for embracing my idea and maintaining a keen interest through every stage of the book's creation; Crissy Calhoun and Laura Pastore for their adept editorial management; Rachel Ironstone for a dynamite cover; and Erin Creasey for her marketing savvy. I am indebted to editor Jonathan Webb, who guided me through the final revisions with great perceptiveness and sensitivity.

I would like to extend my sincere appreciation to all of my family members, friends and colleagues who have enthusiastically followed the progress of this book, sustaining me through words and actions, even when my work left me with too little time for connecting in person.

Above all, I am profoundly grateful to my beloved companion, Mark Zuehlke, for his steadfast support, wise counsel, patience and love: in my world, you're the ultimate Beaver Believer.

Published by ECW Press
665 Gerrard Street East, Toronto, Ontario, Canada
M4M 1Y2
416-694-3348 / info@ecwpress.com

LIBRARY AND ARCHIVES CANADA
CATALOGUING IN PUBLICATION

Backhouse, Frances, author
Once they were hats : in search of the mighty beaver / written by Frances Backhouse.

Includes bibliographical references.
Issued in print and electronic formats.
ISBN 978-1-77041-207-1 (pbk)
ISBN 978-1-77090-754-6 (pdf)
ISBN 978-1-77090-755-3 (epub)

1. Beavers. 1. Title.

QL737.R632B33 2015   599.37   C2015-902767-5
C2015-902768-3

Cover design: Michel Vrana
Cover image: Library and Archives Canada, Acc. No. R9266-624 Peter Winkworth Collection of Canadiana
Type: Rachel Ironstone

The publication of *Once They Were Hats* has been generously supported by the Canada Council for the Arts which last year invested $153 million to bring the arts to Canadians throughout the country, and by the Government of Canada through the Canada Book Fund. *Nous remercions le Conseil des arts du Canada de son soutien. L'an dernier, le Conseil a investi 153 millions de dollars pour mettre de l'art dans la vie des Canadiennes et des Canadiens de tout le pays. Ce livre est financé en partie par le gouvernement du Canada.* We also acknowledge the Ontario Arts Council (OAC), an agency of the Government of Ontario, which last year funded 1,709 individual artists and 1,078 organizations in 204 communities across Ontario, for a total of $52.1 million, and the contribution of the Government of Ontario through the Ontario Book Publishing Tax Credit and the Ontario Media Development Corporation.

Printed and bound in Canada by Norecob   5   4   3   2   1